35776002978660
305.230941 F929v
Frost, Ginger Suzanne,
Victorian childhoods /

D0214293

VICTORIAN CHILDHOODS

Recent Titles in
Victorian Life and Times

Family Ties in Victorian England
Claudia Nelson

Food and Cooking in Victorian England
Andrea Broomfield

Victorian Religion: Faith and Life in Britain
Julie Melnyk

"Gone to the Shops": Shopping in Victorian England
Kelley Graham

VICTORIAN CHILDHOODS

Ginger S. Frost

VICTORIAN LIFE AND TIMES
Sally Mitchell, Series Editor

PRAEGER

Westport, Connecticut
London

Library of Congress Cataloging-in-Publication Data

Frost, Ginger Suzanne, 1962–
  Victorian childhoods / Ginger S. Frost.
    p. cm. — (Victorian life and times, 1932–944X)
  Includes bibliographical references and index.
  ISBN: 978-0–275–98966–8 (alk. paper)
  1. Children—Great Britain—History—19th century.   2. Children—Great Britain—Social
conditions—19th century.   3. Great Britain—History—Victoria, 1837–1901.   I. Title.
  HQ792.G7F76   2009
  305.230941'09034—dc22   2008036906

British Library Cataloguing in Publication Data is available.

Copyright © 2009 by Ginger S. Frost

All rights reserved. No portion of this book may be
reproduced, by any process or technique, without the
express written consent of the publisher.

Library of Congress Catalog Card Number: 2008036906
ISBN: 978-0–275–98966–8
ISSN: 1932–944X

First published in 2009

Praeger Publishers, 88 Post Road West, Westport, CT 06881
An imprint of Greenwood Publishing Group, Inc.
www.praeger.com

Printed in the United States of America

The paper used in this book complies with the
Permanent Paper Standard issued by the National
Information Standards Organization (Z39.48–1984).

10 9 8 7 6 5 4 3 2 1

To Marillyn Frost, my "mum"
and Jackie Dixon, my "great chum"

CONTENTS

SERIES FOREWORD

Although the nineteenth century has almost faded from living memory—most people who heard first-hand stories from grandparents who grew up before 1900 have adult grandchildren by now—impressions of the Victorian world continue to influence both popular culture and public debates. These impressions may well be vivid yet contradictory. Many people, for example, believe that Victorian society was safe, family-centered, and stable because women could not work outside the home, although every census taken during the period records hundreds of thousands of female laborers in fields, factories, shops, and schools as well as more than a million domestic servants—often girls of fourteen or fifteen—whose long and unregulated workdays created the comfortable leisured world we see in Merchant and Ivory films. Yet it is also true that there were women who had no household duties and desperately wished for some purpose in life but found that social expectations and family pressure absolutely prohibited their presence in the workplace.

The goal of books in the Victorian Life and Times series is to explain and enrich the simple pictures that show only a partial truth. Although the Victorian period in Great Britain is often portrayed as peaceful, comfortable, and traditional, it was actually a time of truly breathtaking change. In 1837, when eighteen-year-old Victoria became queen, relatively few of England's people had ever traveled more than ten miles from the place where they were born. Little more than half the population could read and write, children as young as five worked in factories and mines, and political power was entirely in the hands of a small minority of men who held property. By the time Queen Victoria died in 1901, railways provided fast and cheap transportation for both goods and people, telegraph messages sped to the far corners of the British Empire in minutes, education was compulsory, a man's religion (or lack of it) no longer barred him from sitting in Parliament, and women were not only wives and domestic servants but also physicians, dentists, elected school-board members, telephone operators, and university lecturers. Virtually every aspect of life had been transformed either by technology or by the massive political and legal reforms that reshaped Parliament, elections, universities, the army, education, sanitation, public health, marriage, working conditions, trade unions, and civil and criminal law.

The continuing popularity of Victoriana among decorators and collectors, the strong market for historical novels and for mysteries set in the age of Jack the Ripper and Sherlock Holmes, the new interest in books by George Eliot and Charles Dickens and Wilkie Collins whenever one is presented on television, and the desire of amateur genealogists to discover the lives, as well as the names, of nineteenth-century British ancestors all reveal the need for accurate information about the period's social history and material culture. In the years since my book *Daily Life in Victorian England* was published in 1996 I have been contacted by many people who want more detailed information about some area covered in that overview. Each book in the Victorian Life and Times series will focus on a single topic, describe changes during the period, and consider the differences between country and city, between industrial life and rural life, and above all, the differences made by class, social position, religion, tradition, gender, and economics. Each book is an original work, illustrated with drawings and pictures taken from Victorian sources, enriched by quotations from Victorian publications, based on current research and written by a qualified scholar. All of the authors have doctoral degrees and many years' experience in teaching; they have been chosen not only for their academic qualifications but also for their ability to write clearly and to explain complex ideas to people without extensive background in the subject. Thus the books are authoritative and dependable but written in straightforward language; explanations are supplied whenever specialized terminology is used, and a bibliography lists resources for further information.

The Internet has made it possible for people who can not visit archives and reference libraries to conduct serious family and historical research. Careful hobbyists and scholars have scanned large numbers of primary sources—nineteenth-century cookbooks, advice manuals, maps, city directories, magazines, sermons, church records, illustrated newspapers, guidebooks, political cartoons, photographs, paintings, published investigations of slum conditions and poor people's budgets, political essays, inventories of scientists' correspondence, and many other materials formerly accessible only to academic historians. Yet the World Wide Web also contains misleading documents and false information, even on educational sites created by students and enthusiasts who don't have the experience to put material in useful contexts. So far as possible, therefore, the bibliographies for books in the Victorian Life and Times series will also offer guidance on using publicly available electronic resources.

In popular imagination, the phrase "Victorian childhood" evokes conflicting mental images: sentimental greeting cards with sunshine, fluffy dogs, girls in Kate Greenaway dresses playing under the watchful eye of a smiling adult; or the abused and ragged waifs of child-labor exposés and Charles Dickens novels. In *Victorian Childhoods*—notice the plural—Ginger Frost not only provides details about these extremes but also describes many other patterns of life. In addition, she raises questions that have no easy answer. What, for example, is a child? What defines childhood? When does it end? How do a society's beliefs about childhood compare with children's perceptions of their own lives?

As the clear explanations and lively examples in this book make clear, children's experience in the nineteenth century varied enormously not only with their age, class, gender, and family but also with the social, technological, political, and legal changes that transformed Britain between 1837 and 1901. Chapters on home life, schooling, work, play, organizations, and on what Victorian reformers called "children of the state" (orphans, paupers, criminals) are enriched with dozens of quotations and anecdotes drawn from autobiographies, biographies, memoirs, newspapers, and other accounts that present Victorian childhoods in vivid detail and through the eyes of Victorian children.

Sally Mitchell, Series Editor

ACKNOWLEDGMENTS

I must first thank Sally Mitchell, who asked me to write a volume in the series, supported my suggested topic, and then proved a helpful and efficient editor. This book is immeasurably better for having had her guiding hand. I also thank Samford University for financial help in researching and writing the book. I especially owe a debt of thanks to Gail Burton and her staff in the Interlibrary Loan Office of Davis Library. I could not have had any illustrations without their hard work, and they were vital in helping check references during the final stages of preparation. Susan Murphy assisted with the illustrations as well and helped as a sounding board on numerous occasions, and I am very grateful for her intelligence and friendship.

I owe intellectual debts to many historians of Victorian childhood, most of whom are well represented in the endnotes and bibliography. Nevertheless, I especially want to acknowledge the importance of the books by John Burnett, Eric Hopkins, Pamela Horn, and Thomas Jordan, all of whom inspired and illuminated me.

Finally, writing a book about childhood usually causes an author to reflect on her own, and I am no exception. Thus, this book is dedicated to the two major forces of my childhood, my mother, Marillyn Frost, and my older sister, Jackie Dixon. Thanks for always being there.

INTRODUCTION

The history of nineteenth-century Britain fascinates for many reasons. It is long enough ago to be foreign but close enough to be familiar. The period is also associated with one person—Queen Victoria, who served as queen from 1837 to 1901, the longest reign in British history. The influence of Victorianism encompasses an even longer period, from the end of the Napoleonic Wars (in 1815) until the beginnings of World War I (in 1914). The cultural, political, and social forces of the age stretched across one hundred years, in part because so many of them had origins in the eighteenth century and even earlier. All the same, though the continuities were important, the 1800s were also years of dynamic change. The Industrial Revolution began in the late eighteenth century and stretched into the twentieth, generating both enormous wealth and a large working class. Both the overall population and specific urban areas grew exponentially. In 1830, more than two-thirds of the population of 15 million people lived on farms; by 1900, the population was 32.5 million and 80 percent lived in cities. The British Empire also expanded, recovering from the setback of the American Revolution. The British ruled colonies across the globe, most notably in Canada, South Asia (India, Burma, and the future Pakistan), the South Pacific (Australia and New Zealand), and Africa. In addition, the nineteenth century saw political reforms that eventually led to a parliamentary democracy, including a substantial increase in the number of voters, redistricting, and the development of two large party organizations, the Tories and the Liberals. These years, then, were some of the most compelling in British history.

Historians often divide the Victorian period into distinct eras, and this book will follow that example. The early Victorian period includes the 1830s and 1840s, an age characterized by economic, political, and social upheaval. In particular, both industry and agriculture experienced depressions in the 1840s,

mostly because of an industrial downturn and the potato blight. This is the period most casual readers associate with Victorians, represented by smokestacks,
workhouses, and Charles Dickens. However, this was also the time of the early
labor movement and increasing demands for political representation, granted
to most middle-class males in 1832. The mid-Victorian age, stretching from
approximately 1850 to 1875, was a contrast, as this was a period of relative
prosperity. Food prices dropped and wages increased slightly, and the booms
and busts of the early industrial period settled down. Liberalism, or a belief in
laissez-faire economics and limited representative government, was the dominant ideology, and the empire expanded robustly. The first attempt to include
working men in the political nation was mid-Victorian, with a reform bill in
1867. With this act, the Victorian state encompassed "respectable" workers and
set the stage for further changes. Finally, late-Victorian Britain encompassed
the years from 1875 to 1914. This period was one in which the liberal consensus
began to break down. A long agricultural depression began in the mid-1870s
and stretched until 1893, and changes in industry (the decline of old industries,
such as steel, and the rise of new ones, like telephones, chemicals, and electricity) made for renewed labor unrest. In addition, the turn of the twentieth
century saw anxieties about empire and British progress, as well as a strong,
organized movement for women's rights. Though one can overstate the differences between these periods or argue about the dates, the changes over time
were significant and influenced the experiences of children.

Victoria ruled over the United Kingdom of Great Britain and Ireland. Within
this state were distinct countries: Ireland, Scotland, Wales, and England. The
English had conquered Wales centuries earlier, though the Welsh retained a
sense of identity and a separate language. Still, the term "England" in this
period meant England and Wales, and both shared the same law codes and state
church, though the Welsh had a large population of non-Anglican Protestants.
Scotland and England joined together as Great Britain in the Act of Union in
1707. Scotland retained its own law codes and state church but had seats in
the combined British Parliament and recognized the same monarch. The term
"Britain," then, refers to England, Scotland, and Wales. The British had tried
to control and colonize Ireland since the twelfth century with limited success.
The Irish had agreed in 1801 to an Act of Union, thereby forming the United
Kingdom, but religious differences made any real rapprochement impossible.
The majority of Irish subjects were staunchly Catholic and opposed to Protestant
rule, and the sectarian strife did not lessen much even when Parliament removed
some of the restrictions for Catholics in 1829. Because the Irish situation was
contested and extremely complex, this book will concentrate on Great Britain
rather than the United Kingdom. In other words, the following generalizations
about childhood will apply only to England, Scotland, and Wales.

In addition to generation and location, class differences were substantial
during the Victorian period. Aristocrats and other landed gentry, making up
only 2 percent of the population, had considerable wealth and did not work for a

living, instead relying on rents from land and investments. Younger sons might learn a profession, but these had to be gentlemanly, such as high positions in the government, church, law courts, or military. The middle classes consisted of both those who owned their own businesses, such as factory owners, and professionals like teachers and doctors. This class was approximately 15 percent of the population in 1815 and grew to around 25 percent by 1900. Members of this class could afford to hire servants and usually rented housing. Within this class, the major stratification was between the professionals and factory owners and the lower middle class, which consisted of small business owners and white-collar workers like clerks and typists. The latter probably employed only one servant and guarded their class distinctions and respectability carefully. The working class made up the rest of the population. Its members worked for wages and were paid daily or weekly. They too were stratified into various levels; skilled workers, who made better wages, were about 15 percent of the group. The rest fell into the large category of unskilled workers and were particularly vulnerable to economic downturns. However, all workers shared uncertainty about future employment because they had only their labor to sell. Chapter 3 has more about the issue of class; the differences were central to the experience of childhood and appear throughout the book.

Finally, gender distinctions were also significant in this period. One of the results of the Industrial Revolution was the separation of family life from work; although never universal, this divergence meant that middle-class Victorians could see their homes as havens of domesticity and peace in contrast to the harsh business and political world. Victorians idealized the family and, in theory, had strict roles for husbands, wives, and children. It was a middle-class ideal, but it influenced those both above and below on the social scale. One of the major results of this emphasis was a glorification of parental roles, for men and for women. In theory, women were angels in the house, taking on nurturing duties; in contrast, men provided and protected. The legal system supported this dependent role for women; when Victoria came to the throne, a married woman had no custody rights over her children, could not sign contracts as an independent actor, could not own property, and could not sue or be sued. Women also had great disadvantages in the job market and few opportunities for higher education. Though changes occurred throughout the century to improve women's legal position, girlhood remained different from boyhood until well after World War I because of the differing expectations for girls' and boys' futures.

Victorian Britain was a nation of children; until late in the nineteenth century, families were large and life expectancy low. Despite the increase in population and a drop in the death rate, the percentage of children in the population was steady. In 1841, 36.1 percent of the population was younger than fifteen, and in 1891, the figure was still 35 percent. In short, the youthfulness of the population was one of the defining characteristics of Victorian life. The socialization of these future subjects, then, was of great concern and increasingly became the business of more than the nuclear or even extended family. At the end of the century, in fact, the welfare of children was the subject of much political debate. By 1914, Victorians had vastly expanded childhood, by both building on and transcending movements begun in earlier periods.

ISSUES IN CHILDHOOD HISTORY

A central issue for any childhood historian is the question of definition. Who, exactly, was a child in this period? The legal age of majority in Britain was twenty-one; at law, then, anyone under that age was an infant and had to have an adult guardian. Another way to define childhood was by schooling; when a child took a degree or went to work, he or she entered adulthood. A third possibility was to center on the issue of adult supervision; a child became an adult when he or she earned independence from older authorities. None of these definitions is helpful for the Victorian period. In the first place, the age of majority was far too high to comprehend the lives of lower-middle and working-class youths, as these children went to work early, some leaving home in their late teens. Second, the break from childhood to adulthood was not clean. Many children did not receive formal education or did so for only a few years; those who worked full-time at young ages remained at home and under the control of their parents. In addition, those who left home in their teens were often still supervised by employers, church authorities, or the state. Indeed, domestic servants, especially female ones, remained under the control of their employers well into their legal adulthood.

Third, as mentioned previously, childhood differed by class, sex, and generation. In the early part of the century, Britain did not require school attendance for all children, and poor children went to work as early as seven. Upper-class boys and girls, in contrast, stayed in school much longer, and thus were minors until their early twenties. Sex also made a difference, especially in the upper classes, because boys moved on to university or work, while their sisters remained children of the house until marriage. Childhood lengthened during the course of the nineteenth century, too, so late Victorian childhoods were different from early Victorian ones. These difficulties mean that any discussion of Victorian children is contingent on many factors. As a convenience, this book uses the school-leaving age at the end of the century—fourteen—as the cutoff point for defining childhood but will also consider the differences of class and sex frequently in the following pages.

As this problem indicates, the history of children and childhood is distinct from the history of any other minority group. Unlike divisions based on race, gender, or sexual orientation, divisions based on age are both universal and temporary. In other words, every adult has had a childhood, but every adult has also grown out of it. As a minority, then, children have special difficulties in appealing for change or reform, as exploited children in one decade may be the exploiting adults in the next. (Although parents frequently wanted their children to have better lives, they often had little choice in the matter.) Interpretations of childhood, then, are contested and complex and are often cyclical rather than linear; the story of the child does not often make a simple narrative. All the same, the history of childhood has a resonance for all readers precisely because all can relate to the challenges, transitions, and frustrations of being young and vulnerable. This book will try to include the many changes over time as well as the universal experiences of childhood, but the balance between these two factors is always tenuous.

Another problem for the historian is that the Victorian child has a special appeal, because of both the dramatic changes over the course of the nineteenth century and the popularity of many child characters in Victorian literature. In part because of fictional accounts, modern readers often have contradictory views of childhood in the nineteenth century. On the one hand, many see Victorian children's lives as purely negative—slaving in factories, abused by adults, dying of infectious diseases, and exploited in workhouses and prisons. On the other hand, many idealize the Victorian period as a simpler time with conservative values, such as strong religious faith and close-knit, extended families. Each of these stereotypes has some basis in fact, but both are too simplistic. Most lives were mixes of good and bad that avoided either of these extremes. This book takes a thematic and social history approach in an effort to include the multiplicity of experiences, but readers should keep in mind that myths about childhood exert a powerful pull on the contemporary imagination. In other words, one should not read current expectations of childhood into a different context. A modern child's reaction to hard work, brutal discipline, or hunger and cold would be more extreme than a child unaccustomed to anything else. The hardships were real, but the effects varied, depending on the child's expectations.

SOURCES AND STRUCTURE

Victorian Childhoods relies both on secondary works by historians and auto-biographies and biographies of the children themselves. Autobiographies, of course, are limited as a source, because most are written years after the fact, and authors often wished to make themselves look better or genuinely confused memories and events. In addition, an adult's assessment of the happiness or otherwise of childhood is relative to his or her experiences later in life. Thus, I have used autobiographies to illustrate points made by historians working from many additional sources rather than standing on their own. In addition, I have read a large number, as the overall patterns will be more reliable than individual incidents. I have also included some autobiographies from the early nineteenth and early twentieth centuries, encompassing the broader definition of the Victorian era discussed previously; this highlights change over time and also allows study of wider experiences, because otherwise I would have few working-class or female autobiographies. This book takes the position that

Victorians sentimentalized childhood, as in this image of a child at prayer. The romantic view of children as naturally innocent contrasted with the Evangelical assumption that children were sinful, but both could agree on the importance of parental oversight and religion in children's lives. "Children's Thankfulness," in Robert Aris Willmott, *English Sacred Poetry* (London: Routledge, Warne, & Routledge, 1863), 294.

a history from below is invaluable. Rather than a history of narratives and discourses of childhood, this book is told from the child's point of view and emphasizes the experience of growing up during the nineteenth century. Modern Western society reveres and idealizes childhood; children are the center of family life, the economy, and political discussions. In all these things, the Victorians were highly different from, yet also precursors to, twenty-first-century concerns.

This study begins with a chapter on the most important institution for any child, the family. It centers on the experiences of babyhood through adolescence, divided by class and sex. Family life, because it was the most idealized part of childhood in the Victorian period, was also the one in which disillusionment was the most possible. Relationships with mothers, fathers, siblings, and other kin were all vital to a child's development. Children's roles in the family helped shape their opportunities in other institutions; elder children had fewer options than younger ones, boys had more than girls, and well-off children had more than the poor. Nevertheless, the most important issue in family life was whether a child had a sense of belonging; most families had lines of obligation that were both vertical and horizontal. Children, in fact, were crucial to the smooth working of the family economy and often continued to support their families years after gaining employment.

Chapter 2 concentrates on the other major socializing force in children's lives, the school. Over the course of the nineteenth century, both the quality and the quantity of schooling increased for most children, but the role of school in children's lives remained less significant than in modern times. Only a minority used education to advance economically; the vast majority stopped schooling as soon as possible to go to work. Throughout the century, in fact, Britons debated the advisability of requiring children to go to school for a set number of years rather than laboring full time. Thus, the third chapter centers on children's work in the nineteenth century, one of the best-known but least-understood aspects of Victorian life. This chapter points up class differences most distinctly, as middle- and upper-class children did not take employment until they had finished with secondary school, while poor children worked as early as the age of seven or eight. Still, child labor was not new in the Industrial Revolution, nor did most children work in factories. What changed, then, were the types of labor and the visibility of children in dangerous occupations. As a result of a number of factors, the British Parliament passed acts to regulate child labor over the course of the century. Most were limited in scope and impossible to enforce, but they did help shape the debate over the suitability of having young children working long hours. In the end, most children completed between three and six years of schooling before full-time work, but they had part-time jobs while doing so.

The amount of discipline in children's lives was great, from parents, employers, and teachers. Still, children found time for imagination and play, the subject of chapter 4. The amount of leisure a child had varied mostly by class, but older children also had less leisure time than did younger ones, and sometimes girls had less than boys because of gendered domestic duties. Even the poorest child, though, had a few toys and books, and over time, Victorian businesses began to devote entire industries to children's needs. The late-Victorian period saw the growth of department stores and mass readership in popular literature, both of which influenced children's playtime. All the same, play was not entirely frivolous in this period; much of the literature and games was educational, and even well-off children were not spoiled. The Victorian period, then, saw only faint beginnings of the child-centered economy and society common today.

Instead, the Victorians believed in filling leisure hours with improving activities, including religious and patriotic organizations and games, the subject of

Over the course of the century, children had more time for play, even if they had to
improvise the equipment. The children in this illustration made a swing out of a lamppost
and rope. This image is surprisingly happy, given that it is from a book about "street arabs,"
a term usually reserved for homeless children. From Dorothy Stanley, *London Street Arabs*
(London: Cassell & Co., 1890).

chapter 5. Compared with secular societies today, the Victorians were highly
religious. Both England and Scotland had state churches, the Anglican Church
in England and the Presbyterian Kirk in Scotland. Both were Protestant denominations, though the Anglican Church had more ritual and hierarchy. Non-
Anglican Protestants in England, called "Dissenters" or "Nonconformists," included Baptists, Methodists, and Congregationalists. By the nineteenth century,

Britain tolerated the open worship of all religious groups, including Catholics and Jews, but restricted office holding to Anglicans for some decades because of a required loyalty oath. All legal disabilities against Catholics were removed in 1829 and for Jews in 1858; from that time on, all denominations could serve in government and attend university on the same footing (though atheists did not get similar relief until 1888). Thus, a child's experience within his or her religion was most influenced by the religiosity of the parents and the informal pressure of neighbors rather than the law. By the late nineteenth century, fewer families were fervently religious and church attendance had declined, but religion remained vitally important. Large numbers of children attended Sunday school, and even nonreligious parents married in the church and baptized their children. In addition, the late-Victorian period partly substituted fervent nationalism for religious enthusiasm, particularly in imperialist groups like the Boy Scouts and through organized sports. The emphasis on empire and jingoism made for new holidays, like Empire Day, and popular support for troops during late-Victorian conflicts acted as a unifying force in ways that, in theory, overcame differences of class, religion, nationality, or gender.

The first five chapters, then, give an overview of major aspects of so-called normal childhoods, ones that followed more or less regular patterns. Chapter 6, in contrast, turns to atypical boys and girls, those who lived in state institutions for most of their lives. The two most important state-run organizations in the nineteenth century were the workhouse and the prison. Workhouses served pauper children, those whose parents could not or would not support them. Children in workhouses may well have had more to eat than those outside, but these institutions were grim places to live given the Victorian stigmatization of poverty. Similarly, early Victorians made little distinction between children and adults in the treatment of criminals and might sentence children as young as seven to prison terms or to transportation to the colonies. Over time, conditions in both institutions improved. Nevertheless, the difficulties of children without traditional families indicate the vital importance of a family to a child's development. Many institutionalized children suffered lifelong difficulties from their sense of not having a right to exist, and only limited reforms benefited them. Victorian authorities feared that lessening the shame of pauperism or crime would result in increased laziness and violence, results deemed more serious than occasional psychological harm to any individual child.

In part because of this attitude, one can make a plausible argument that the Victorians did not serve children well, wasting talent and potential along the way. However, the first and often most intense critics of the Victorian attitude toward children were the Victorians themselves, and many of these critics took decisive action to make things better. Thus, the last chapter of this book looks at the child-saving efforts of numerous men and women and how much they accomplished. Though these reformers retained strong class and gender biases, they achieved an impressive array of legal reforms and created scores of associations to benefit children. By 1900, arguments about the importance of rearing healthy and educated future subjects were commonplace, and the Victorian state intervened in the lives of children in unprecedented ways. Both good and bad consequences flowed from this fact, but undoubtedly fewer children faced starvation or neglect by the beginning of World War I than at the end of the Napoleonic conflicts a century earlier.

Many historians debate what these changes meant. Did the Victorians pioneer a new attitude toward children and childhood? Or did they build on long traditions of concern for children? How much was a romantic view of childhood, and how much was a continuation of Evangelical religious beliefs? No one century can claim a discovery of childhood; historians have found varying attitudes toward children from medieval times to the twentieth century. On many issues, Victorians continued innovations of the early modern period, especially the eighteenth century; in addition, many Victorians retained their old-fashioned views of children and tolerated neglect and cruelty that would be unacceptable now. Few modern Western states, for instance, would allow the levels of child hunger and adolescent employment still common in 1900, nor would they shame children for being illegitimate or disabled. All the same, the Victorian era was crucial to the development of modern childhood. The amount of attention to children's needs, the range and number of reforms, and the many parliamentary acts to increase the legal rights of children all point to the significance of the nineteenth century in improving children's status. In other words, even if the ideas or impulses were not new, their implementation and reach were innovative and had far-reaching effects. As a result, the experiences recounted in the following pages help to give a history and context to contemporary child rearing; like the nineteenth century, the twentieth century was both a continuation of and reaction against the era that preceded it.

s in the early part of Victoria's reign were large, but most were
composing two generations, parents and children). Because of lower
tancy, few children knew their grandparents well and even fewer lived
e generations in a household. Thus, the large families of the early
h century were due to the high birthrate; women born between 1781
had an average of six children each. Later in the century, the birthrate
by roughly half, most of this reduction occurring in affluent families.
nce, the average birthrate for mothers in Hampstead, a fashionable part
n, declined 30 percent between 1880 and 1900; in Poplar, a working-
rict, the decline was only 6 percent.[2] The typical family, then, contained
and a widely varying number of children, depending on class and
on. Some households might also include other kin, such as an unmarried
a grandparent, but more often servants (in the upper classes) or lodgers
lower classes) joined the nuclear family if its members did not live

ORKING-CLASS FAMILY

within families varied sharply between classes. Working-class women
always gave birth at home, often with the aid of a midwife rather than
r. Newly born babies entered households ruled by economic difficulties.
omes were small, difficult to keep clean, and had minimal furniture,
cial room for a baby was impossible. Instead, infants stayed with their
s a good deal of the time. Breast milk was by far the most economic food,
hers nursed children for at least six months and sometimes for two years.
tion, mothers carried babies with them as they did their chores, feeding
whenever they cried, and keeping them in the parents' room at night.
e all this attention, infant mortality was high. In poor districts of towns,
cent of babies died before the age of one, and 25 percent of children were
y five years old. If a child survived past five, life expectancy increased,
ral children were slightly better off in this regard. Still, as late as 1900,
cent of babies died in the first year in London, ten times the number in
nporary times. Children's health improved after 1850, but babies were
rable to fatal infections until the twentieth century. Cholera, smallpox,
bing cough, diphtheria, typhus, scarlet fever, and tuberculosis all remained
rous despite improvements in sanitation and health care.[3]
e second stage in a child's development was the transition from baby to
er, a difficult and sometimes perilous period. What moved a child out of
hood was usually the birth of a younger sibling. This new infant absorbed
ilk of the mother's care, while the older boy or girl became the ex-baby,
umatic event in some children's lives. A. S. Jaspar (b. 1906), remembered
ief when his mother had a new baby: she "told me I would have to sleep
my sister Jo' as I was now getting a 'big boy.' . . . I cried and cried my eyes
Eventually, his sister reconciled him to the change, but he never forgot

1

Children and the

Myths about the Victorian family are almost as
American West. Many regard the institution as
of dutiful children and loving parents. Others se
rigidly patriarchal, unloving, and riddled with
Both views, though too generalized, contain som
tremendous variety of family lives during Que
bad, families were the most important factor in a
things influenced the upbringing of children, in
urban settings, presence or absence of extended
gender. In particular, a child's experience depend
status of the family and on the child's sex, for bot
his or her future prospects.

As Claudia Nelson demonstrated in her volume in
Victorian ideology of the family, permeated the cult
the middle classes but eventually influencing all. Fat
homes, providing financially and acting as the ult
tended to the emotional and physical needs of the
own desires for others' well-being. Victorians partic
as ennobling and stressed the importance of women
children, but fathers also took an active interest in th
the other hand, were dutiful, obedient, and thankful
and care. In short, all worked together toward a har
life. This ideal, obviously, was possible only for the m
poor mothers and fathers had limited time and resour
was a goal toward which many families worked, and
children in their assessments of their own childhoods

12

Famili
nuclear (
life expe
with thr
nineteen
and 1831
lowered
For insta
of Lond
class dis
parents
generati
aunt or
(in the
alone.

THE W

Life
almost
a docto
Poor h
so a sp
mothe
so mot
In addi
them
Despit
20 per
gone l
and ru
15 pe
conter
vulne
whoo
dang

Th
toddl
baby
the b
a tra
his g
with
out.'

that first major step away from infancy.[4] Mothers also had trouble controlling toddlers, who were learning to walk and were far more likely to get hurt than were babes in arms. Some mothers tied toddlers to their high chairs or locked them in small rooms for hours at a time to avoid accidents. Moreover, children were also more likely to be under the care of siblings when they reached two or three years old, which put a great deal of responsibility on older children. Eventually, children grew enough to have some freedom before school and/or work claimed them. Probably the most carefree time in children's lives were the years between three and six, when they were old enough to walk, talk, and play but still too young for the most onerous chores.

As children grew older, they became aware of their surroundings and physical needs. Lack of comfort was standard for poor children throughout the century. Urban families lived in unsanitary row houses or rented rooms in tenements or basements. In the 1840s, these rookeries in newly industrial towns were notorious centers of disease; lack of running water and indoor privies meant that cleanliness was all but impossible. Rural families were not much better off; many tenants rented small, run-down farm cottages. Though they had more access to fresh air, they too suffered from substandard housing and lack of indoor plumbing. In short, in both city and country, large families squeezed into tight spaces with minimal privacy. Most families had few beds, so the children slept together, sometimes on pallets in the kitchen. Houses were also full of insects and had little effective heat or light.

Other discomforts were also common. Though children wore a great deal of clothing, most of it was used (often handed down from older siblings) and carefully patched and darned. Good shoes were particularly hard to find. Many poor children went barefoot or wore wooden clogs; younger siblings had to wear their brothers' and sisters' castoffs, even if they fit poorly. Warm coats were all but unknown, so children were cold all winter, especially those in northern England and Scotland. Nor did many children eat well. Large families and small incomes meant that the family ate potatoes, bread, cheese, and tea for most meals, though Sunday dinners were usually more lavish. In homes with unemployed or absent fathers, the food was even scarcer and less nutritious. One complaint common to almost all working-class autobiographies was the constant, low-level hunger, and, as a result, autobiographers' most sensual descriptions were about food. Though some improvement in living standards occurred over the course of the century (the low point was the 1840s), the dips in the business cycle and the long agricultural depression of the late-Victorian period meant that the majority of children lived in poor environments.

In these circumstances, a child's well-being depended on the ability of the parents to make ends meet. Unlike in affluent families, both working-class parents often contributed to the family income, though the mother perhaps worked only part-time. The father was away from the house for long periods, so he could be a distant figure to his children. Mothers, then, were the towering figures of their children's lives. Mothers had the unenviable task of keeping the home and children clean, housed, and fed, on whatever portion of the husband's earnings he gave her. This was usually an immense struggle, involving hard work and much sacrifice; even at the end of the century, poor women in London had to keep their children fed and housed on around a pound a week, the barest subsistence for a large family. As a result, though working-class parents certainly loved their children, they rarely expressed their emotions openly, and they were sparing with praise or physical affection. Instead, they proved their love through their hard work.

Unsurprisingly, then, children's first major memories were of their mothers working ceaselessly in the house, providing food, caring for babies, sewing the clothes, and tending the sick. In addition, poor mothers worked part-time outside the home or slaved in home industries like matchbox making or laundering. Many mothers sacrificed their own health to feed their broods, and the children noticed. Many autobiographies record children's strong attachments to their mothers; even if they received little overt love, they felt obligated to someone who worked so hard for them. Thomas Okey, born in 1852, described his mother's workload as "heroic" because "all the work of the house, the nursing and care of the children in health and sickness, the providing, the preparation and the cooking of the food, the making and repairing of the clothing, and, hardest of all, the balancing of the domestic budget, fell on her." Numerous examples exist of children who remembered their mothers as pillars of strength who held the family together through countless hardships. George Ratcliffe, born 1863, insisted, "There have, of course, been millions of good mothers, but somehow I have never been able to repress my feelings that my mother was the very best of them all. Quietly, she went about her work . . . and at night time, when we were all together, she seemed like a mother hen gathering her chickens under her wing."[5]

Despite the children's loyalty, most mothers had faults and limitations. Overworked and exhausted, they could not always find the energy to be loving and kind. Kathleen Woodward, born in London in 1896, had a deep bond with her mother, but she seldom received open affection or caresses, explaining

[My mother] sweated and laboured for her children, equally without stint or thought, but was utterly oblivious to any need we might cherish for sympathy in our little sorrows, support in our strivings. She simply was not aware of anything beyond the needs of our bodies . . . She had no love to give us and, thank God, she never pretended what she did not feel; but children miss the presence of love and wilt, when they are not embittered, in its absence. At home it was always wintry.[6]

Even children who revered their mothers admitted that they could be harsh or indifferent to their children's needs for individual attention. In addition, parenting commonly included slaps and even beatings of young children; mothers assumed that children needed strict discipline. Mothers showed their love by

This postcard from around 1900 shows a mother with her four children.
The children are dressed in their Sunday best, the boys in matching outfits
and the girls with ribbons in their hair. Mothers were the center of family
life in the working-class home, and most children's earliest memories were
of their "mums." Collection of the author.

providing food and paying the rent every week but seldom with words or
tenderness. Many children eventually understood this, as the mother's vital
role made her the center of home life, whether or not she had an emotional
connection with all of her children.

Fathers had important family roles, too, mainly as providers. Technically, they were the heads of the households, but men worked long hours and also spent much of their leisure time in pubs. As a result, children had less contact with them. Arthur Harding, born in 1886 in the desperately poor Jago district of London, explained, "When I was young I didn't see much of father. He wasn't home much and when he was at home you tried to keep out of his way. He only lived for himself." Men had special privileges as breadwinners; for example, some had armchairs in the sitting room that they alone could use, and others demanded quiet at the dinner table or when they wanted to rest. Grace Foakes (b. 1901), who was fond of her father, nevertheless remembered him as distant; her clearest memory of him was when he slapped her in the face when she accidentally woke him from his Sunday nap by singing in the sitting room.[7]

The rampant alcohol abuse that was a common part of working-class life did not help to endear some fathers to their children either, and fathers were far more likely to be alcoholics than mothers. Fathers' drinking led to violence, and it meant that the family had less money for food and other necessities. Many poor children remembered fearing their alcoholic (and sometimes abusive) fathers and sympathizing with their mothers who fought to preserve some of the family income from the pub. A few children even coaxed drunken fathers to bed several nights a week, as a matter of course. Grace Foakes's best friend Winifred persuaded her drunken father to bed at the age of ten: "talking to him all the while as if he were a baby, she took off his clogs and socks and led him into the bedroom, where she managed to sit him on the bed and undress him." Then, Winifred played with Grace until the latter had to go home, as if nothing untoward had occurred.[8] Some children's perceptions of both parents were indelibly marked by their fathers' alcohol abuse, as the following passage by A. S. Jaspar shows:

> What a tower of strength my mother was! There was no help from my father; he carried on in his own drunken way and had no feeling for any of us. To us, the children, he somehow didn't exist. We seldom saw him. It was only at week-ends that his presence was felt. He would start on us over something trivial and we would go and stand round Mum. We knew we were safe when she was around.[9]

For all these reasons, fathers were less well remembered than mothers, though, of course, experiences were so different that exceptions occurred.

The majority of children, then, whatever their sex, were closer to their mothers than to their fathers. Nevertheless, relationships between children and each parent were sometimes gendered. Sons predominated in descriptions of idealized mothers; although daughters also felt bound to their mothers, they were more realistic about them. Daughters worked in the home and so knew their mothers intimately and with more complexity. In addition, as boys grew older they began challenging their fathers more, which led to conflicts, especially if the fathers were drunken or unemployed. Still, the gender roles were complex. Some working-class girls left home early, rebelling against fathers they considered failures. Interestingly, tender fathers also received criticism for not being firm enough in the home. Hannah Mitchell (b. 1871), daughter of a Derbyshire farmer, described her father as gentle and kind, but he did nothing to protect his children from their mother's wrath:

> My father always seemed to me one of nature's gentlemen. . . . His only weakness was his submission to mother's temper, which grew worse with the advent of each child. She would fall into violent passions about the merest trifles and drive us all out of the house for hours; sometimes we would have to spend the night in the barn sleeping on the hay. My father seemed totally unable to combat these storms, or even to protect us. He was always the first to leave the house when they broke out, and the last to return. . . . He was so kind a parent, so gentle in sickness, so indulgent in letting us off some of the hard work which even children had to do on these remote farms sixty or seventy years ago, but he could not shield us from my mother's virago-like temper.[10]

For whatever reason, children were often more ambivalent about fathers than about mothers, but sons and daughters did have different reactions, depending on the circumstances.

Because of the large families, children received limited attention from their parents, for good or ill. Mothers practiced benign neglect, shooing children out of the house and expecting siblings to look after one another. The only time that children received undivided attention was when they were sick, a common occurrence in an age of poor hygiene and limited medical care. When children fell ill, death was a real possibility, but most children were too young to be afraid. Instead, many rather enjoyed being sick, because they could lie in bed and get all their mothers' attention. Grace Foakes, who grew up in a tenement in London, liked feeling unwell; she could sleep late, and "Mother would come and give me hot bread and milk sprinkled with sugar. It never failed to make me feel better. I think the extra bit of loving helped me as much as the bread and milk." Even George Acorn's mother, not an affectionate woman, showed a different side when his brother fell deathly ill in the late-Victorian period. She worked tirelessly to earn money for him and comforted the boy in his pain in a show of tenderness that astonished her eldest son.[11]

As with parent-child relationships, children's treatment in the family varied according to their sex and age. Girls did more domestic chores than boys and usually received less schooling. Especially the oldest girl had the responsibility to be "little mother" and help care for younger siblings. Arthur Harding's older sister, Harriet, called "The Mighty," was the rock of his family, taking care of her brothers and sisters and eventually running the house herself:

I was brought up more by my sister than I was by my mother. My
earliest recollection is of being taken round by her. Later she used to take
me on errands and to look after me in the street . . . when she began selling
lemons in the market she had a bit of money and she would buy me treats
sometimes, and take me to the theatre. When my mother began drinking
she kept the house together.[12]

Nevertheless, any older child had to mind the younger ones at some point,
and boys changed diapers and fed babies as well as watched toddlers. Many
times the oldest children grew weary of the expectations their parents had of
them in caring for younger siblings, a new one of which seemed to come every
one or two years. Birth order determined the level of responsibility as well as
the amount of schooling and affection a child could expect; younger siblings
minded other children less and received more attention. The oldest children of
any family had the shortest childhoods; not only did they act as babysitters,
but they also went to work as quickly as possible to bring in more income.
Once several children were earning, the mother's difficulties in making ends
meet significantly decreased, so the youngest also enjoyed the improved family
income.

Though burdened with adult responsibilities, older siblings sometimes welcomed younger children as playmates and enjoyed taking care of them. The
key to the relationship was often how close the children were in age. Usually,
children bonded with siblings who were only a few years apart. Alice Linton
(b. 1908) was best friends with her brother Albert, who was three years her elder. He went everywhere with her and "was always kind and generous." Similarly, Emma Smith's closest childhood companion was her brother Harry, who
was two years younger than she (both were born in the 1890s). Of course,
children did not always get along perfectly with their siblings, even when they
were close. Jealousies and difficulties in tight quarters and limited incomes were
inevitable. Emma loved Harry, but she admitted that the two of them bickered
at every meal, convinced that the other had the larger share. Unsurprisingly,
then as now, some older siblings were bullies or bossy, and younger ones were
sometimes spoiled. But most autobiographies emphasize the crucial role of close
siblings in making one's way in life. Brothers and sisters were the first playmates and protectors when necessary. Especially older siblings often assumed
responsibility for younger ones, and they continued to send money to their
parents to help rear the family after they had left home.[13]

Though some conflicts emerged, all members of poor families worked together to keep the family fed and sheltered. They had a sense of obligation to
one another in both their vertical and horizontal relationships. Parents carried
the heaviest burden, but they expected their children to help as soon as possible, and brothers and sisters accepted their roles. Paid employment, discussed
in chapter 3, was the most useful addition. But all children had chores around
the house as soon as they were able, fetching water, running errands, or helping do laundry. If children lived on farms, they were especially likely to start

Older sisters often helped mothers care for babies and toddlers, as in this image. Note the baby doll on the floor, and that the child is in a cradle in the parents' bedroom, indicating that this is a better-off home. Siblings were crucial socializing figures in all classes, however. From Dorothy Stanley, *London Street Arabs* (London: Cassell & Co., 1890).

chores early, but all poor children did so. Without family cooperation, most working-class households would have faced grim times indeed.

Work in the house was always gendered to some extent and became more so late in the period. Early in the century, boys (and some girls) went to work full-time as early as the age of seven. And even in the 1890s, when child labor was restricted, boys found part-time jobs by the time they were nine or ten years old. In contrast, girls largely did domestic duties unless they were the only children in the home. Though both sexes worked hard, then, privileges—reduced chores and more prestige—went only to wage earners. In other words, usually boys' workdays had a definite end, and they also got pocket money; girls, in contrast, did unpaid housework into the evening, even if they had other jobs. Nor was such work an easy option in an age with few labor-saving devices. Hannah Mitchell's mother, for instance, expected superhuman efforts of her small daughters; the sons, on the other hand, got to rest after their day's work, as she explained:

> It was a hard life for us all, especially the girls, as my mother was a harder taskmaster than my father. She never seemed to realize how small and weak we were. She made us sweep and scrub, turn the heavy mangle on washing days and the still heavier churn on butter-making days. Stone floors had to be whitened, brasses and steel fire-irons polished every week. On winter evenings there was sewing by hand, making and mending shirts and underwear. At eight years old my weekly task was to darn all the stockings for the household, and I think my first reactions to feminism began at this time when I was forced to darn my brothers' stockings while they read or played cards or dominoes.[14]

Children's reactions to the work expected of them depended on its intensity but also on their feelings for their parents. Those with troubled relationships with mothers and fathers resented the tasks set before them, as Hannah did. Similarly, George Acorn did not appreciate the constant financial demands of his parents who beat him unmercifully and never supported any of his interests.[15] In contrast, children who revered their parents, or even just one of their parents, were happy to contribute. Many children sympathized especially with their mothers, as they saw the daily struggle to keep the family fed and housed. More than one child felt proud of any action that eased the burden on his or her "mum."

Both parents and children made heroic efforts to support large broods. Nevertheless, many children experienced the loss of a family member before they left home. Life expectancy in 1850 was only forty years; in 1912, it had risen to fifty-two for men and fifty-five for women, numbers that were still relatively low.[16] Thus, orphans and half orphans were common. The loss of a father usually meant a tremendous economic struggle for a widow with children and even, at times, the breakup of the home, but the loss of the mother was often just as severe. One reason that remarriage was so common in this period, in fact, was that children needed both parents; only if the eldest daughter took over the role of "little mother" did fathers wait to remarry. Many children, then, grew up with stepparents and often stepbrothers and sisters as well. The Victorians, in short, had many blended families. Stories of wicked stepparents abound in Victorian literature, and some evidence supports this anxiety; for example, criminal cases disclose nasty instances of violence against stepchildren. However, loving stepparents also appear in many sources, and most were similar to birth parents in their dealings with children. At the least, the timely remarriage of a parent meant the home stayed together.

The loss of siblings was not as disruptive to the household as the loss of a parent, but it was emotionally difficult. Walter Littler, born in 1882, was the fourteenth of sixteen children, including two sets of twins. Between 1867 and 1879, eight of the children died, all but one from infectious diseases (scarlet fever and measles). Walter, born after this horrific period, does not record his parents' grief, but it must have been profound. Similarly, Grace Foakes's mother gave birth to fourteen children, but only five survived childhood, three boys and two girls, an almost unimaginable loss to modern eyes.[17] Parents faced such grief with resignation, but when siblings died, children were both frightened and saddened, a state sometimes aggravated by the Victorian custom of keeping the body in the parlor or kitchen until burial. The death of a contemporary was a shock, one that forced children to face the reality of mortality. Alice Foley's brother Jimmy died of appendicitis when he was sixteen and she was a few years younger. Her sadness was compounded by religious fears, as the nuns at her school told her Jimmy would be in purgatory for a long time because he had missed Mass the week before he died. Alice was sick with grief for weeks.[18]

In working-class districts, parenting was often communal. People in urban areas lived in overcrowded housing, so neighbors looked after one another's children. Some children also knew and appreciated their grandparents and other extended kin. Again, these relationships with the older generation were more common at the end of the century, when adult life spans had increased. Allan Jobson, for instance, born in the late nineteenth century, visited his mother's parents in the country every year for three weeks to see the blooming of the cowslips; like modern children, he looked forward to these trips, partly because he loved the farm so much.[19] Still, extended kin had limited responsibility for children. Sometimes grandparents or aunts and uncles (or even neighbors) took in orphans, but other times relatives simply could not afford to do so. In fact, poverty was so endemic in old age that grandparents often needed help themselves. Thus, parents had the main responsibility for any children they brought into the world. In other words, children without responsible parents had extremely difficult childhoods; family, for good or ill, determined much about a poor child's well-being.

MIDDLE- AND UPPER-CLASS FAMILY LIFE

The middle and upper classes in Victorian England had both the income and the leisure to pursue family lives as they pleased. The nobility and gentry were distinct from the middle class with respect not just to income but also to domestic customs. Noble families lived on large estates, had armies of servants, and often left the day-to-day care of children to nannies and nurses. Some mothers did not even breast-feed infants but hired wet nurses to do so, though social pressure for mothers to nurse their own babies mounted during the nineteenth century. In short, many well-off children, even infants, saw their parents for only a few hours a day. As they got older, children saw their parents at specially designated times, such as during the midday meal or in the parlor in the afternoon. This is not to say that parents did not love their children, but quite often both mothers and fathers became close to them only after they were grown. In this world, adults were the important figures, and the rhythm of the household followed the parents' schedule. The children's closest relationships, then, were often with their nannies. Still, even here the notions of domesticity began to penetrate over time; many children in landed families recorded loving relationships with their parents by the late-Victorian period. But from babyhood until they left home, they had parenting from many sources.

In contrast, the middle-class family matched most closely the domestic ideal for Victorians—the loving, hardworking father; the nurturing, angelic mother; obedient and dutiful sons and daughters; and the hearth surrounded by the glow of mutual affection. Few families lived up to such a high standard, but many tried to emulate it. In particular, children growing up in the middle classes expected a great deal of attention from a fond mother, whose primarily role in life was to rear her children. Middle-class mothers breast-fed their children if they were able to do so and oversaw their development from infancy to adulthood. They had this luxury because they could afford to hire servants to do other domestic chores and because they did not have to work for wages themselves. Although many fathers worked long hours away from home, they were also vitally concerned with their children's development and welfare. Like the working class, the middle class wanted to train children to obedience and duty, but they were more likely to be openly affectionate while doing so.

Most of these children grew up in nuclear families but with at least one servant in the household. Despite the drop in the birthrate after 1880, middle- and upper-class families were large for most of Victoria's reign. Famously, William Gladstone, the Liberal prime minister, had eight children with his wife, Catherine Glynne (married 1839). Her sister Mary married Lord Lyttleton the same year and had twelve of her own, which meant that when the two families socialized, they had twenty children underfoot. Because of remarriages, blended families were also common. Alfred Graves had five children with his first wife (married 1874) and five more with his second wife (married 1891), which made for quite a brood when they were all together.[20] Nevertheless, the drop in the birthrate occurred first in better-off homes, and the trend was clear by 1900. Many families were still large, but middle- and upper-class children were more likely to be only children, or one of two or three, than were their counterparts in the lower classes. Schooling for these children was expensive, and girls required dowries for marriage while boys needed help getting into professions. Thus, the upper classes were quicker to limit births.

This is a typical depiction of the mother-child bond, a sacred one
to the Victorian middle class. Middle-class mothers were openly affectionate with their children and pursued close relationships with
them. In return, children remembered their mothers in idyllic terms.
"To a Child Embracing His Mother," in Robert Aris Willmott,
English Sacred Poetry (London: Routledge, Warne, and Routledge,
1863), 280.

Unsurprisingly, children in these classes grew up with much better housing,
even rooms of their own, and did not suffer hunger on a regular basis. They
had new clothing as they grew and decent shoes. Moreover, they had fewer
responsibilities in general, both because servants did the housework and because
they had no need to go to work at young ages. In short, they had hours of leisure
unknown to poor children. Still, most parents, especially in the middle classes,
were determined not to spoil their children, so they did not indulge every
whim; in fact, most parents encouraged children to self-denial, self-control,
and religiosity. Middle-class children received a great deal of attention from
both parents, but this did not mean that they got all they desired. In addition,
because of close monitoring, they had far less freedom of action than did their
poor counterparts.

For different reasons, children in the middle and upper classes often idolized their parents. Middle-class children spent leisure time with mothers and fathers and developed close bonds, but even noble children who rarely saw their parents would often love them passionately, as idols worshipped from afar. As in the lower classes, mothers received more devotion than fathers. Victorian gender ideology stressed that women should defer to the interests of others, a self-abnegation that made mothers beloved. H. A. L. Fisher (b. 1865), a future Liberal cabinet member, described his upper-class mother in a typical passage as "a saint. A more selfless unworldly being never drew breath. Her life was a perpetual surrender of ease and comfort to the service of others."[21] In addition to their self-denial, middle-class women, especially, took mothering seriously. Few of them had numerous servants; some had only one, a maid-of-all-work. In consequence, they reared their children themselves; those who did have many servants at least oversaw the child care. The vast majority were their children's first teachers and tended them in hurts or illnesses. Mothers were also vitally involved in religious training; those with strong faiths had much anxiety about their children's spiritual lives.

Fathers, again, had the role of providing for the family and acting as the ultimate authority. They were revered as the heads of the households, and their needs came first. They could be strict, especially with sons, but they were also loving, for example tending children when they were sick. In addition, fathers were sometimes the more playful parent. Sylvia McCurdy (b. 1876) remembered her father taking his children on outings and playing blindman's bluff with them—without the blindfold: "He used to pretend he couldn't see you and when he caught one of you he said you were someone else.... It was our favorite game and we played it every Christmas and birthday until my mother said it must stop as it was too exhausting for father." Eileen Baillie, the daughter of a vicar in the Edwardian period (1901–1910), adored her father as "the instigator of all our amusements and the originator of all sorts of adventures." Middle-class fathers were openly emotional with their daughters, on whom they doted, but they could also be close to sons. Eric Bligh (b. ca. 1886) was "passionately devoted" to his father, a doctor, and they had a warm relationship, reinforced by daily time together. Thus, though some children reported the stereotypical distant Victorian patriarch, others were close to both their parents.[22]

Especially in upper-class households, servants shared the parenting chores with mothers and fathers. For many aristocratic children, their nannies were the centers of their lives. Famously, Winston Churchill (b. 1874) adored his nanny, Mrs. Everest, who gave him the love and attention he did not receive from either of his admired but distant parents. Nannies could be strict, but they became attached to children under their care and gave unconditional love. They took the most difficult and labor-intensive parts of child rearing from mothers, allowing the latter to focus on early education, religious instruction, and play. Unfortunately, nannies were employees, not members of the family, and thus

Middle-class fathers took parenting duties seriously and wanted close
relationships with sons and daughters. In addition, fathers could also be
fun parents. In this sentimental picture, "An Autumn Sabbath Walk," a
father spends special time with his children in the countryside. Robert
Aris Willmott, *English Sacred Poetry* (London: Routledge, Warne, and
Routledge, 1863), 217.

they could be temporary. Eileen Baillie, the vicar's daughter, considered her
nanny "all-sufficing, constant, stable as a rock in a world of uncertainties." Yet
when her parents fell on hard times in 1913, they had to cut expenses, including
laying off the nanny. Eileen "was inconsolable for months."[23]

Parents, nannies, and nurses shared disciplining duties with respect to children. In the upper classes, physical punishment, particularly of boys, was common. Alfred Graves's father, a member of the gentry, whipped him and his
brother when they accidentally destroyed hollyhocks while gardening overen-
thusiastically. In the same household, the governess boxed the boys' ears when
they damaged the chairs in the classroom. In some families, both boys and girls
received physical chastisement.[24] Parents assumed that firm correction was a
sign of their love for their children and certainly not abusive; on the contrary,

those who spoiled their children were far more likely to encounter societal disapproval. Fathers, mothers, nurses, nannies, and even governesses all might hit children if necessary, as Agnes Hunt related in her autobiography:

> My mother and father had a firm belief in the old proverb that to spare the rod was to spoil the child, and right royally they lived up to it. Indeed, one of my first recollections is of an indignation meeting held in the schoolroom, presided over by my eldest sister, May, to consider the number of people who were allowed to beat us, and if anything could be done about it. The entrance of my mother broke up the meeting in disorder.[25]

On the other hand, many middle-class parents ruled through love and guilt rather than blows. Punishments included being locked in a cupboard, being sent to one's room, or losing pocket money. Parents also relied on religious training and repentance to impress on children the need for virtue. Molly Hughes (b. 1866) described how she tried to get their cook into trouble by telling her mother that the woman would not give her a glass of water. Her mother, rather than spanking her, made her write in her precious diary "I told a lie to-day." This was punishment enough for Molly to regret the falsehood. Laura Troubridge (b. 1858) described how her nurse "always had a birch rod hanging over the chimney-piece in the nursery, as a sort of emblem of authority, for she was never allowed to use it and could only crash it down on to the unoffending table when we disobeyed her."[26] In short, parents rarely needed crude methods of control. Their overt love for their children, and their disappointment when the children did not live up to expectations, kept boys and girls in line. G. B. Grundy (b. 1861) expressed this best in his memories of his mother:

> What made my mother's teaching so effective was the fact that her children were so absolutely devoted to her—a devotion she deserved if ever a mother did. She never showed anger. That was not necessary. I was not always a good child. I certainly never attained more than the bare average of the goodness to which young boys attain. But when my mother expressed a calm disapproval of what I had done or was doing I did not repeat or continue it.[27]

Well-off children did not face hunger or poverty, but many parents believed that they should learn to deal with hardships without demur. Agnes Hunt (b. 1867) said nothing about the two abscesses that she developed on her shoulder because "children in Victorian days were not encouraged to complain." She was equally silent about a blister on her foot; by the time her parents realized something was wrong, she had blood poisoning and ended up partially disabled. Even after this, her parents would not let her siblings fetch and carry for her; they did not want her to fall into self-pity. Similarly, Mary Carbery (b. 1867) crushed her toe under a table when she was six or seven, and when her father rushed to her, his first words were "'Never blub . . . Stand up, Bumble. Put your foot down. Now then, march.'" When Mary could not do this, her father still refused to carry her because "he thought I had better not give in." Instead, "he hopped me along the passage and landing . . . both of us singing at the top of our voices."[28] Though such behavior borders on negligence to modern eyes, Victorian parents believed they were teaching their children self-reliance and strength of character. This was also why most children got very limited pocket money, perhaps two pence a week. Parents wanted their children to learn the value of money and the importance of thrift.

Because of the presence of servants, nannies, and tutors, siblings did not have to act as parents to the younger members of the family. However, girls often did help their mothers as they got older. Edwin Waterhouse (b. 1841) recorded that his oldest sister, Ellen, was "much her mother's daughter, taking a share in household duties, and doing something towards the education of her little brothers, until a tutor was found for them." Ellen was eighteen when she took these expanded roles, though, considerably older than caregiving children in the working class. Still, if the mother died, the oldest daughter took over the household, sometimes when she was in her teens. Indeed, depending on the family and the age difference, older siblings could rule the roost. Agnes Hunt recorded that her older brothers and sisters "exercised a very rigid discipline over the younger ones." More often, though, siblings divided into groups, with those near one another in age spending the most time together. Since middle- and upper-class children had more leisure time, they formed strong bonds with their brothers and sisters, and these crossed gender lines. Francis Ommanney (b. 1903), part of the upper middle class, was closest to his sister, who was two years younger. Mary Marshall (b. 1850) had an older sister and a younger brother, and she spent most of her time with her brother, who was "my great chum."[29]

Well-off children had restrictions on their playmates; their parents did not want them associating with just any children. In addition, some lived in the countryside for at least part of the year, with only the family party around them. As a result, relationships with siblings were intense, with both good and bad consequences. Some children remembered loving relationships. Molly Hughes, the only girl in a family of five, remembered all of her older brothers with great fondness, and the boys indulged her as much as possible. Maud Ballington Booth (b. 1865) was so close to her sister Florrie that the two of them were all but inseparable, and many historians have noted the lifelong bonds of sisters. On the other hand, conflict was also common. Especially when they had greater age differences, older sisters were likely to find younger ones annoying. Eileen Baillie's sister, who was five years older, "never tired of teasing me relentlessly." Eileen suspected that the age difference was simply too great: "our relationship was inevitably one of patronage and supplication, and doubtless my infantile importunings were often tiresome."[30]

Brothers could also be close, especially if they could get into mischief together. Molly Hughes's four older brothers, for example, were all good friends and spent hours playing games together. Nevertheless, as with sisters, the intensity of the relationship could also lead to conflict, though for different reasons. Francis Ommanney was deeply hurt when his older brother refused to associate with him at their school, because of Francis's poor performance in school games. His brother, a star athlete and a prefect, could have made things much easier for Francis. Instead, he "seldom took any notice of me at all, but, when he did, it was to chase me across the junior football field and kick my bottom for not attending to the game or punch my head for leaving my gym shoes lying about the boot-hole."[31]

Gender differences were strong in the middle and upper classes. The middle class believed that men were suited to the public sphere because of their strength, intelligence, aggressiveness, and independence. Women, on the other hand, belonged in the home, and were weak, emotional, nurturing, passive, and dependent. As a result, boys and girls received different educations almost from the beginning. Most important, boys went through several transitions during their childhoods, all meant to make them "manly." Until the age of four or five, boys wore the same clothing as girls and received the same treatment. At that point, they were "breeched," meaning that they began wearing pants instead of skirts and assumed masculine roles in the house. Although breeching was less important in the late nineteenth century than it had been in previous times, the transition to school age remained vital. Boys either began studying with tutors or went away to boarding schools by the age of six or seven, pulling them away from the influence of women and into the masculine, public realm. Girls, in contrast, rarely left home to go to school until later, and their focus remained domestic.

In addition, boys had scope for exploration and rough games, while girls were supposed to be ladylike. For instance, Sylvia McCurdy recalled that her nurse scolded her for being dirty after working in the garden, because "it was natural for boys to get dirty but little ladies should like to be clean." Any girl who played too physically was considered a tomboy or hoyden, neither of which was a flattering term. And, as in the working class, girls helped around the house more than boys. Molly Hughes's mother insisted that her daughter fetch and carry for her brothers, regarding this as natural:

I suppose there was a fear on my mother's part that I should be spoilt, for I was two years younger than the youngest boy. To prevent this danger she proclaimed the rule "Boys first." I came last in all distribution of food at table, treats of sweets, and so on. I was expected to wait on the boys, run messages, fetch things left upstairs, and never grumble, let alone refuse. All this I thoroughly enjoyed, because I loved running about, and would often dash up and down stairs just to let off my spirits. Of course mother came in for some severe criticism from relations in this matter, but I have never ceased to thank her for this bit of early training.[32]

In short, boys were clearly superior to girls, and parents did not apologize for the obvious favoritism. Families spent far more on sons' educations and even on their rooms than they did on their daughters, preparing the girls to be self-sacrificing and to perpetuate the cycle into the next generation.

Both boys and girls learned these gender distinctions from a young age. Several girls noticed that men had far more freedom and longed to be boys (in contrast, I have found no examples of boys who expressed a wish to be girls). Mary Carbery prayed for years that God would turn her into a boy, only stopping when her mother told her it would never happen. Emily Lutyens (b. 1874), daughter of a diplomat, grew increasingly frustrated with the different treatment her younger brothers both expected and received, writing

> Much as I love Neville he occasionally drives me absolutely wild by his utter selfishness. It is impossible to knock into his head that it is a duty ever to think of other people. I am sure it is the ruin of boys to have sisters, for a sister is always a slave. I sometimes sigh for a family of boys and girls that I may bring them up properly, the boys waiting upon the girls instead of the girls upon the boys.[33]

On the other hand, most parents assumed that girls were superior morally, which gave them some advantages. Greville MacDonald (b. 1856) claimed that his sisters were not punished because his parents thought they were naturally good, unlike the boys in the family. His younger brothers resented this assumption, but Greville believed it. He thought men were so inferior, in fact, that he could not understand how his beloved mother could have married one.[34]

The death rate in middle-class families was considerably lower than in the working class, and these families had the resources and time to travel. Thus, they were more likely to know their extended kin, especially grandparents, aunts and uncles, and cousins. Grandparents stepped in readily whenever the parents needed help or when tragedy struck. The Troubridge children lost their parents in one six-week span in 1867, and both their maternal grandmother and paternal grandfather offered them homes. Similarly, Leah Manning's parents emigrated to Canada in 1892, when she was six. They left her, the youngest, to live with her grandparents and her three uncles, all of whom still lived at home.[35] Close relationships with relatives could help in building businesses and in finding future spouses, so there were practical and emotional reasons for extended families to stay in touch, and doing so became much easier with the development of efficient railways and the penny post.

Even in the better-off classes, parents lost children to infectious diseases and accidents, though. For example, Samuel Bligh, a doctor, lost four of his

This postcard of an older woman with children from around 1910 could
be of a mother with children but probably is of a grandmother, perhaps one
who has stepped in to help rear her grandchildren. Middle-class children
had a better chance of knowing their kin because of longer life expectancy.
Collection of the author.

eight children at young ages, his medical training unable to save them. Sylvia
McCurdy had two brothers and a younger sister, but the sister died when Sylvia
was only four; Sylvia herself had a bout of scarlet fever a few years later and was
quarantined for a month. Accidents were also surprisingly common for children
who were supposedly closely monitored. Maud Ballington Booth, daughter of

a rector, almost drowned in her bath at two (her five-year-old sister pulled her out); similarly, Alfred Graves fell into a nursery fireplace at eighteen months, and his three-year-old sister saved him.[36] Any of these accidents could have been fatal. Far more frequently, children lost one or both of their parents, as with the Troubridges. When parents knew they were dying, they took formal leave of each of the children, commending them to good behavior and saying farewell, a custom that seems gruesome to modern eyes but one that comforted the bereaved. Most families also had the consolation of religion during these terrible times, as well as support from friends and kin.

Children in the upper and middle classes had longer childhoods than their poor counterparts. Working-class children went to work as early as age seven in the beginning of Victoria's reign, and certainly by fourteen at the end. In contrast, upper- and middle-class boys and girls stayed minors for much longer. Boys went to boarding school and then to university to be fitted out for careers. Some boys might skip university to go into the family business, but rarely as early as fourteen. Girls stayed at home as "children" of the house until they married, which could be into their twenties or even longer. Rather than enter a profession, older girls helped their mothers run the house and took part in social rounds. Only if the family lost its money did sisters take jobs or learn trades, unless they were highly unusual women. In short, affluent children legally came of age at twenty-one, but they remained dependent on their parents for longer than this.

Generational conflict (e.g., between fathers and sons) was a perennial part of growing up. In the late-Victorian period, this process became overt and some-what politicized. Under the influence of the labor and women's movements of the 1880s and 1890s, some children began to question or even reject their parents' values. This process was famously highlighted in Edmund Gosse's *Father and Son*, published in 1907, in which Gosse traced the way his mental development and widening interests pulled him away from his deeply religious father. The final confrontation was one of great emotional strain for both:

> There was a morning, in the hot-house at home, among the gorgeous waxen orchids which reminded my Father of the tropics of his youth, when my forbearance or my timidity gave way.... My Father had once more put to me the customary interrogatory. Was I "walking closely with God"? Was my sense of the efficacy of the Atonement clear and sound? Had the Holy Scriptures still their full authority with me? My replies on this occasion were violent and hysterical. I have no clear rec-ollection what it was that I said,—I desire not to recall the whimpering sentences in which I begged to be let alone, in which I demanded the right to think for myself, in which I repudiated the idea that my Father was responsible to God for my secret thoughts and my most intimate convictions.[37]

Similarly, John Tosh has noted the difference in attitudes between Edward Benson, Archbishop of Canterbury in the mid-Victorian period and a firm family man, and his three sons, none of whom married.[38]

Though struggles between fathers and sons were more prominent, mothers and daughters also differed. With the advent of colleges and schools for girls and widening work and leisure opportunities, some young women broke free from the strictures of life for "proper" ladies. Most of these rebellions consisted of having careers as single women, wearing looser clothing (no corsets) and riding bicycles, or abandoning the use of chaperones. But a few women went further, becoming suffragists or labor leaders. The so-called revolt of the daughters was never as great as the public discussion indicated (few things frightened Victorians more than independent women), but alternatives to Victorian gender roles did exist by 1901. Still, these were exceptions to the rule; most middle- and upper-class children remained dutiful to their parents and followed the expected family roles until at least the First World War.

CONCLUSION

Whatever the class or gender, children's memoirs show commonalities. In all classes, other people than parents took part in rearing children, be it neighbors and siblings or nannies and nurses. Also, gender differences were vital. Girls had more domestic duties, less schooling, and more restrictions than boys. Working-class girls worked longer hours and made less money, a circumstance that made some bitter. But in the upper classes, girls' restrictions meant they had longer childhoods than their brothers. Boys might go away to boarding school as early as age seven, but girls remained at home much longer, some until they married; in short, they had far more leisure but less independence. In addition, the quality of the relationship with parents made all the difference to a child's assessment of his or her childhood. Some of the happiest memoirs are those of poor children whose parents gave them love and security despite the physical hardships, though middle-class children were more likely to idealize childhood in general.

Finally, children went through a difficult process of growing apart from their parents as they matured. In the working class, children started jobs as early as possible; for most of them, childhood ended there. But the process of leaving home was usually fraught, as parents did not want to lose the income, and children felt a strong obligation to repay their parents' efforts. In a similar way, middle-class boys had to negotiate their growing independence with respect for their fathers and mothers. This could be especially difficult with author- itative fathers, who were used to obedience and little else, which is why so many memoirs from the late-Victorian period record tensions with patriarchs. Working-class girls usually had a more abrupt ending, either marrying or going into domestic service and thus leaving the home altogether, but some of them sent money back as well. As with their brothers, poor girls left childhood much earlier than did their upper-class counterparts. Better-off women remained at home until marriage, except for a few daring women who forged careers on their own.

These examples of difficult transitions show how closely children's family lives related to the worlds of school and work. How long a child remained a child depended in part on job opportunities and educational requirements. In other words, two activities took up the bulk of a child's time during the Victorian years—education and employment. Here, too, great differences by class and gender existed but some similarities crossed these barriers.

2

School Days

Modern children in the Western world expect to go to school for a minimum of ten to twelve years, and many continue on to university to pursue undergraduate and graduate degrees. In 1837, however, most children received a minimal education, for a number of reasons. First, free schools were not always available, and poor parents could not afford to pay fees. Second, many poor children had to go to work at young ages to help support their families. Third, girls consistently received less education than boys, as they had fewer career prospects. Slowly, all these factors changed during Victoria's reign. By 1900, the majority of Victorians agreed that children belonged in school, but the move to mass education was a long and uneven process.

SCHOOLS FOR THE POOR, 1800–1850

England had no national system of schools before 1870, did not require school attendance until 1880, and did not make schooling free until 1891. Scotland, too, lacked a truly national system, though it made schooling to the age of thirteen compulsory in 1872, abolished fees in 1889, and had a longer tradition of supporting academic achievement. Nevertheless, in both countries, a child's education depended on class, sex, and generation. Early Victorians had fewer choices for schooling, and quality varied widely. Small private schools, called "dame schools," taught the most basic reading skills. Charity schools were usually associated with religious denominations; some, known as "ragged schools," were for the very poorest children and offered free food to those who attended. Almost all children went to Sunday school, which taught basic literacy and gave religious instruction (for more on this, see chapter 5). Night schools were available for those children who still had energy to take classes after a long workday. Still, all of these alternatives offered only basic skills rather than intellectual enlightenment or a path to advancement.

Most working-class parents wanted their children to learn to read and write but did not have greater aspirations for them. Children started school as early as three or four years old in England, and slightly later in Scotland, but they left school when their families needed their labor and income. The Scots often differentiated themselves from the English by stressing that their education system rewarded merit, not class privilege, and a larger percentage of poorer scholars went to university. However, there too the amount of time a child stayed in school depended on the family's economic situation and opportunities for child labor in the vicinity. Charles Shaw's education was typical of the first half of the nineteenth century. Born in 1832, he began at a dame school when he was three or four. He learned to read, but not to write, and to knit stockings. When he started work in the potteries, at age seven, his formal education was over, but he did go to Sunday school until he was ten. Tom Barclay, born in 1852, received even less education. He never attended a day school, instead going only to Sunday school as a child and night school as a teen. His part-time schooling was the result of his parents' poverty; he went to work at a mill from the age of eight. Other factors also limited formal education. Marianne Farningham's mother taught her in the 1830s, because the only school within walking distance was associated with the Church of England, and her parents were Baptists. She only went to day school when she was nine and a Baptist school opened nearby.[1]

Historians can only guess as to the number of children who went to school or how much they learned during these years. In industrial centers, literacy appeared to drop in the first half of the nineteenth century, due to child labor and the fact that the number of schools built between 1800 and 1850 did not keep up with the increasing population. In one northern industrial town, for instance, the literacy rate, measured by those who could sign marriage registers, dropped from 48 percent in 1823 to 9 percent in 1843. Going to school was not universal even without child labor. According to the 1851 census, only two million of the five million children between the ages of three and fifteen were in school. The rest were working (about six hundred thousand) or not listed at all; the latter probably received homeschooling or helped with domestic industries. Most Victorians assumed that poor children would leave school by the age of ten and did not consider that fact regrettable, citing the need for labor. As a result, early Victorians did not always have even basic literacy. The 1841 census indicated that only 67 percent of men and 51 percent of women were fully literate, which meant that they could sign their names.[2]

When children did attend school, they did not receive quality teaching. Most schools were not free, but the costs were low, so classes were large. Teachers chose older children to be monitors who helped instruct the others. Some children claimed never to have seen the schoolmaster or schoolmistress but only the monitors, whose academic abilities were limited. For instance, more

Schools available for poor people were not always high quality. Here George Bartley imagines "A London Dame School in 1870," led by an older woman of limited intellect. Note the boy in the back releasing a mouse while the teacher and her cat doze by the fire. From George C. T. Bartley, *The Schools for the People* (London: Bell & Daldy, 1871), between 500 and 501.

than seven hundred "teachers" in 1851 could not sign their own names on their reports to educational authorities; they simply put a mark. Similarly, many dame and ragged schools were little more than babysitting services. Though Scottish teachers were better educated because of Scotland's tradition of university-trained schoolmasters, their teaching was limited by the size of classes; in addition, the Gaelic-speaking Highlands and the Catholic population in Scotland often had to take whatever teachers they could get. In some areas of Wales, as in Scotland, the children did not know English and learned the most basic skills only. Robert Roberts, born in Wales in 1834, went to school when he was eleven. Out of the fifty to sixty children in the class, aged five to twenty, a mere six could read phonetically (in Welsh). The schoolmaster was energetic and caring, but the amount he covered was inevitably small.[3] Moreover, early schools often had difficulties with order. Roberts himself eventually became a teacher in Wales in the 1850s, and he found his charges thoroughly uncooperative, indeed violent. Children did not assume that school was a natural part of life any more than their parents did, and the expansion of adult discipline was a transition for both:

> [T]he Caernarvon boys were so thoroughly savage in their manners, and behaved so rudely to the "Trainers" as they called us, that our attempts at teaching them were on the whole a grievous failure, and the week at the school was a weariness of spirit. If we attempted to chastize [*sic*] any of these promising pupils, we were sure to have a crowd about us on our way

home; enraged women volleying Billingsgate, and their precious offspring volleying stones after us. Appeal to the Head Master was useless, for he would say that this unpopularity only indicated our want of efficiency as teachers.... As we saw that it was becoming intolerable, we signified to the Headmaster that we must henceforth take canes in our own hands, and fight them into good behaviour, cost what it may. We had a tremendous conflict for about a week, but our determination carried the day; and we had something like peace.[4]

EDUCATION FOR THE MASSES?

The idea that children needed basic literacy gained ground after 1850, especially when voting rights expanded to include many working-class men in the reform bills of 1867 and 1884. Victorian authorities agreed that potential voters needed to be able to read and do basic math, but reforms began slowly. Parliament gave grants to private charities to build schools in 1843 and passed a program for training teachers in 1846. As a result of a report by the Royal Commission on Popular Education in 1861, the government began the payment-by-result system in 1862 (which lasted until 1895); during these years, schools received grants depending on annual reviews of the children. In other words, schools received money according to the number of students who passed yearly exams and moved on to the next standard. Most significantly, Parliament adopted the Education Act of 1870 in England and the Education (Scotland) Act of 1872. These laws established national systems of schools so that every child lived close enough to attend one. At least one local school per area was the national or board school (overseen by an elected school board) and followed a set curriculum; these were usually associated with the established church, Anglicanism in England and Presbyterianism in Scotland. If such a school was not available, though, the local authorities had to find—or build—a substitute.[5]

Successive governments eventually made education universal in Britain. After 1872 in Scotland, and 1880 in England, attendance at school was mandatory. In theory, all children under a certain age were in school, but enforcement was difficult. Mothers kept older daughters at home to help care for babies, and agricultural districts, such as the Highlands in Scotland, saw poor attendance during harvests. Moreover, loopholes allowed children to leave school as early as ten years old, as long as they passed a proficiency exam. Some industrial areas (e.g., Bradford, a manufacturing district in northern England) continued to allow half-time schooling, with children working half a day and then going to school for the other half. Fees were another problem: between 1880 and 1891 in England, and 1872 and 1889 in Scotland, parents without a free school nearby had to pay for each child's enrollment. Truant officers compromised with poverty-stricken parents as a result. George Ratcliffe's parents were so poor they could not pay the fees for their eight children in the 1870s, when his father was out of work. After weeks of trouble, the school board found a charity to pay the fees until Ratcliffe's father could find employment.[6] This problem ended in 1889 and 1891, when the British government made free schooling available to all. Thus, by the end of the century, children received a minimum of three years of free schooling and most received six to eight years.

After 1870–1872, children, theoretically, followed a similar path. In schools that served large populations, they started school at the age of four or five, when they went to an infants' class to learn basic skills. Schools would, however, sometimes take children as young as three or even infants if they would otherwise be at home alone. George Acorn, for instance, went to school at the age of three, mainly so his mother could get him out from under foot. Walter Southgate fussed so much about his sister going without him that the schoolmistress agreed to take him at four years old. Unfortunately, she changed her mind when he almost set the classroom on fire by lighting a match during lessons: "She sent me home immediately with my sister and a note to mother that, under no circumstances, could the school admit me until I was five."[7] After a year or two, children went to standard 1 (first grade) and would move steadily up through standard 7, adding subjects and complexity as they passed the yearly examinations. When they reached a designated age, they entered full-time employment. The school-leaving age changed over the course of the century, from ten in 1876 to fourteen in 1914, so an increasing number of students reached standard 7.

Naturally, not all schools followed the norm. Small villages had a single elementary school with one classroom that mixed sexes and ages. The local schoolmistress or schoolmaster struggled to teach children of all ages in a single room, and so had to be more flexible in her or his curriculum. In addition, even in larger schools, students did not always progress smoothly through the standards. Pamela Horn has pointed out that in 1877–1878, the inspectors tested 1,335,118 students, 655,435 of which should have been in standards 4 to 6, as they were older than ten. In reality, 390,575 of them were in the lower standards; of these, 72,125 were still in standard 1, where the pupils should have been seven years old. In industrial centers, where children were working half-time and going to school half-time, educational progress was painfully slow.[8]

In addition, instruction was not inspiring. Large board schools had fifty to ninety students per class. Rather than hiring an appropriate number of teachers, school boards preferred to use cheaper pupil-teachers as assistants and never hired enough of them either. Small schools were also understaffed; one village school in 1880 had a single master and one pupil-teacher serving one hundred children. Personal instruction, then, was impossible, and teachers taught toward the yearly inspections. They concentrated on reading, writing, math, and basic religious instruction; other subjects, such as science or history, received cursory treatment. Even when they taught a broader array of subject matters, teachers stressed the dullest aspects. For example, instructors taught music through

Children often began school at the age of four or five, going to the infants class. Here the students do simple tasks, looked after by four teachers. In reality, most students were in large classes, primarily taught by pupil-teachers rather than the schoolmaster or schoolmistress. The term "kindergarten" came from Germany and was used in Britain as early as the 1850s, though "infant school" remained the most common term. "Kindergarten Infant School," in George C. T. Bartley, *The Schools for the People* (London: Bell & Daldy, 1871), between 40 and 41.

singing scales and geography through memorizing maps. Ethel Mannin (b. 1900) memorized sections from her history books verbatim and "learned multiplication tables parrot-wise, without ever understanding them." This system was most unpopular in Scotland, as Scottish schools had traditionally concentrated on giving an equal and academic education to all. Nevertheless, the lure of grants forced some homogenization by 1890. Rote memorization was the normal method for teaching, due both to the class size and the physical proximity of the different standards. Unsurprisingly, children were heartily bored and remembered little of the material. Alice Foley, born in Bolton in 1891, went to a Catholic school and recalled that "instruction was for the most part perfunctory and uninspiring; grammar was taught via the blackboard, mainly parsing nouns and verbs; history, that might have been exciting, began with the Roman Conquest and seemed to end mysteriously with the Reformation."[9] Walter Littler began school when he was four (in 1886) and could not concentrate for long enough to absorb the lessons:

[After telling the story of Sodom and Gomorrah, the] teacher began to talk about something else, numbers such as 1 and 2 and 4, but my mind was far away. I remember her saying: "Why aren't you listening Walter Littler?" (for some reason in the Infants' School we were always addressed by our full name). I brought my attention back with difficulty to my present surroundings. "I was thinking about that poor woman who was turned into salt," I explained. I tried to listen to what she was telling us about numbers but I soon lost interest and got up and began to walk away. "Here, where are you going?" the teacher asked. I said politely that I had now had enough and was going home. To my surprise I found that this was not allowed. It was my first taste of any discipline other than parental.[10]

Older children did not fare much better. On exams, they parroted back memorized rules or spellings or math problems, but they had no understanding of the theories behind them. Thus, the knowledge did not last, and skills they did learn were slapdash. Lack of comfort also influenced children's poor performance; all students sat for hours at wooden or iron desks. Normal school hours were from 9 A.M. to 12:30 P.M.; town children usually went home for lunch, though rural children stayed at school to avoid being late back from break. Schools had two-week holidays at Christmas, a week at Easter, and three or four weeks in late summer (July to August). Thus, for a large part of the year, children sat in poorly built rooms that were freezing in the winters and sweltering in the summers. An infants' school in Edmonton was so cold in January that the teacher had the children march around, singing hymns, until they got warm enough to sit down. Other schools lacked equipment, such as slates and books. None of these factors encouraged academic achievement.[11]

Unsurprisingly, reports of school inspectors showed minimal learning. Teachers drilled answers into students, but these methods often backfired. John Kerr, a school inspector in Scotland in the 1860s and 1870s, blamed student errors on rote memorization. On a science exam, for example, one girl in secondary school wrote, "The philosopher Sir Isaac Newton was the first to make the great discovery that when an apple becomes over-ripe it falls to the ground," while another boy, in writing an essay on salt, reported, "Salt is a stuff which, if it is not boiled with potatoes, makes them nasty." Ethel Mannin summed up her experience in early education of geography thus: "I learned that the world is round like an orange, and that there are five continents and a North and South Pole, which I, of course, thought of as poles sticking up at the top and bottom of the world."[12] Katherine Warburton, who taught a Catholic charity school in London in the 1850s and 1860s, feared the yearly inspections because student misunderstandings were so common, despite her fervent efforts:

My anguish over the school examinations, which were held once a year by the Government Inspector, was very great, but the inspectors were always kind and made allowances, for which we were deeply thankful. Every now and then one of the clergy came in to give an examination in Scripture and religious instructions, and I felt I could have cried when one of the big girls, whose class I had been working up specially hard for this examination, announced that "S. Mary Magdelene [sic] helped Moses across the Red Sea"; and when asked who appeared to our LORD and the

Lesson 2.

Please to give me a plum.   Here is one.
I want more, I want ten, if you please.
Here are ten.   Count them.   I will.   One (1),
two (2), three (3), four (4), five (5), six (6),
seven (7), eight (8), nine (9), ten (10).

This 1885 spelling lesson by William Mavor emphasized various ways to learn, including rote memorization and building up from small to larger words. Most
of the lessons in the Victorian period were of the dullest
variety, but this spelling book included several charming images to keep students' attention. "Lessons of
one Syllable: Lesson 2," in William Mavor, *The English Spelling Book* (London: George Routledge & Sons,
1885), 21.

Apostles on the Mount of Transfiguration another girl replied "Ananias
and Sapphira." The little ones said that Adam and Eve were turned out
of the Garden of Eden for "thieving apples"; and perhaps the answer was
not so wide of the mark after all.[13]

The natural results of such boredom and restlessness were truancy and
disruptive behavior. Teachers, then, maintained strict discipline, caning students' hands for talking, lateness, passing notes, not following instructions, and

numerous other infractions. Faith Osgerby, born in Yorkshire in 1890, had a schoolmistress who caned for trivial offenses: "I remember one very heavy swish I had from her was one day when we were marching round the room in twos and I had dared to join hands with my neighbour and walk along with arms swinging." Other punishments included raps on the knuckles or standing in front of the classroom; Emma Smith recalled a teacher threatening to cut out her tongue for talking, which left her terrified for several hours. Despite these experiences, children only rebelled with excessive correction. In the 1860s, Alfred Ireson, son of a stonemason, refused to hold out his hand for caning for lateness, as his job had caused the problem. The teacher beat Alfred on the back with a stick, and his parents threatened a lawsuit until the man apologized. Such treatment did not make Alfred, an inveterate truant, more likely to attend classes. Similarly, George Ratcliffe, born in 1863, saw a teacher abusing his sisters and slapped the teacher in the face. His schoolmaster later hided him for it, but George insisted he "felt glad of it."[14]

Without such discipline, teachers could not have maintained order, but they also caned children who were slow at learning. Charles Cooper, born in 1872 in a mining village in Yorkshire, was a pupil-teacher from the age of twelve. He recalled, "Children were not regarded as mentally deficient. The idea was that every child could do the work if he tried hard enough. And he was made to try by threat of punishment." The method was self-defeating; beaten children became paralyzed rather than knowledgeable. Walter Littler's teacher slapped him for making his stitches too small in sewing class and then slapped him again when he made them too big. Not surprisingly, he did not learn how to sew at school; his mother taught him at home. Children accepted the beatings with resignation, because most parents supported the system, assuming that their children needed correction.[15] Boys, in particular, did not get too angry unless the beatings were excessive or malicious, as Albert Lieck indicates:

> There was a good deal of caning, but it was applied scientifically and with a purpose. Flogging as a sanction of the criminal law strikes me as foolish, and I suppose it has nothing much in its favour anywhere, but I am not conscious of any resentment or damage when I look back at myself and other boys being urged along the path of learning with blows. We took it as a matter of course, though I suspect now that if it made the bright ones quicker, it dulled the stupid with greater stupidity. However, there it was, and if the answer 2s. [shillings] 9d. [pence] to the question what was the cost of a dozen reels of cotton at 2 $\frac{3}{4}$ d., was not given without appreciable pause, one was for it like a flash of lightning, which indeed a slash with the cane often resembled.[16]

Girls received the same punishments as boys and endured as their brothers did. Complaints became serious only with an unusually harsh schoolmistress.

Daisy Cowper, born in Liverpool in 1890, was terrified of her teacher: "It was the big girls of the school she vented her sadistic instincts on, and she would bring down her beastly cane on the palms, one on each hand, with such a full-arm action and sickening thwack that I was terrified that the hand would drop off at the wrist, and lie there, cut off, on the floor!" Teachers' discipline was at odds with modern principles, but not surprising in an age where beatings were common and when most parents also used corporal punishment. An occasional guardian protested specific types of discipline; Anna Davin, for example, documented London parents complaining about detentions, which disrupted work and home schedules, as well as other issues. One woman in East London pulled her daughter out of school when the daughter had to write one hundred lines for writing on the doors. School boards also got letters from annoyed parents; one late-Victorian mother wrote, "It appears to me that you have taken an Unwarrantable Liberty by Chastising my child James. . . . It is for you to instruct and not to crush Infancy." Relatives rarely were satisfied when they protested. Only the occasional teacher received a reprimand; in addition, schools often excluded students whose parents protested too vigorously. And many parents supported the strictness; one father insisted to the board, "I Agree with discipline being maintained and am not screamish [sic] over a slap," and blamed his wife's "softness" for any difficulties controlling his children. In addition, parents sometimes came to see the school as a way to cope with problem children and so positively encouraged strictness. Thomas Gautrey, a London school board member for thirty-five years, received the following note in the late-Victorian period: "Sir Will you please cane Charley Parkyn for . . . taking money out of the till and locking up his brother's Medals and taking pictures and photos[?] . . . He is a fair little devil."[17]

As with discipline, schools made little difference in curriculum between the sexes. The infants' schools were mixed sex, and both boys and girls learned sewing and knitting. In small schools, boys and girls stayed together until standard 7. In large schools, they might separate at standard 2, but schools had too few teachers and rooms to segregate the genders entirely. In the 1890s, the national curriculum dictated that boys learn drawing and military drills and girls learn sewing. In larger schools, girls sometimes did domestic economy, which meant laundry or cooking, rather than Latin or mechanics or even English literature. These differences, though, caused controversy. In Scotland, parents resisted sewing classes for girls, and schoolmasters resented losing time to nonacademic subjects. Thus, even the grants could not produce total sex segregation. The main difference, then, was that girls missed school in greater numbers than boys. Families needed girls' domestic (or other) labor and did not think girls needed much education. The authorities, too, worried more about boys' truancy, and sometimes did even not remark on girls' absences in their reports. In London in the 1880s, girls' attendance in local schools was consistently five to six percentage points below boys in every standard, yet the local

inspector tacitly approved parents' desire to teach girls homemaking skills by
not making an issue of it.[18]

A tiny minority of poor children became monitors and then pupil-teachers.
Pupil-teachers made minimal pay, so they had to continue to live at home;
thus, they were usually in the skilled working class. Pupil-teachers worked at
the school all day and then studied secondary subjects early in the morning,
in the evenings, or on Saturdays. At eighteen, they took an examination, the
queen's scholarship. If they passed, they went on to a training college to become
teachers. Working-class students won scholarships to grammar schools and
university in other ways as well. Frederick Hobley, born in 1833, worked his
way up from poverty by singing in the church choir. His payment for those
services made his education possible; he graduated from Oxford and became a
schoolmaster in 1851. All the same, in 1914, the odds of a poor child winning
a scholarship to a grammar school was forty to one, and many could not have
accepted a scholarship if offered. The majority of poor children left school as
soon as they could because of sheer economic necessity.[19]

SCHOOL STORIES

School was a child's first extended foray into a wider social world, which led
to anxiety for most children. The poor lived in fear that their shabby clothing
or lack of shoes would cause derision. In the early twentieth century, Alice
Linton rejoiced when her mother made her a new shirt, wearing it to school as
soon as her mother finished it. Instead of admiring her finery, two of the girls
made fun of her, accusing her of making "a blouse out of her dad's old shirt."
Alice remembered, "I was really mortified. For once I had thought I looked
really smart." Similarly, Alice Foley was humiliated when her classmates saw
her secondhand clothes:

> I never had any new clothes but always wore my sister's hand-me-downs;
> my school attire was not unlike Joseph's coat of many colours, but the
> patch-work effect was scrupulously hidden by a large white pinafore.
> One luckless day, whilst artlessly pirouetting in the school-yard, pinafore
> lifted high like a floating ballet skirt, the joy of life was suddenly darkened
> by the presence of a group of well-dressed girls chanting in unison the
> coloured sections of my frock. Down came the pinafore like a drop scene
> and a dismayed child slunk away conscious of not being quite like other
> people.[20]

These fears meant that some truly destitute children did not go to regular
schools of any sort. Jack Lanigan, born in 1890 in Salford, wore sacks on his
feet in winter and went to a ragged school, and all the children there lived up
to the name: "You never saw such a bunch of scruffy kids in all your life. If we
had been bunched together you could not have made a suit from the lot."[21]

The only children worse off than Jack were workhouse children and illegit-
imates, discussed in chapter 6. But many of the poor suffered humiliations.
In the early twentieth century, the British government passed laws to offer
free meals for poverty-stricken children and to institute health inspections,
but these were often embarrassingly administered. Children who received free
meals were called out in front of the entire student body. The health inspectors,
in their turn, focused on finding nits and lice. Ethel Mannin remembered that
"the girls who were verminous had to be segregated and sat at benches together,
shamed outcasts. They were generally known as 'the dirty girls.' The teachers
themselves used to refer to them as such."[22] In short, sensitivity was not the
strong suit of the Victorian educational system, and children remembered the
resulting playground taunts for years.

All the same, not all school stories were negative. A minority of children
gained a lifelong love of learning. Daisy Cowper, bored and frightened by her
cruel schoolmistress, changed completely when she switched schools. She had
inspiring teachers and eventually became a pupil-teacher. Some children did
not even mind the grinding repetition; Walter Littler, for instance, supported
the rote memorization of the national schools, arguing that children liked it.
Frederick Rogers (b. 1846) claimed that the teaching method in his school was
to "memorize passages from the grammar or geography, and repeat them at
the proper time," but this had helped him, because it "laid the foundation of the
excellent memory I have had all through my life." For all its faults, the Victorian
system did achieve basic literacy; by 1900, 97 percent of both men and women
could sign their names in marriage registers. And, as most of youngsters had
to leave school as soon as possible, the dullness of the curriculum at least made
the transition to work easier.[23]

EDUCATION IN THE MIDDLE AND UPPER CLASSES

Middle- and upper-class children stayed in school longer, but their instruction
was divided by gender. Boys usually went to private schools, first grammar,
then public schools (despite the name, these were privately funded secondary
schools), and then university. Some boys went to day schools, living at home,
while others attended boarding schools, where they came home only on school
holidays. Thus, an aristocratic boy might leave home as early as age seven
and stay in school until his twenties. In contrast, girls either had governesses
or went to less exalted day and boarding schools. Parents assumed that girls
would marry and so did not spend extravagantly on girls' education. Late
in the century, girls went to boarding schools for secondary education more
regularly and a few studied at universities. Still, the number of women who
took advantage of these opportunities was always small in comparison to men.

Mothers and nannies were the first teachers of sons, but only to the age of six
or seven. Then boys went to private primary schools, often a mix of boarders
and day pupils. George Grundy's experience was typical; his mother taught him

until he was six, then he went to the grammar school where his father was head-master. (Afterward, he intended to go on to Rugby, a public school, and then to university, but his father's financial problems scuttled the plans.) Grammar schools were plentiful; the headmasters and teachers were university-educated men who prepared boys for the public schools academically and socially. The prestigious public schools at the beginning of the nineteenth century included Charterhouse, Eton, Harrow, Rugby, St. Paul's, and Winchester, among others. By the end of the century, public schools had proliferated, including some new-comers, like Marlborough and Cheltenham, which had glowing reputations. Nobles and gentry sent their sons to these establishments, as did an increas-ing number of wealthy industrialists and professionals. The number of boys from the middle class entering Winchester, for instance, went from less than 3 percent in the 1820s to almost 14 percent in 1900. Still, the landed classes predominated.[24]

Most middle-class boys went to local secondary schools, and the curriculum at these schools was modern, meaning that they included more math and science. Many were day schools rather than boarding schools, and boys typically left at age sixteen to go into business or professions. Still, some of the schools had excellent records of preparing boys for further study. Fleet Road Board School in the fashionable Hampstead district in London, for example, was known as "the Eton of the board schools" because so many graduates went on to university. Boys got the chance to continue schooling by taking exams, offered by Oxford and Cambridge in various localities from the 1850s. However, not all areas or towns had any high schools, much less elite ones. In poorer districts, decent secondary schools were scarce. These problems did not receive government attention until after Victoria's death, with the Education Act of 1902.[25]

Boys from elite families went to public schools. Conditions at these institu-tions were notoriously bad in 1800; instruction was indifferent, living conditions were poor, and gangs of bullies ruled. In the 1830s and 1840s, several schools went through reforms, led by Thomas Arnold at Rugby. Arnold stressed order and character building. Students came as young as the age of seven, and the headmaster determined their level of competence and put them in the correct grade or "form" (the public school version of "standards"). Most schools had between seven and nine forms, and boys progressed after passing yearly ex-aminations. Arnold argued for education of character rather than intellect, and he stressed teaching boys religion and the code of the gentleman. This meant, in practice, that the curriculum was dull, focusing on Latin and Greek, taught tediously. George Grundy's training in Latin, for example, consisted of memo-rizing a grammar textbook, leaving him with no understanding of the language. Alfred Graves learned almost nothing of Latin or Greek at Windemere College, as the subjects were "badly and carelessly taught" in the 1850s.[26] But the point was not so much the usefulness of the subject matter but the character-building experience of the school.

Here is a main schoolroom (built 1803) at the public school Charterhouse. Note the spacious interior, beautiful furnishings, and skylight. The accommodations were highly superior to most national or board schools, as befit the sons of the landed classes. "School-Room," in William Haig Brown, *Charterhouse: Past and Present* (Godalming: H. Stedman, 1879), 155.

Public schools had two levels of discipline. The boys ruled themselves when not in class. Arnold, for instance, chose older boys (fifth or sixth form) to be prefects in each house and to supervise the others. Academic skills did not gain one authority; instead, leadership in cricket, football, or rugby was the key to popularity. Anyone who did not like games, or who enjoyed learning too much, was a target. At Marlborough, John Betjeman (b. 1906) remembered boys threatening to put him "in the basket," which meant being stripped, stuck in a wastebasket, and smeared with ink, because he was not good at sports. In fact, at most public schools, new boys were fair game to teachers, prefects, captains of teams, and anyone large enough to threaten harm. Robert Graves (b. 1895) faced so much petty persecution at Charterhouse that he began to fake madness. Seniority did confer more status, even on bookish boys, but the school leaders were the athletes.[27]

Discipline within the classroom came from schoolmasters, and caning for most offences was the rule. Greville MacDonald, born in 1856, was caned only once at his school, for something he did not do, yet he considered it "a most horrible outrage, restraining all outcry, and preventing my ever alluding to it at home, though I had to hide my hands at the tea-table." Many times the canings were routine, and boys exchanged tips on how to counteract the pain, including rubbing an orange peel on the palm of the hand or laying a horse's tail there (the latter was supposed to split the cane). Neither of these methods worked, even had orange peels and horses' tails been available at the crucial time, but boys nevertheless passed the lore down to future generations. In regular circumstances, the punishments were routine, but some masters were frankly abusive. In the early twentieth century, Francis Ommanney's sadistic headmaster "cuffed and struck out at the small boys without any apparent reason. Or he would pull viciously at the short hair above their ears or twist the ears themselves until tears started into the eyes of even the strongest." Fortunately, this kind of cruelty was not the norm; boys could generally accept caning as a routine practice without personal rancor.[28]

Other problems were inherent in any boarding situation. Boys lost touch with the everyday events of their parents' and sisters' lives. Coming home for holidays meant a disorienting period of transition, only to return to school and start the process over. Relationships with families inevitably changed. Boys who had been close to their sisters saw little of them, and they became more distant with their parents. Indeed, hazing experiences taught boys to avoid showing emotions or connections with family. Still, parents believed that boys needed the school's hardening process to learn to stand up for themselves and work with others. Public schools qualified boys for universities or professional training and offered vital contacts for later in life. Thus, parents sent generations of their sons to school "for their own good." Some boys saw advantages to this type of education. H. A. L. Fisher, the future Liberal cabinet member, could not remember much of the teaching at his grammar school, which he attended in the 1870s, but he did think "the competition was good for me, helping to shake me out of my early habits of vague musing and to teach me the art of attention and critical reading." He later went to Winchester, which he loved, despite the uneven quality of the teaching.[29]

The final step in a boy's education was university. Several universities in Britain were venerable; Oxford and Cambridge had the brightest reputations, but Durham, Dublin, and St. Andrews also had long traditions. Newer excellent institutions included the Universities of London, Liverpool, and Manchester. All the same, Oxford and Cambridge dominated, as their graduates received a disproportionate share of public positions. Students applied to one of twenty or so colleges associated with the university, usually gaining admission through personal contacts and their schoolmasters' recommendations. Once there, the college assigned tutors to all students; the former arranged personal programs of study with each undergraduate. The calendar year consisted of three terms of eight weeks; students could attend lectures, but this was not required. During the first term, students took preliminary exams. If they passed, they continued reading and meeting with tutors for three or four years. They received degrees if they passed final examinations in their subjects. This kind of program required great self-discipline; students commonly met with tutors only once or twice a week. Failure in exams or disciplinary problems resulted in expulsion.

As in public schools, academics was not the focus of life at university. Most boys studied the classics, which were of little practical use, though after

Oxford University's extensive cricket field showed the importance of sports for building manly character in undergraduates. Like grammar and public schools, universities stressed classical education and games. "Oxford Cricket-Ground and Club-House," in Caspar W. Whitney, *A Sporting Pilgrimage* (New York: Harper and Brothers, 1894), 327.

midcentury both Oxford and Cambridge added modern subjects to their curricula. The point of the university education was to make contacts and build character. When a man reached twenty-one, he began professional training (for the church or in law) or took a position in the civil service or taught at grammar or public schools. Even aristocratic or independently wealthy young men often attended, though they frequently did not earn degrees. Most graduates began serious work only after they left university, meaning that their childhoods lasted until they came of age. Typically, then, by 1901, an aristocratic boy stayed in school until twenty-one, a middle-class boy anywhere between sixteen and eighteen, and a working-class boy no later than fourteen.

EDUCATING WELL-OFF GIRLS

Educational opportunities for middle- and upper-class girls were uneven in the Victorian period. Girls learned first at home, so the quality of their early education depended on the skills and attention of nurses, nannies, and mothers. Molly Hughes, who grew up in a middle-class family in the 1870s in London, received her education from her mother until she was in her teens. Eileen Baillie, born in the Edwardian period, learned reading, writing, and basic math when she was four, from her nanny. Once she needed more advanced subjects, her mother took over. Learning at home had advantages, but it was not systematic. Molly learned much about literature but virtually no math; Eileen knew history and geography but no math or science. Girls usually excelled in literature and history, subjects that were easy to absorb from reading in family libraries, but needed more specialized help for any advanced study of "modern" subjects. Mary Marshall (b. 1850), for example, studied at home until she was nine. She learned languages very well—her family even spoke German at the dinner table—but her science textbook was completely out of date. Girls occasionally received extra training from their brothers' teachers at a young age, but this stopped when brothers left for school.[30]

Once girls reached the age of six or seven, parents had the choice to send them to private schools or to hire governesses and tutors. The choice depended partly on class; middle-class girls tended to go to day schools, while gentlewomen had governesses. Most communities had at least one small private girls' school, often run by widows or spinsters; other places, especially at the seaside, had numerous choices. Parents looked for respectability and personal attention rather than academic achievement in girls' schools. They preferred small schools with limited clientele. These schools stressed accomplishments, like piano playing and French; they also put much emphasis on good works, encouraging pupils to sew or knit items to donate to charities or to volunteer in missions or at Sunday schools. Only when a girl reached adolescence was she likely to go to a boarding school—in England or abroad—for "finishing."

In contrast, noble and gentry houses often employed governesses. Because they lived in larger houses, these families could set aside a room as a schoolroom. In fact, all children learned there when they were very young; once the boys left for school, governesses concentrated on the girls' education. The quality of the teaching was uninspiring. Louisa, Lady Antrim, who was born in 1855, remembered that in her time "education for girls of the leisured class was decidedly indifferent. Governesses were chosen for their refinement and high principles, not because they were qualified to teach." Indeed, Lord Lyttelton, who worked tirelessly to increase educational opportunities for Victorian women, nevertheless paid little attention to the schooling of his own four daughters. In response, Meriel, his eldest daughter, teased him by describing her own training as "slip-sloppy and feminine as if you had never cared a rap for girls' education!"[31]

Girls' curriculum in both schools and with governesses concentrated on English literature, math, science, geography, history, and modern languages, but it could also include music, art, and dancing. Margaret Gladstone went to a small private school in the 1880s and had regular lessons in math, French, geography, history, grammar, literature, and Scripture, and half days of music, drawing, and painting. In the 1860s and 1870s, the Troubridge sisters had a governess who taught them the basic lessons, but they also had tutors for music, drawing, dancing, math, geography, and Bible studies, later adding German and Italian. Most families could not afford so many different teachers, and their girls learned from a combination of mothers and governesses. Mary Marshall, whose mother had trained her for some years, began studies with a German

Girls' education was inferior to that of their brothers. Most schools (and parents) were less concerned with academics than with deportment and manners. As shown in this image from 1863, the girls' moral development was also a key concern. "Evening Prayer at a Girls' School," in Robert Aris Willmott, *English Sacred Poetry* (London: Routledge, Warne, and Routledge, 1863), 277.

governess when she was nine. The governess, like her mother, was skilled in history, geography, music, and several languages but not in science or math.[32] The informality of girls' schooling gave them substantial time off from lessons; for instance, Sylvia McCurdy and her sister, both born in the 1870s, had afternoons free. Nevertheless, Sylvia later regretted that her education was so slight:

Looking back on my childhood after so many years some anomalies strike me. My parents were intelligent, devoted and well-to-do. Yet they left the education of my sister and me in the hands of a young woman whose only qualification for the post was that she had gained a Certificate from the College of Preceptors. As well as the three Rs she taught us to play the piano. My mother said that as she passed the schoolroom door she heard the same wrong notes played day after day. Yet she, who had been her singing master's favourite pupil, did not provide us with a better teacher. She and my father went, season after season, to the Saturday afternoon Concerts at Queen's Hall—called the Saturday Pops—yet our musical training was entirely neglected.[33]

Girls received corporal punishment less often than boys, but they did not run free, and some suffered from abuse. Mary Carbery's governess during the 1870s, Miss Moll, became "a tyrant" and punished wrongdoing by refusing the girls food (including denying Mary supper for two weeks because she forgot a date in a history class). Lady Antrim had a German governess who made her miserable, but neither she nor her sisters complained to their mother:

> It seems strange that we who were idolised [*sic*] by our parents, and indeed much spoilt by them, should never have told them how unhappy we were with our Fraulein. I suppose we took it for granted that governesses were immovable institutions and fancied that if we complained we should suffer for it afterwards. At any rate we said nothing though once an elder sister Victoria was made to walk for miles with a broken chilblain on her heel, and Mary, learning to read, was often battered and pinched until her poor little arms were pulp. I remember feeling like murder, and clenching my hands with suppressed rage until the nails ran into the palms at this ill-treatment of my sisters. It must have been bad for us to hate as we did then. So miserable were we that Victoria used to pray to die in the night; I used to pray that Fraulein might die![34]

Discipline was a regular part of children's lives, and parents discouraged complaints; girls also feared retaliation. Not all governesses were cruel, but even loving ones did not indulge young people for fear of spoiling them. In the late-Victorian period, Elizabeth Bibesco's governess loved her fiercely, "but she was very severe with me. I was never allowed to be pleased with myself."[35]

Later in the century, parents in both the middle and upper classes sent girls to day or boarding schools more often but at a later age than boys. Girls went for secondary education. Again, the quality of these institutions varied widely. Some had good reputations for teaching particular subjects, such as foreign languages, while others taught mainly manners and deportment. Mary Marshall went to a "select school for young ladies" at age thirteen. She learned "'Mangnall's Questions', the 'use of the globes' and deportment. Our education was then 'finished' and for the next two or three years we read and did much as we chose." Similarly, Leah Manning went to "the Misses Thorn's Select Academy for Young Ladies" in the 1890s, where she learned to play piano, draw, and embroider. Leah later argued that she would have learned more had she read books at her parents' house. Such schools did, however, give more opportunities for girls to socialize with those outside their families and so had intangible benefits. In fact, Molly Hughes insisted that this was the only advantage to the "Establishment for Young Ladies" she attended at the age of twelve: "It must have been to give me some companionship, for I can conceive no other rational motive for the step. Indeed, I have come to think that the main value of school life is to prevent one's getting on too fast in the natural surroundings of home."[36]

Upper-class girls' education improved over the century. Secondary schools for girls, called "high schools," opened in many towns in the 1870s and 1880s. Parents preferred day schools for their daughters so they could monitor their social contacts. Mostly girls of twelve to eighteen attended; the fees were relatively low, so a wider social class attended than in grammar or public schools, which caused some parental concern. Education reformers like Frances Buss and Dorothy Beale opened schools that trained girls for university; these institutions had the same curriculum as boys' public schools. At both the high schools and the new rigorous schools, though, girls did not always approve of the curriculum. Helena Sickert went to the Notting Hill High School in the 1870s, at thirteen, and complained that girls had to study the same amount of Latin and Greek in three years as the boys did in eight. Molly Hughes went to the North London Collegiate College when she was sixteen and described the education as "a feeble imitation of what the boys were doing." She also resented the overly regimented way of life required of the girls. Still, the opportunity to go to university was a real advantage, and many of the students saw themselves as pioneers for women's education.[37]

In the 1870s and 1880s, select female pupils studied at Newnham and Girton Colleges at Cambridge (1873 and 1875), Somerville and Lady Margaret Colleges in Oxford (1879), and the University of London. Scottish universities opened their doors to women on equal terms with men in 1892. The number of women at colleges in the Victorian period was small, and their days were more structured than those of male undergraduates, including set times for prayers and special lectures by the dons who traveled to the women students rather than the other way around. (Women could only attend regular lectures while chaperoned, for fear of misbehavior by the male undergraduates.) Women took the same examinations as men after 1872, but the college administrators did not list their results with those of men. In time, the women's results received addenda, explaining where they placed in relation to the men, and women did well. For example, in 1887, a Girton student came first in the classics tripos (honors examination). More impressively, in 1890, Philippa Fawcett placed first in the prestigious mathematics tripos; had she been male, she would have had the title "senior wrangler," the highest intellectual achievement at Cambridge. In comparison, Karl Pearson, a future professor of mathematics and the father of statistical studies in England, placed third in the mathematics tripos when he took it in 1879.

The improvement in educational opportunities helped a minority of women enter academia and break out of expected gender roles. Mary Marshall excelled at Latin, history, literature, and logic at Cambridge, a wider range of subjects than governesses or high schools taught. Leah Manning also went to Cambridge; her years there formed the basis for her career as a teacher, union activist, and Labour member of Parliament (in 1929). In short, girls' education improved greatly from 1830 to 1900. Nevertheless, they were "special" students, and they had both social and academic limitations. Oxford and Cambridge did not grant women university degrees until the twentieth century.[38] In addition, though some women had fulfilling careers and lived on their own in the 1890s, the majority remained at home as "children" of the house until they married, in contrast to their brothers.

CONCLUSION

The overall trend in education was one of convergence. By 1901, working-class children stayed in class longer, and girls' opportunities for advancement had improved. In addition, national systems and payment by results made the Scottish and English systems similar. Variations remained, though, and much of the teaching stayed woefully poor. The curriculum for the majority of the population reflected the belief that most pupils needed only the most basic education, and girls' opportunities lagged behind those of boys. In short, most children's futures were mapped out from their births; only a few broke through class and gender barriers. Still, Victorian authorities valued children and invested in their development, if only to create an informed electorate and to help self-improvement.

Schools added an extra layer of discipline to children's lives, so that they had strict controls both at home and school. The punishments meted out by teachers reflected parents' desires that their children learn self-control and obedience. At times, parents came into conflict with schoolmasters over truancy or beatings, but most did not. The level of control varied, however; schools trusted upper-class boys to discipline one another, something they did not try with poor boys. In addition, parents kept girls closer to home in all classes. Thus, for a few children, schooling led to more freedom and opportunity, but for many others, school meant another set of rules, limitations, and expectations.

The importance of education increased during the century, but schools fought a tug-of-war over children with employment (paid and unpaid), a battle waged throughout the century. Schools received grants based on attendance, so school-masters had every incentive to get as many children as possible into the class-room. Eventually, education won the battle, but the workplace remained a formidable factor in children's lives, as the next chapter shows.

3

Child Labor in Victorian Britain

Horror stories about child labor during industrialization began in the late eighteenth century and have continued to the present. Critics point to the long hours and poor wages of youngsters as a blot on Britain's history. This picture has some validity, but it is incomplete and lacks context. The vast majority of children had always worked, as most grew up as peasants and helped on farms as soon as they could. What differed in the industrial age, then, was not the fact of the work but its character. Factory jobs meant a long day of almost constant toil, paced by steam-driven machines, under the supervision of strangers, and in unhealthy conditions. These problems—and not the idea of children working for wages per se—garnered the negative attention. In addition, most Victorian child workers labored in small workshops, agriculture, domestic industry, and domestic service, not in factories. And change over time was crucial to a child's experience, because conditions had improved greatly by 1900.

Children's labor was necessary because of the low wages of most workers. At midcentury, the highest-skilled workers (e.g., ship engineers) might make as much as one hundred to two hundred pounds a year; on this they could support a family in relative comfort. However, most skilled workers (e.g., carpenters, jewelers) earned seventy-five to one hundred pounds a year, and their children began apprenticeships or became pupil-teachers by age twelve. Semiskilled workers earned around fifty pounds a year (twenty to thirty shillings a week); these included hatmakers, butchers, and bakers. Their children would help out at younger ages, especially if their families were large. Unskilled laborers—such as dockworkers, millers, and textile workers—earned eighteen to twenty-three shillings a week (or forty-five pounds a year); the lowest of all, at eleven to twelve shillings a week, went to farmworkers. In these two poorest groups, child labor was essential to family survival. At the end of Victoria's reign, 60 percent of male workers made twenty-five shillings a week or less. Because of the fall of food prices late in the century, a small family could manage on eighteen to twenty shillings a week but had no margin for error. A large family, however, suffered hunger on this wage, and any accidents, illnesses, or layoffs led to utter destitution. Thus, children began earning as soon as possible in most working-class families, rural and urban.

AGRICULTURE

In 1801, 36 percent of the British labor force was in agriculture; by 1851, the percentage was declining, but 20 percent of workers were still on the land. Pay was extremely low, so children began work early and had long hours. During planting and harvesting, the workday went from sunup to sundown, but even in less intense times, farmwork was heavy manual labor. Often, a child started at four or five years old scaring off crows from the corn, tending sheep or pigs, or picking stones out of the ground. Boys did these jobs more often than girls, who instead helped with the dairy and vegetable gardens and assisted their mothers in gleaning (gathering up the wheat stalks left behind by the harvesters). At the age of eleven or twelve, boys started full-time work, plowing or shepherding. George Mockford, born in 1826, first worked at the age of eight, scaring off crows, seven days a week, for a shilling a week. (A shilling purchased a four-pound loaf of bread and around a pound of meat, so it was a helpful supplement to a family's wages.) When he was ten, he stopped going to school altogether and became a shepherd. Working outside had its dangers. George got chilblains in the winter, which burst, became infected, and left him bedridden for a week. Later, he came down with bronchitis. Yet his father insisted that he get up on cold mornings and pull up the frost-covered turnips without gloves, because he had to become hardened to the work to survive.[1]

Victorians worried less about children's farmwork, because such labor had occurred for centuries and because the work, though monotonous, was not especially dangerous. Instead, rural communities caused concern because of poverty and poor housing; low wages and large families meant that children grew up hungry and cold. One type of rural labor that did receive national criticism before 1850 was the gang system. Particularly in East Anglia, employers used gang masters, who put together large groups of women and young children to work in fields, often far away from their villages. If the master did not provide carts, women and children walked miles to and from the fields. Children as young as five or six joined these gangs, working long hours for minimal pay. They were regularly beaten for small infractions and went out to work in any weather. A parliamentary investigation in 1843 harshly criticized this system, though the government did not abolish it entirely until the Agricultural Gangs

Children went to work on farms as early as possible. In this 1863 picture, a boy helps his father plow. The author, Robert Aris Willmott, imagines plowing the land as "A Hymn," but rural children remember farmwork as hard and sometimes dangerous. *English Sacred Poetry* (London: Routledge, Warne, and Routledge, 1863), 162.

Act of 1867.[2] Mrs. Burrows described her experience in gangs in the 1850s and 1860s below:

> On the day that I was eight years of age, I left school, and began to work fourteen hours a day in the fields, with from forty to fifty other children of whom, even at that early age, I was the eldest. We were followed all day long by an old man carrying a long whip in his hand which he did not forget to use. A great many of the children were only five years of age.... In harvest-time we left home at four o'clock in the morning, and stayed in the fields until it was dark, about nine o'clock.... For four years, summer and winter, I worked in those gangs—no holidays of any sort, with the exception of very wet days and Sundays—and at the end of that time it felt like Heaven to me when I was taken to the town of Leeds, and put to work in the factory. Talk about White Slaves, the Fen districts at that time was the place to look for them.[3]

Agricultural labor was resistant to reform and hard to regulate, but compulsory schooling did make inroads. After 1872 in Scotland and 1880 in England, more children delayed full-time employment until they were twelve or fourteen years old. Instead, they first took part-time positions that fit around the school day. Kate Taylor (b. 1891) and her sister Ethel were the daughters of an agricultural laborer in Suffolk, two of his fifteen children. Both had heavy workloads as soon as they were physically able, which meant they missed more school than other children. Their part-time jobs were onerous enough to require constant juggling:

> Ethel left home at 6 A.M. to start work at 6.30. After doing housework and helping with the dairy work, she delivered milk, in cans, eggs, butter, cream, and sometimes prepared chickens in baskets on her arms, to at least six of the big houses in the parish, taking back the cans she delivered the previous day.... Owing to this work Ethel was excused an hour's schooling, reaching school at 10 A.M. instead of 9.00. Exactly the same conditions applied to me when I was old enough to do the work.... The day girl's wage was 9d. [pence] per week. On a Saturday, after the milk delivery, there was the dairy, the kitchen and the larder to be scrubbed, and the dining room to be turned out and thoroughly cleaned. Ninepence per week didn't pay for the amount of shoe leather we wore out as the roads then were rough, muddy and stony, and we frequently had our feet bound in rags which would flap in the mud.[4]

Kate left school at thirteen to work as a general servant on a neighboring farm, where, after twelve hours of manual labor, she did the mending. For all this, she received no pay at all for the first six months and fifteen pence a week afterward (a shilling was twelve pence). This was a pay rise from her part-time earnings, as she also got room and board, but the job did not allow independence.

Farmwork changed less than many other types of child labor, with few safety precautions and low wages into the 1890s. Tom Mullins, born in 1863, left school at ten to work as a carter's lad; he was paid three pounds a year and room and board. He helped drive the horses, "and when there were two I had to walk between them while leading and often got trodden on." He eventually went to a bigger farm and began plowing at age eleven and tended seven cows at age thirteen. (Though not generous, Tom's wages were considerably higher than farm girls received, a typical Victorian gender bias.) As agriculture consolidated and mechanized in the 1880s and 1890s, families struggled as laborers, so poverty remained endemic and truancy was common. A carter in 1903 in Gloucestershire had twenty-one children and an income of twelve shillings a week. As Thomas Jordan put it, "Not surprisingly, the boys were put to work in the fields by the age of ten. Compulsory schooling based on laws passed in Westminster meant little in the country when a family had mouths to feed."[5] Agriculture employed a declining number of workers by 1901 (around 12 percent), but those who remained used child labor as much as they could.

WORKSHOPS AND HOME INDUSTRIES

The major industrial employers of children in the early Victorian period were not factories but small workshops with fewer than ten employees. In businesses such as painting or metalworking, boys still went through apprenticeships in the early nineteenth century. The parents paid a fee to the master, and children worked from two to seven years to learn the trade. When they became skilled, they went to full-time employment. By 1820, few businesses continued the traditions of formal movement from apprentice to journeyman to master, and most apprentices lived with their parents rather than with masters. Apprenticeships offered legal protections, but an expanding number of trades stopped using them by the 1830s. Anyone without such formal agreements, usually orphans or pauper children, went to work as early as seven and suffered violence from drunken or cruel masters. For instance, one thirteen-year-old testified to an 1842 parliamentary commission that his "master often beats him with a whip with four lashes to it, and tied in knots: his master beats him for not doing enough work, and he could not do more." Others complained of beatings with straps and whip handles, among other instruments. Even without violent abuse, these workshops were unhealthy—ill ventilated, overcrowded, bitterly cold in the winter, and miserably hot in the summer. A particularly egregious example was a nailing business in the Black Country in the 1840s that was consistently flooded by a local cesspool. Rather than make the necessary repairs, the owners brought in duckboards, and the employees stood on them as they worked. Moreover, the hours were long, in some trades up to sixteen hours a day, though the most common shift was twelve hours. Few shops had washing facilities to clean up before meals or privies separated by sex. Despite these conditions, the usual age for a child to begin full-time work was seven or eight, depending on the skills and strength needed for the work. John Shinn, born in 1837 in London, went to work with his father, a cabinetmaker, at age ten to learn the trade. He worked from 7 A.M. to 8 P.M., Monday to Saturday, a seventy-eight-hour week.[6]

The kinds of work children did in these shops varied. In nail making, boys used the hammers while girls worked the bellows, keeping the fire going in the middle of the room. In lace making, children wound bobbins or threaded needles. In cutlery, they did the finishing work—putting the various parts together and then polishing—or they were grinders, sharpening the knives on a grindstone. In fireclay brickyards, children brought the clay to the molders, who actually shaped the bricks, and then took the bricks to the fire to harden afterward. Some carried as many as one thousand bricks a day in twelve-hour shifts (a wet brick weighed approximately nine pounds). In glass working, boys acted as takers-in, carrying the glass goods to the fire and back; if they did well, they might progress to glass cutting when older. In all these workshops, the main problems were terrible building conditions and long hours rather than cruelty. Masters sometimes beat slow children, but not excessively, except in certain locales, like the Black Country. In fact, in some businesses, like hosiery or glove making, the workers still lived with the master, and a family atmosphere prevailed.[7] Many of these businesses were overtaken by industrial production in the last part of Victoria's reign.

Most children who worked in industry in the nineteenth century worked in small workshops. This image shows boys of various ages soldering pots and pans for market. Note the fire at the back; all metalwork required constant fires, which meant workshops were always hot. "In a Birmingham Soldering Shop," in Robert Harborough Sherard, *The Child-Slaves of Britain* (London: Hurst and Blackett, 1905), between 124 and 125.

Girls also labored in workshops, but they more often went into "female" trades. In the 1840s, girls apprenticed to dressmakers or lace makers as young as twelve years old. During the season, the period of parties and balls for the upper classes in London, dressmakers worked fifteen to eighteen hours a day finishing ball dresses for wealthy young women. Out of season, dressmakers worked twelve to fifteen hours a day, six days a week. An owner of a dress shop or a celebrated dressmaker earned a decent living, but apprentices received no pay for the first two years and seven to twelve shillings a week thereafter. Louise Jermy's family spent three pounds for her apprenticeship in dressmaking in the early 1890s. After her probationary period, she made seven shillings and six pence during slack periods and ten shillings in season, not enough money for Louise's stepmother to think the investment was sound, nor for Louise to live independently. Eventually, Louise gave up and went into domestic service.[8]

Other trades also had sweatshop conditions. Caroline Chatwell started lace making at age ten, in the early 1840s, working for nine and a half hours a day in a closed room for two pence a week; the rationale for her low pay was that she was learning a trade. She could earn better pay after leaving the lace school but not enough to live alone. Straw plaiting (treating and braiding straw for hats or textiles) and hatmaking were also low-pay employment. Lucy Luck tried straw plaiting in the 1860s and could not make ends meet. Mrs. Scott, a future justice of the peace, worked making hats from the age of twelve (ca. 1890s). She and the other girls sat at long tables; some put together the basic structure while others trimmed. Sewing through the hard parts of the hat was difficult, and any crooked stitches had to be removed and redone; this was especially onerous in leather bindings. After years of experience, Scott made thirteen to fifteen shillings a week; she could not live on this alone, so she boarded with an uncle. Except in certain areas, such as Lancashire (cotton mills) or Dundee (jute manufacture), girls had few well-paid options. The 1867 Factory Act regulated such sweated industries, but enforcement was difficult; only industrialization of the work ended sweating, but with a consequent loss of employment.[9]

Into the late-Victorian period, much of children's industrial labor was hidden in homes. In unmechanized businesses, families produced or finished goods by hand, paid by the piece. A worker could stitch a pair of trousers for six and a half pence; heavy overcoats earned four shillings; 240 stitched gloves earned around eighteen shillings; and a gross of matchbook covers paid only two and a half pence. Ironically, as a result, children tended to have longer hours when they worked for their parents than when they did not; one thirteen-year-old in 1902 told an investigator that she worked sixty-one hours a week at matchbox making and housework for her mother. Goods produced by hand included shoes, clothing, gloves, paper bags, artificial flowers, brushes, tennis balls, and curled feathers for hats. Children not only helped with the work but also bought the necessary materials and delivered the goods to and from the warehouse, carrying heavy loads in all weather.[10] Payment by the piece meant low wages and brutally long hours, and the production materials cluttered up the family's limited living space. Many children were truants from school because their mothers would not have the money to feed them the evening meal without their help in producing these goods.

In the home, children also took part in service work, such as charring (rough cleaning), minding their siblings, or laundering. Laundering was especially work intensive, involving hauling water, scrubbing on washboards, mangling (putting clothes through a hand-cranked wringer to remove most of the water), hanging up clothing to dry, and ironing or starching the cleaned clothes and linen (if necessary). Louise Jermy left school in 1888, when she was eleven, and worked for her stepmother, turning a mangle and bringing and carrying back the loads of wash. After two years, Louise got a tubercular hip disease and had to stop; her description of the work shows why:

> So when we moved to the new house the mangle went too, and my school days were over. Some cards were printed and I had to take them round, and soon we had all the work we could possibly do, and four days out of six I had to stand and turn that mangle, some days there was hardly time to get our food.... If my father had any love for me he certainly didn't show it, and sometimes when we were still at work in the evenings, I would leave off turning and go into the sitting-room and ask him if he would . . . not come and turn for a bit as I was tired. He always teased me before he came, but I didn't see any fun in it, I was so tired.[11]

If not laundering, then women and girls cleaned, which involved scrubbing hearthstones, kitchen grates, windows, and floors, as well as dusting any furniture and beating rugs. Girls could start cleaning while in school; step girls, for instance, whitened the stone steps at their neighbors' front doors for a few pennies. None of these jobs paid highly, and the physical labor was considerable.[12]

STREET WORK

Like home industries, street work received limited attention from Victorian legislators, but many children worked long hours in petty trading, street sweeping, and scavenging. Henry Mayhew, who wrote a four-volume investigation of working people in London in the 1850s, interviewed many street sellers, called "costers," who sold goods from barrows to passersby. The children of these traders assisted their parents or had their own barrows of matches, flowers, fruits, vegetables, or novelty items. A girl of eight who sold watercresses told Mayhew that she bought her stock and tied it in bundles before breakfast. She then spent the day selling; on a good day, she earned a shilling. A girl of nineteen began selling flowers when she was nine; she rarely got home before 9 P.M., but she got no dinner unless she had sold out. Children also swept the streets of London or became mudlarks, wading into the muck of the Thames riverbed to dig up salvage goods. Boys whose fathers were scavengers joined in the job of cleaning the London streets, taking out the garbage in large piles; they might also train as dustmen, taking chimney ashes away for resale.[13] These jobs were on the fringes of the economy and involved self-employment rather than a potentially villainous employer, so they attracted limited attention.

Other work that resisted regulation included performing at various levels. The British theater employed numerous child actors, for instance. Because of their odd hours and frequent travels, few went to school. If a child worked in a respectable company, he or she at least had decent pay and some career prospects. Ellen Terry, the most famous Victorian actress, began as a child performer in the 1850s, as did her sister Kate. They learned lines and rehearsed plays rather than go to school; a law setting ten as a minimum age for actors did not pass until 1903. Still, most child performers were at the lowest end of the profession. Mayhew interviewed an array of street performers, including circus clowns, sword swallowers, street patterers, and musicians. Most street performers knew that having a child along increased their earnings, as a result of the sympathy the latter engendered in the crowd. Emma Smith, born in the 1890s, went to work rather than school when she was six. Her foster parents outfitted her in a ragged dress, and her "father" played the hurdy-gurdy while she picked up the pennies. Her guardians managed to avoid sending her to school for a year through such "tramping."[14]

Street selling, like performing, continued despite compulsory schooling. Rather than stopping work entirely, these children sold their goods at night, making for even longer days. John Kerr discovered a young boy selling matches at midnight in winter in the 1870s in Scotland, and he expressed his indignation in his memoirs:

Many children were street sellers throughout the nineteenth century. Such labor was difficult to regulate and had potentially unlimited hours. This picture shows a flower girl; most began work as early as eight or nine and worked from early morning until late at night. "A London Flower Girl," in Robert Harborough Sherard, *The Child-Slaves of Britain* (London: Hurst and Blackett, 1905), between 80 and 81.

I remember seeing a boy of not more than seven years of age selling matches at the Register House in Edinburgh at nearly twelve o'clock at night. There was a cold wind blowing, and the poor little fellow had availed himself of a projecting part of the building as a shelter from the wind. He looked so pale, worn, and dejected that I spoke to him, bought a box of his matches, and asked him why he was out on the street so late. "I daurna," he replied, "gang hame till I have selled a' my matches." I bought all he had left, and asked at what time he went to bed. In a piteously languid tone he replied, "Just ony [any] time." Hardly anything could be more pathetic than the hopeless sadness of the answer, as if, infant as he was, the iron had already entered into his soul, and there was nothing for it but passive acquiescence in the hardened neglect of his parents. Abandoned thus morally and physically, what did mature age, if he should ever reach it, promise for such a child but a permanently twisted and debased nature?[15]

Like many middle-class reformers, Kerr blamed the boy's parents, but economic necessity was a much more likely culprit. Legislation for such children did not come until an 1894 act limited street trading to those eleven or older and restricted their hours, but, as usual, the provisions were all but impossible to enforce. Until parents made sufficient wages, long hours for children before and after school were inevitable.[16]

DOMESTIC SERVICE

Domestic service was a major employer, particularly for girls, throughout the century. Indeed, the number of young women servants expanded; in the 1890s, a third of all girls between the ages of fifteen and twenty were servants. Servants lived with their employers, received tips and uniforms, and had regular meals. Wages were low, but because servants had few expenses, they could save money or send part of their earnings to their parents. All the same, the work was hard. In large establishments, servants' daily tasks included cleaning out numerous coal grates, dusting and polishing furniture, airing and making beds, preparing food for scores of people, cleaning and stacking the dishes, and serving at table. Weekly, they laundered, ironed and mended mounds of clothing and linen, polished silver, and washed windows, walls, drapes, and curtains. Even with a team of other servants, the work was extensive. Most girls, though, did not get jobs in large establishments but instead were maids-of-all-work for middle-class homes, which meant that they had to do all domestic chores by themselves or with, at most, two other servants, usually a cook and a nursery maid. Servants were also on call twenty-four hours a day with highly limited days off.

Mrs. Layton, born in London in 1855, first worked as a babysitter at ten years old. She made a shilling and sixpence and received one meal, and she worked from eight to eight all but the two nights a week when she went to night school and got off at seven. She quit when her employer insisted she stop schooling, and, at thirteen, she became a nursery maid. By fifteen, she worked as a maternity nurse at three shillings a week; although she enjoyed it, she was exhausted from doing all the child minding and housework, and she sometimes fell asleep on the stairs on her way to bed.[17] Lilian Westall, born in 1893, left school at fourteen and worked as a nursery maid to three children, then for a dentist as a maid, then as a waitress, and finally as a kitchen maid. She left all these jobs in short order, unable to manage the housework and child care for, at the most, five shillings a week. Her description of her work as a maid shows the onerous nature of domestic work:

> I was the only servant. I had to be up at six in the morning, and there were so many jobs lined up for me that I worked till eleven o'clock at night.... I had to clean all the house, starting at the top and working down, sweeping and scrubbing right through. Hearthstoning the steps from the front door to the pavement took me an hour alone.... I gave in my notice in the first week, but a servant was obliged to stay at least one month in those days, and wasn't paid, of course, until the end of that time. I found out that a succession of girls before me had stayed only one month, but there were enough youngsters looking for work to ensure that a regular supply was maintained.[18]

Changes over the century made for better wages in the 1880s and 1890s. In the 1840s, for instance, the average housemaid earned twelve pounds a year; in 1890, she received nineteen pounds. Similarly, nursery maids went from eleven pounds to twenty pounds during the same period. The job of domestic labor, however, declined in status during the century; men, in particular, found it degrading. Thus, domestic service increasingly became a woman's job, though butlers, footmen, coachmen, or valets remained in the wealthiest households. For many girls, domestic service was the only unskilled job with a living wage, and, despite the limitations, some saw it as a step toward independence. Louise Jermy tried laundering and dressmaking, but, in the end, became a servant, where the pay was sufficient and she could escape her nagging stepmother.[19]

FACTORY WORK

Though large sections of child employment were outside of the factory, the enduring image of the Victorian economy was of smokestacks and steam-driven machinery. Between 1800 and 1850, Britain was at the climax of the first phase of the Industrial Revolution, characterized by cotton mills, iron and steel production, and railways. The first business to industrialize was textiles; others with numerous child employees were coal mining, ironworks, and pottery making. Later in the century, chemical works, electricity, and gasworks were the leading industries, while older businesses declined relative to the new economic powerhouses of Germany and the United States. Due to a variety of factors, children's participation in the industrialized workforce lowered over the course of the century. Children were less crucial to later phases of industrialization, but between 1800 and 1850, they helped make Britain's economy the most advanced in the world.

The work conditions in many early factories were poor by modern standards. Factories that continued work around the clock often had two twelve-hour shifts (with two meal breaks), but others had longer hours, for example from 6:00 A.M. to 8:30 P.M., with only ninety minutes or two hours for three meals. Masters were strangers who had no hesitation in beating children, and pay was low. Industrial accidents were not uncommon; newspapers printed a steady stream of tragic incidents involving lost limbs and lives. For example, one twelve-year-old working in the mills in Rochford in the mid-Victorian period was dragged into the engine and had multiple fractures; he died within hours after an amputation. Steam-driven machinery set the pace of work, forcing children to stay awake and alert beyond their natural capacities. Most of the horror stories of children's factory work come from this period, when the government had few regulations, and the poverty of the workforce made it vulnerable to exploitation.[20]

Charles Shaw's experience with industrial work was typical for the 1830s and 1840s. He went to work in the potteries in the 1830s when he was seven. His hours were from 6:00 A.M. until 8 or 9:00 P.M., six days a week, and his work was physically demanding. He was a mold runner for a muffin maker. He took the newly formed clay plates and rushed them to the oven. He placed them on the edge of the hot stove to make sure they got the full heat. When the lower shelves were full, he used a ladder for the higher ones. Once the plates were dry, he took them back to the master. In between these trips, he wedged clay, an onerous process requiring stamina and brute strength:

> Wedging clay, for a boy, was as common as it was cruel. What is now done by hydraulic pressure was then done by the bone and muscle of, perhaps, a half-fed boy. He had to take a lump of raw clay upon a plaster block, cut it in two with a piece of wire, lift one half above his head, and then bring it down upon the lower half, to mix them, with whatever force he could command. This had to be repeated till the clay was brought to the consistency of something like putty. Doing such work as this was "rest" from the mould running.

At a young age, then, Shaw did heavy manual labor, and if he were too slow at these tasks, his master beat him. He went through this exhausting process for a shilling a week. His pay supplemented a tight family budget, but it was hard earned.[21]

The major employer in Lancashire was the textiles industry, and boys and girls worked in cotton, wool, and silk manufacture. Tom Barclay, born in 1852, went to work in a wool mill at the age of eight to turn a wheel. He described his experience thus: "Unwashed, ill-clothed, ill-fed, untaught, worried by vermin, I worked in all weathers, and not without scolding and threats of violence, seventy hours a week for—how much? One shilling and sixpence. About a farthing [a fourth of a penny] an hour, think of it." Children did various tasks in mills; commonly they threaded the bobbins or acted as a piecers, repairing the broken threads by piecing them together. As they became older and more skilled, they graduated to spinning or weaving themselves. Children were always in danger of falling asleep and having potentially fatal accidents, as well as stunting their growth and breathing in unhealthy substances. Beatings with straps, sticks, and factory implements were common when youngsters had difficulty concentrating for twelve to sixteen hours.[22]

Another major employer of children was the metalworking industry. Children as young as eight or nine worked in iron or copper factories. They did various tasks—keeping the coke fires going, breaking up the limestone, or dipping the plates into metal. Many assisted puddlers, who kept the iron ore at the correct heat so the skilled workers could remove the iron at exactly the right moment. Children also took out the ashes from the furnaces and collected the coke (a type of coal) for the next day's fires. The shifts were twelve hours, seven days a week, as the furnaces had to keep going; workers also worked night shifts every other day. Because of the fires, the factories were hot all the time, and accidents were common. Many workers suffered burns, and others got caught in the rollers and lost limbs. For this dangerous work, boys received three to four shillings weekly in the beginning (girls less); by the age of fifteen, boys' pay had risen to twelve to eighteen shillings. Because of the long hours required for the two shifts, the number of young children in metalworking declined after compulsory schooling.[23]

If factory work was unhealthy, so too were the jobs related to the Victorians' main fuel, coal. Coal mines employed children as young as four, though most were nine or ten. The youngest were trappers, who pulled the door to the shaft open and shut to regulate the oxygen below and to let coal carts through. Others pushed the carts of coal up the shaft, helping their mothers. Older boys were putters, who hauled the coal the last part of the journey. Putters dragged six to eight hundredweight of coal at a time; they started at the age of twelve, working in teams, and were paid by the load. Some boys even did the mining, as they were small enough to crawl into the narrower shafts. The normal working day was twelve hours, but this did not factor in the trip to and from the mine, or the walking beneath the ground to get to the seam, which increased the workday as much as four hours. Cave-ins and explosions from the buildup of gas were also possible; in 1838 alone, fifty-eight children under the age of thirteen died in mining accidents. In addition, children suffered from diseases such as black lung, caused by inhalation of coal dust. Miners made fifteen shillings a week and trappers ten pence a day (less than five shillings a week); together, this was a living wage. As a result of an investigation in 1842, Parliament passed a law barring children under ten and women from working underground, though it was difficult to enforce because of the poverty of mining families. In addition, women and girls continued to work in mining above ground, sorting the different grades of coal.[24]

Chimney sweeping was equally controversial. The coal fireplaces of Victorian homes needed the soot cleaned twice a year, and adults were too large to do so. Thus, boys went down the shafts, some as narrow as nine square inches, and cleaned them out by hand. Injuries were frequent: chimneys collapsed while boys were in them; boys breathed in soot or sulfur and fainted; others slipped in wet shafts and fell. William Wright, born in 1846, experienced several close shaves. He got stuck in a chimney in a paper mill and did not get out until the foreman knocked out some of the bricks. Later he almost burned to death when his father lowered a candle on a birch rod into a boiler flue William was cleaning and caught William's tool sack on fire. Small injuries, such as scrapes on the back, festered with soot embedded in them and left lifelong scars. In addition, the master sweeps were often brutal. George Elson, one of the last sweeps in England, complained that "the master sweeps spent most of the money the boys earned for them in riotous drinking, consequently their wretched apprentices were compelled to beg their food and clothing off the benevolent, and, moreover, were brutally kicked and beaten if they failed to obtain such by some means, fair or foul." Parliament outlawed the use of chimney sweeps in 1842, but the illegal use of boy cleaners continued. Elson, who eventually became a master chimney sweep, was still cleaning out chimneys by hand when he was eighteen, in 1851.[25]

REGULATING CHILD LABOR

Parliament investigated conditions in small workshops and in agriculture in 1840, 1843, and 1867, but children working long hours in factories or mines provoked far more concern. The 1867 commission on child labor in agriculture, for instance, did not deplore children working as much as it did their lack of schooling. In contrast, opponents of child factory labor attacked the fact that children worked in such conditions at all. They argued that factory children were overworked, stunted, and prematurely aged; in addition, their low pay depressed adult wages. As the old laws protecting workers (based on the notion of apprenticeships) were not adequate to the new conditions, successive British governments studied the problem. All the same, factory laws did not make a smooth, linear progression. Parliament tended to center on those industries with the most visible child labor (textiles) or the most accidents (lucifer matchmaking or cartridge making), as they garnered sensational newspaper headlines. Other regulated businesses had cruelly long hours, such as paper staining, in which some unfortunate children worked twenty hours a day. Children continued to do heavy manual labor in industries that stayed out of the public's eye; only if muckraking reformers wrote exposés did the legislature act, and then often ineffectually. For instance, George Smith wrote an account of children working in the brick trade in the 1870s, showing children as young as nine carrying wet clay weighing forty-three pounds over twelve miles. Parliament responded by passing an act to regulate brickmaking in 1871, but it was, as always, difficult to enforce.[26]

Still, over the course of the century, Parliament passed factory acts in 1833, 1844, 1847, 1850, 1867, 1871, 1874, and 1891. The government passed so many bills because each one was highly limited; rather than tackle juvenile work overall, individual laws restricted child labor to certain ages in specific industries. For example, the Factory Act of 1833 covered cotton and wool textile mills but not silk mills. It prohibited employment of children under nine, and those nine and eleven could work only eight hours a day (forty-eight hours a week). Until the age of eighteen, no one could work longer than twelve hours a day, and those between the ages of nine and thirteen had to go to school for two hours. The Factory Act of 1844 actually lowered the age of employable children to eight, but reduced the hours of all workers between the ages of eight and thirteen to six and a half or seven hours, with three hours of schooling. Parliament added other industries, such as potteries and matchmaking, in 1864 and metalworking in 1867. The latter act also added workshops with fewer than fifty employees. In short, these laws constricted children's hours and raised the age at which they could work full-time from eight in 1844 to eleven in

George Smith's muckraking reports on children's work in brickyards pressured Parliament to regulate such businesses. In one of his many illustrations, a young girl carries heavy loads; she was paid by the task, which limited her earnings. "A Girl Carrying Clay 'by the Task' to Make the 'Tale of Bricks,'" in George Smith, *The Cry of the Children from the Brick-Yards of England* (London: Houghton & Co., 1879), between 26 and 27.

1891, though in a piecemeal and inconsistent manner. Nevertheless, improvements occurred; for example, by the end of the century, children were banned from night work. Moreover, factory owners had to do administrative tasks if they employed children, especially during the period in which children went to school part-time. Some businesses stopped hiring children younger than thirteen to avoid the complications. In theory, children should have been working much shorter days in factories by midcentury, and particularly by 1890.[27]

In reality, enforcement was problematic. The Factory Act of 1833, for example, provided for only four inspectors, and penalties for flouting the laws were slight. In addition, the law covered only a few businesses, and even after the number of covered businesses expanded (as in the Ten Hours Bill of 1847), small concerns, domestic labor, theatrical work, or home industries were all exempt. Parents and doctors colluded to pass off underage children as old enough for work; they did this with impunity, as the law did not require the registration of births until 1874. Children also worked illegal overtime after their half day of schooling; chances that the inspectors would uncover such practices were slight.[28] Lucy Luck worked in the silk mills at the age of nine and rarely received any schooling, showing how little her employers feared discovery:

> I was too little to reach my work, and so had to have what was called a wooden horse to stand on. At that time children under eleven years of age were only supposed to work half-day, and go to school the other half. But I did not get many half-days at school, as Mr D— was a tailor by trade, so I had to stop at home in the afternoon to help him with the work. But I have never been sorry for that, for I learned a lot by it. Neither was I eleven when I had to work all day at the mill.[29]

In addition, the attempt to impose a half day of schooling on exhausted children was unrealistic; most were too tired to learn anything. Because of these factors, many historians have argued that the reduction in child labor resulted from compulsory schooling rather than factory legislation.

Nevertheless, children working in the 1870s and 1880s were older and had shorter hours than those working in the 1840s. In 1871, hardly any children between the ages of five and nine worked full-time, though almost a third of boys between the ages of ten and fourteen did so and about a fifth of girls of that age. By 1901, even older children who worked full-time were a minority—22 percent of boys and 12 percent of the girls between the ages of ten and fourteen. Of course, these figures undercount domestic labor, but the downward trend was clear. After 1872 and 1880, then, most children fit in their jobs around the school day. There were occasional exceptions to this; poor families could petition to have a child leave school early as long as he or she passed a basic skills test. Jack Lanigan (b. 1890) went to work part-time as a lather boy (helping a barber to shave) as his first job. Once he reached ten, though, he took the school-leaving examination and worked as an errand boy full-time. Jack's mother was a widow, so her sons left school as early as possible. But most late-Victorian families relied on part-time jobs for their children.[30]

PART-TIME TO FULL-TIME

A variety of part-time positions existed for children in the 1880s and 1890s. Some were in traditional trades such as dairies or barbering, but others were related to the growth of retail and white-collar employment. Expanding jobs included shop or office clerks, typists, telephone operators, and secretaries. Clerks, for instance, were only 0.04 percent of the workforce in 1851 but 4 percent by 1901. While some clerk positions offered chances for advancement (as in law), most working-class boys had less exalted positions. A boy usually got his first part-time position at the age of eight or nine, as an errand or delivery boy. These jobs were part-time only by Victorian standards. Walter Southgate's first job in the 1890s was as a barrow boy for a milkman. He delivered milk before school, and then polished churns and did general cleaning after school and on weekends. He worked forty hours a week, earning 3 shillings and six pence per week, and went to school full-time. He endured this exhausting schedule for two years but admitted, "I sometimes experienced great fatigue, dropping off to sleep about 3 o'clock on Sundays and sleeping round the clock until five o'clock the next morning." A variety of unskilled positions existed, and boys changed jobs frequently. William Luby (b. 1883) found work at nine years old leading around a blind man for six pence. He also sold wax lights and newspapers, worked as a candymaker, and later was an errand boy for an upholsterer, all by the age of sixteen.[31]

Most such jobs had no hope for advancement. A few businesses still offered apprenticeships, but even these did not guarantee a steady income, as employers kept boys only as long as they were cheap labor. Allan Jobson (b. 1889) became an apprentice to a furniture maker where his "early training . . . consisted in cleaning and scavenging and portering heavy loads that all but broke my back and my spirit." He dusted, swept, and polished in twelve-hour shifts for three years, "receiving a shilling a week for the first year, three shillings for the next and five shillings for the last." If he broke anything, his employer took it out of his wages; if Allan looked at the clock, the boss kept him after hours for spite. After three years of this "living death," Allan's employer fired him to hire another boy at one shilling a week. Allan went through three more employers in the next few years; one fired him when he asked for a raise. He finally got a permanent position as World War I began, only to leave when he joined the army in 1916.[32]

Some jobs opened up for girls at the end of the century, especially in retail and clerical work, such as typists or telephone operators. These jobs tended to go to daughters of lower-middle-class or skilled working-class parents. Typists made only ten shillings a week in the 1890s, not enough to live independently, but operators could work up to a living wage (a pound a week) after five years.

In the late nineteenth century, boys often found part-time jobs as early
as nine, including selling newspapers. This image shows an older boy
distributing papers to younger ones; note the raggedness of their clothing
and lack of shoes. Such work was not a living wage but would supplement
a family income. "Edinburgh Street Hawkers," in Robert Harborough
Sherard, *The Child-Slaves of Britain* (London: Hurst and Blackett, 1905),
between 172 and 173.

Still, most poor girls ended up in service or in factories. For instance, Alice
Foley left school at fourteen (in 1905) and went to work as a shop assistant,
cleaning, polishing the cases, dusting, and marking the prices. Nevertheless,
her employers let her go after a month's trial, so she went to the cotton mill, as
had her sister Cissy. Also in contrast to boys, girls moved in and out of formal
employment. Grace Foakes (b. 1901) left school at fourteen and worked as an

errand girl for a restaurant. She left this job when her mother fell ill with cancer and her father needed her to run the house.[33] Indeed, most girls expected to leave work upon marriage, so only a minority stayed long enough to earn a decent salary.

In addition to these formal jobs, boys and girls earned a penny here or there by watching babies, raising rabbits, or running errands. Kathleen Woodward, for instance, sold salt with a neighbor, helped another old woman on her frequent trips to the hospital, and removed sawdust from the floor of the local pub in the early 1900s. Arthur Harding (b. 1886) started a variety of semilegal money-earning schemes. He and his siblings collected waste potatoes (those too damaged or small for the regular harvest) and begged for coal from the gasworks and leftover wood from sawmills. He also went to the train station and carried luggage for passengers for tips. Other children in his neighborhood swept the pavements in groups or busked in the street (singing or dancing for pennies from the crowd). Few of the activities could turn into a career, but they brought in much-needed funds for poor homes and fit around the required hours in school.[34]

LEAVING SCHOOL AND LEAVING HOME

In the 1880s and 1890s, most children went to work full-time between the ages of twelve and fourteen, depending on the poverty of their families. The majority of boys continued to live at home and contribute to the family until they married. If girls found jobs in factories or trades like dressmaking, they too remained at home until marriage; if they were servants, they lived with their employers. Children's emotions about going to work were usually mixed. Almost universally, they put the end of their childhood at the moment they started full-time employment. Most hated the long hours and tedious tasks, and some remained angry for years at cruel masters or bore scars from accidents. In short, most jobs were boring, dangerous, and without hope of advancement. Allan Jobson's remark that his first job was "a living death" was matched by Kathleen Woodward's description of millwork as "a new slavery." For ambitious, smart children, a life of tedious manual labor, beginning at adolescence, was frustrating. Victorian autobiographies are full of stories of parents thwarting their children's desire for education, demanding that the children go to work instead of "wasting time on books." Charles Dickens's dismay at being pulled from school to work in a blacking factory is only the most famous example. Hannah Mitchell, whose mother had contempt for her daughter's love of books, never forgave her mother for turning her into a household "drudge." Even those children who had excellent relationships with their parents might regret their lost opportunities.[35]

On the other hand, many sons and daughters were glad to contribute to the family's well-being. If their jobs were no more stimulating than school, at least they paid for food and clothing. Hunger was a powerful motivator in reconciling young people to labor, and many took pride in their achievements. Boys, especially, had privileges when they became earners, including leisure time, pocket money, and freedom from chores. Jack Lanigan, who worked full-time at the age of ten, did not regret leaving school. His mother bought him a new suit, and Jack swelled with pride: "I now wanted to tell the world I was now a man, working and helping my mother." Because his older brother was also earning, Jack's mother could stop laundering, and they had enough to eat for the first time in Jack's memory. Even Kathleen Woodward, who hated her job, noticed that "the change in my status [at home] was swift—marvellous," from her mother's delight in being able to stop laundering. Girls, though, continued to have to help with domestic labor, a crucial difference from their brothers.[36]

Most children took it as a matter of course that they would work as soon as possible. Because they had no expectations of anything different, they were not disappointed. As stated in chapter 2, periodically particularly bright working-class children gained scholarships to grammar schools, and their parents allowed them to continue schooling. And some unusual children rebelled against their fates and fought to make things better for working people; these individuals usually grew up to be leaders of trade unions or the Labour Party. John Wilson, born in 1837, resented the conditions in the mines so much that he helped lead a strike at age sixteen; he had a long career as a labor leader and eventually won election to Parliament in 1885. Hannah Mitchell, who so much resented her mother's demands, joined the Independent Labour Party as an adult and demonstrated violently for women's suffrage between 1905 and 1914 as part of the Women's Social and Political Union.[37] But these reactions were unusual. Lifelong, poorly paid labor was not ideal, but most people had no choice.

CONCLUSION

The need to work at a young age sharply divided the working class from the middle and upper classes. A child in the lower middle class, the son or daughter of a shop owner or middling farmer, might help out in the family concern, but he or she did not leave school early to do so full-time. Well-off children avoided all paid employment until they had finished high school or public school and even university. Boys in this class trained for careers, and girls left home only upon marriage. Because most children saw the end of their childhood with the beginning of work, the class difference in the length of childhood was considerable. Gender differences were also important; girls had limited opportunities and had to fit in school and work with domestic responsibilities. Nonetheless, the necessity for work broke through gender barriers to some extent. Most upper-class girls assumed they would not have to work to make their living; working-class girls never made such an assumption.

Attempts to regulate child labor, feeble as some of them were, showed that the Victorian state valued children as national assets. The laws were not effective until compulsory schooling began in 1872 and 1880, and even afterward, children spent many hours at their part-time jobs. Nevertheless, the government set down the principle of universal education, and this inevitably restricted child labor. Politicians hesitated to interfere in business, worried that overregulation would harm profits, but the majority eventually accepted some curtailment of the exploitation of children. Observers assumed poor children should work but also learn to read and write. These two goals conflicted with each other throughout the nineteenth century; in the end, schooling won the battle.

Both the workplaces and the schools added extra layers of discipline to children's lives. Children faced strict controls in their homes, at school, and at work; indeed, in some workplaces, the masters used corporal punishment. Parents could clash with employers about the treatment of their children, but they often supported the training in hard work and self-control, and they also did not want to lose the income. Thus, the time that children had for leisure was especially valuable, giving Victorian children the chance to relax and be childlike. Fortunately, despite child labor, the nineteenth century also saw the expansion of leisure hours and whole industries devoted to children's pleasures.

4

Victorian Children at Play

Leisure time in the nineteenth century was not abundant for many children, but even the poorest played with games and toys and attended fetes and national celebrations. As with education, some convergence occurred over the nineteenth century; by 1900, a rhythm of life with set times for school, work, and play was standard, with the weekends the main time for relaxation. Increasing numbers of families enjoyed holidays, with Christmas as the central festival. Along with this came the commercialization of childhood, led by industries and publications devoted exclusively to children. Thus, though the amount of time for play differed sharply between the rich and poor, all children had moments of enchantment and whimsy.

PLAY AROUND THE HOME

The home was one site for leisure. Nearly all children had one or two toys, even if they were secondhand or in poor shape. Louise Jermy (b. 1877), for instance, had an old wooden doll with no legs and flaking paint that she nevertheless enjoyed. Costers sold cheap toys like tops and marbles, and unless the economic downturn was severe, they always had some business. Poor families also often had games, such as draughts (checkers), Snap, and Happy Families. And children collected a variety of cheap goods; Walter Southgate (b. 1890), despite having virtually no pocket money, collected cigarette cards, along with almost all of his friends, remembering, "We pestered the life out of passers-by for them." Almost all of these activities were inexpensive; in fact, probably the most popular game of all was simply playing make-believe, a universal activity for the young and one that cost no money at all.[1] Better-off children had more elaborate playthings. Typical toys included a Noah's ark (a replica of the ark with pairs of toy animals), toy soldiers for boys and baby dolls for girls, and wooden rocking horses of varying sizes, some so large they could carry five children at a time. These children had board games, like Snakes and Ladders, but also elaborate educational toys. For example, English county cards listed all English counties with geographic and historical facts (like the largest city or battles fought there). Others games taught scientific principles or mapped out the British Empire, all to improve young minds.

Children of all classes had intense relationships with some of their toys, much as children today favor certain dolls or stuffed animals. Indeed, because even well-off children had fewer possessions in general, their favorites were doubly precious, linked in their minds with happy occasions or parental attention. Mary Carbery, born in 1867, adored her German doll, Otto, despite the fact that he "was a wooden head with a kid body like a grub, armless and legless." When she discovered that her siblings and cousins had buried Otto during a game of "funeral," she wailed so loudly that her nanny forced the nursery maid and her older sister to resurrect him. Greville MacDonald's favorite toy in the 1860s was a wooden horse; the end of that toy was a turning point in his childhood:

> I loved it as much as any girl her doll, so that at last it must break my heart. It slept with me and fed with me, helped me to carry things away from their right places and compel them to some fairyland service.... But there came a day when our nurse had to caution me to be gentler with Dobbin or I should break him. Indignant with her narrow views as to his mortality, I exclaimed, "*He* won't break! He's *wood*, not china!" and, to prove my claim, I threw him against the nursery wall. Dobbin's back was broken: there he lay in two pieces, dead for all eternity. I think I was too much amazed to weep; yet the tragedy did, I know, leave my conscience with a wound I would not touch, knowing it could never be healed. Dobbin was dead: one door into the kingdom of magic was closed for ever.[2]

In all classes, children's first playmates were their siblings, especially those closest in age, as stated in chapter 1. Maud Ballington Booth (b. 1865) and her older sister Florrie were inseparable; as Maud put it, "My beloved sister was the center of my world." Sylvia McCurdy (b. 1876) did everything with her sister and two brothers, including playing hide-and-seek and tobogganing down the stairs in their large house.[3] Additional mates soon followed. Working-class town children quickly met neighboring children, as their mothers sent them outside to play, and gained more friends at school. Several autobiographers remember having best friends of the same sex. Arthur Harding, growing up in the tough Jago neighborhood of London in the 1890s, had two close male friends with whom he got into frequent scrapes. John Paton grew up in Aberdeen at the same time as Harding and did not spend much time with his two brothers. Instead, his friends were of his own age: "In a street such as ours, where children swarmed, playmates never lacked."[4] In the countryside, poor children might

Children had favorite toys and cared for them as if they were pets. Frances Freeling Broderip's collection *Tales of the Toys*, published in 1869, was built entirely around this notion, showing the growing importance of consumer goods to children. In this story, the doll's "illness" distresses her owner. "Dolly's Attack of the Measles," in Frances Freeling Broderip, *Tales of the Toys* (London: Griffith & Farrar, 1869), 94–95.

meet others in the local village, but they primarily played in the fields and woods with siblings, swimming, climbing trees, or picking mushrooms and berries.

Because of lack of funds and poor weather, working-class families spent some leisure time inside together. On Saturday or Sunday evenings, for instance, they might have a sing-along, inviting close neighbors, especially if the latter played instruments or sang. Other families told stories; Irish and Welsh parents knew many fairy tales and ghost stories. In the 1890s, Alice Foley's father recounted Irish folklore, including the tradition of leaving a basin of water for the fairies at night—a mistake, as Alice woke up the entire house at 4:00 A.M. the next morning in her effort to see if it were true. In addition, he had formerly worked in the theater as a sceneshifter, and, in her words, "Often, with unexpected dignity, he stalked round the house declaiming magnificent passages from the plays. On occasions, when quoting the Moor's noble lines, I was used as the unfortunate Desdemona, flung on to the old horse-hair sofa, and half suffocated by a sweaty cushion."[5]

Though well-off children had far more time and toys, they also had less freedom. Upper- and middle-class children played in their gardens or in special rooms set aside to hold their toys and books, and many of them could not venture out alone. Instead, families depended on one another for fun. Parents often amused their children; fathers, particularly, had designated times to romp with them. In the 1870s, Laura Troubridge's father spent the hour after tea with his children, drawing, making shadow puppets, singing, or telling stories. Most of the time, though, the children spent their leisure hours with one another. When they did see playmates outside the family circle, they paid formal visits. In the early twentieth century, Eileen Baillie had her friend Maggie Saunders over for tea parties from two until six in the afternoon. Their activities included playing "hunt the slipper," dressing up, making scrapbooks, and pretending to cook dinner. Children's parties, again with invitations and careful arrangements, offered other socializing possibilities. When young, these might coincide with birthdays; when older, they were more about sports, such as croquet or tennis parties.[6] Overall, well-off children had more leisured, but also more regulated lives, as Sylvia McCurdy explained:

To the child of today, accustomed to freedom from parental control from a very early age, our life would have seemed intolerably restricted. Until we went to school when Nigel was nine and Irene and I were ten and eleven, we had never left the house unaccompanied by a grown-up person. When Nigel refused to walk to school with us, after the first few days, because the other boys would laugh at him, it caused so much astonishment in the household that our cook used to get on a chair, in order to see through the area railings so young a boy going off by himself. As for Irene and me, the schoolroom maid took us to school and was at the school-gate to walk home with us.[7]

Class issues were not the only factor; play also differed by a child's sex. Girls had toys and games that fitted them for their future in domesticity, most obviously dolls. Girls also played "house" or "school" or "shopping." In general, girls pretended more than boys, perhaps because their parents discouraged them from too much physical activity, but this was not universal. A. S. Jasper (b. 1906) remembered playing "mothers and fathers" with his siblings in abandoned houses in their neighborhood. Because his father was an alcoholic, he would "play the drunkard husband. . . . Some girl would be mother and all the smaller kids would be our children. I would come home and want to know why the dinner wasn't ready and start to clump kids and be the tyrant father."[8] As this example shows, such play helped children cope with problem parents as well as offering a diversion. At any rate, "mothers and fathers" worked better if at least one boy participated, though many girls managed without male assistance.

The emphasis on gender difference was greater in the middle classes. Parents expected girls to be ladies, and so daughters could not participate equally with their brothers in rough play. Many remember being reprimanded for tomboyish behavior, especially if they dirtied their clothing in the process. Girls also learned accomplishments that they frequently enjoyed; they spent hours gardening (usually flowers rather than vegetables), drawing, or playing the piano and singing—all activities that promoted education as well as pleasure. Boys, on the other hand, had toys with mechanical or military overtones, especially toy soldiers. If they could not get actual soldiers, they substituted as best they could. James Laver remembered cutting soldier figures out of illustrated magazines in the early 1900s: "I cut out so many of them that I had a permanent callosity on my second finger." Francis Ommanney had a model train, an air gun that shot rubber darts, and a "Red Indian outfit which had no charm for me because I never wanted to feel like a Red Indian."[9]

In addition, social gradations existed within as well as between classes. Respectable working-class families, no matter how poor, shunned both workhouse children and those born out of wedlock. Catherine Cookson, the famous novelist, was the illegitimate daughter of an alcoholic barmaid in East Jarrow in the years before World War I. At a young age, she discovered that she was not "respectable" when she was the only child in her neighborhood not invited to a schoolmate's birthday party. Stubbornly, she arrived at the party anyway, and the young hostess refused to let her in, telling her she was not welcome because she "had no da." Families with drunken parents or semicriminal leanings were not in the same social segment as those with steady (if small) incomes and clean clothing. Walter Southgate's parents lived in a slum but maintained standards of decency and good behavior. They thus forbade their children to go into the rough Jago area nearby. Walter admitted, "I defied that restriction once, and I found the area cordoned off because of an outbreak of smallpox or cholera, so I quickly decamped and said nothing."[10]

Social restrictions were greater as one moved up the scale; the middle class was particularly careful. One lower-middle-class grocer forbade his daughter to play hopscotch on the sidewalk; instead, she could play only with children invited to the family garden. Eileen Baillie's rector father, serving in the poor East End of London, did not want her socializing with the local children. She remembered, "I could not for the life of me be made to understand why I must not play with the children in the streets. I could see for myself that they were dirty, their clothes ragged, their hair matted, and their noses constantly running. But . . . they were cheerful, often high-spirited; they screamed with laughter." Nevertheless, when she persisted in putting her hands through the iron railings to greet these children, her father put up a high fence to separate her from them.[11] In the 1880s, Eric Bligh's father, a doctor, restricted his son's access to parts of his work space specifically to avoid class mixing:

> I was strictly forbidden to go into the front surgery, partly on account of the danger of "catching something," and partly for the undemocratic reason that I was not to hold conversation with the surgery boy. The surgery boy was always a lazy little brute who was supposed to keep the dispensary dusted, and to deliver bottles to outlying patients. . . . We never got a satisfactory boy; and the poor, who drank our soup and our drugs, did not requite us well with their sons. I managed to spend many dubious hours standing wide-eyed before these nasty little oracles. I always expected, as a nemesis, to come out in spots, but the only time I ever did so was when my father coerced me to going to his Sunday school. . . . I caught measles, and I think my mother saw the humour of this.[12]

As this quote makes clear, this segregation did little to promote cross-class understanding, but it was ubiquitous. Upper-class children saw playmates when their parents arranged meetings or parties or at school. By limiting contact, parents controlled the social level of their children's friends and ensured that their children did not pick up diseases, bad language, or unrespectable habits.

OUTSIDE PURSUITS

In the cities, poor children lived in crowded, tiny homes without gardens, so their main playground was the street. Given the general youth of the British population, the streets in working-class districts were crowded to bursting whenever school was out; in fact, various commentators complained about the number of children blocking traffic. In South London, Ellen Chase collected rents in a working-class housing project in the late 1880s, and she could barely walk down the streets during school holidays:

> You had to wedge past knots of girls waiting their turn to skip-rope and to dodge flying balls and shuttle-cocks, and be wary lest you get a stray crack from a youngster busy at whiptop or wildly speeding a hoop. Sometimes

Poor children's main playground was the street, and they participated in games with neighboring families. This image shows the game blindman's bluff, one that did not require any equipment except a handkerchief and could include players of both sexes. From Dorothy Stanley, *London Street Arabs* (London: Cassell & Co., 1890).

five or six tiny lads played horse, tandem fashion, the end boy acting driver, while all the mothers looked on with amusement as they idled at their doors. Oftener still the lads were squabbling over tip-cat—a form of hockey—to the peril of our window-panes; or were wholly absorbed in a game called "Banger." This could be played in different ways; but in any case the point was to bang some small object, generally a jagged bit of slate, glass, or tin, up against a side wall with intent to displace, by the rebound, some marbles or a companion bit of tin in a circle chalked on the pavement. The children's toys were generally home-made. Joey Alford's ring-toss, for instance, was played with brass rings broken from buttons, which were pitched at a large nail stuck into a small block of wood.[13]

Most commonly, children played hockey, cricket, and football (soccer), or chalked the street for marbles or hopscotch. Some girls stretched their jump ropes right across the street, blocking any chance for traffic to flow smoothly. Playing in the middle of the road was dangerous, but poor children had little choice; public parks or playgrounds were not accessible.

Working-class children remembered a wide array of games, including tag (sometimes called "tig"), and other chasing games like capture. In the latter, one child was the keeper who stood in the middle of the playing area. The other children made two lines opposite one another and then ran across; during each pass, the keeper tried to catch one player. As children were caught, they joined the keeper in the middle of the playground until all were out. The last to be caught became the keeper for the next round. This was a very popular pastime;

variations on chasing games were legion. Numerous games also centered on collecting small tokens. In the 1870s, W. Pett Ridge played a game of marbles in which the first boy shot a marble into a dry gutter. The next boy tried to aim at it and hit it; if he did so, he got the marble. Children also used rocks, tin cans, and buttons as tokens. Ridge also played tipcat, which involved throwing around pieces of wood that had been sharpened at one end, a hazardous game from which he emerged unscathed.[14]

Both boys and girls participated in games like red rover or hide-and-seek, and other types of play were also mixed sex. In the Edwardian period, Edward Ezard remembered playing a game of tracking with his sister and her friends. Boys were hounds while girls were hares. The hares got a five-minute start to run away, but they were supposed to leave clues so that the hounds could track them. He and his friends had little luck catching his sisters: "Surprisingly fast runners, they might take us twice round the park at a cracking pace, then on the last corner before the Park gates we would find scratched a circle with a dot in the center, the agreed sign for 'Gone Home.' The girls, all unconcerned, were footing it out across the Circus. Reproach on our part led only to derision." Boys and girls both also played the most popular game, called Knock Down Ginger, which involved knocking on doors and then running away. Grace Foakes (b. 1901) described it as "the best game of all": "About a dozen of us would get into a line and run quickly along a street knocking at each door as we raced along. We must have been a great annoyance to the people who lived inside the houses but this was our favourite game and never once did we get caught."[15] Teasing neighbors did not lose its appeal; in fact, George Ratcliffe (b. 1863) appeared to have done little else with his free time:

[In the game cockleshells,] one lad would knock at a door, asking if Mrs. Swanston lived there. While the door was ajar, another lad would place three or four half-cockleshells above and below the hinge. When the door was shut, small but startling explosions seemed to take place.... [Long-tailed pony] consisted of tying a rope around the lad's body, fastening the other end to the door of any house, leaving some yards of slack rope, then giving a rat-tat-tat on the door. When the inmates tried to open it, the boy with his long leverage was as powerful as they; the door would open and shut, to the great amusement of the boys. When this see-saw had gone on long enough, the rope was cut, and the Long[-]tailed [p]ony was free, scampering away with the rest of us.... [In the game tip-tapping, a] lad would stand on the shoulders of another, and fasten a pin into the woodwork at the top of a house window with a piece of thread a few inches long, at the end of which a little stone had been tied. The end of a reel of black cotton was fastened just above the small stone; and after crossing the road and finding a hiding place, the thread was pulled, the stone tap-tapping on the window. Invariably some member of the house came out, looked about, and seeing nothing, went back.[16]

In all likelihood, contemporary British neighbors would report these activities to the police, who would arrest George or cite him for antisocial behavior. Victorian neighbors largely tolerated these high jinks, involving authorities only in cases of vandalism or property damage.

Despite some mixed-sex activities, gender differences in street play were also common. For instance, girls' tops had whips while boys' tops had pegs; boys rolled iron hoops and girls used wooden ones. Boys did not play hopscotch or skip rope, and girls avoided tipcat because it was not ladylike. Games exclusive to boys, in fact, often involved fighting and potentially serious injuries. Walter Littler (b. 1882) described playing a boys-only game called "fighting on horse-back." A strong boy was the horse with a lighter boy as a rider, and pairs of boys fought each other. He explained, "The horse had the job of keeping his feet, which was by no means easy, while each rider tried to pull the other from his mount." Even more peaceable games carried serious risks. Several boys played a game that involved half the boys lining up, bent over, while the other half tried to jump on their backs, the object being to get as many boys on the backs as possible with each boy taking only one jump. Any number of injuries could have resulted from a game of Jump Jimmy Knacker, but men remembered it fondly. As John Paton put it, "Most of our games were rough, involving at some point fierce scuffling and much incidental tearing of clothes." Indeed, straight-up fighting was common among boys; being willing to fight was one way a boy showed his manliness and gained prestige. In Aberdeen, boys fought frequently, but, according to John Paton, the fights "were harmless affairs and left no rancour."[17] One reason for the lack of hard feelings was that the fights had strict rules, as Walter Littler explained:

Once the fight had started, it was conducted in accordance with a few simple rules. The thumb had to be held touching, but outside of, the fingers of the clenched fist, not between the second and third fingers which would give a projecting thumb nail know[n] as "Coward's fist." If you had the good fortune to knock your opponent down, you must not hit him again until he had regained his feet. If on the other hand you could hook your left arm round his neck and force his head downwards, you had achieved a very strong tactical position. . . . With your right fist you could punch his imprisoned face for all you were worth. At any moment the fight would stop if one of the contestants shouted "Will you give in?" and the other agreed to do so. He retired perhaps with a bleeding nose, a black eye and a torn collar, but with honour untarnished.[18]

Playing in the streets was only one form of outdoor activity. Enjoying nature was common to all classes and both sexes. Rural children roamed over woods, streams, and fields in all seasons. Sandy Toye, born to a Cornwall farmer in 1877, became a champion swimmer and hiked through the countryside for hours at a time. J. R. Mortimer (born in the 1820s) ice-skated on local lakes, kept hawks and ferrets to hunt down rabbits, and went rook shooting with his uncle.

Boys and girls both played with hoops, though boys had iron ones and girls had wooden ones. Here a boy appears to be offering to show the girl how to use it. Note that they are standing in front of a display window, another indication of the growth of the retail trade in the Victorian period. From Dorothy Stanley, *London Street Arabs* (London: Cassell & Co., 1890).

An occasional poor town child had relatives or friends in the countryside and so could visit, and they too basked in the surroundings; usually these holidays were only possible in the late nineteenth century, when the rising standard of living allowed working-class families more time off. Edward Ezard's family borrowed a cottage in Surrey for the month of August when he was a boy, and he regarded it as idyllic: "Spreading fields in which to play, instead of our street beside the railway: mysterious woodlands to explore . . . and sometimes the winding paths went steeply down to rippling brooks where we tried to trap

In the countryside, upper-class children learned to ride horses, including "riding to hounds" (foxhunting). In this drawing, one horse runs loose, a danger in a hard-riding sport, provoking the warning cry, "[Be]ware the Horse." Despite potential accidents, both boys and girls learned to ride, though girls would do so with sidesaddles. From Caspar W. Whitney, *A Sporting Pilgrimage* (New York: Harper and Brothers, 1894), 19.

tadpoles with our handkerchiefs." He loved it so much that he wanted to stay and become a farmer, but his parents refused.[19]

Landed families frequently moved between homes, going to town (London) for some months of the year and to the country in the summer or at holidays. While in the country, both sexes learned to ride horses; many also practiced ice-skating, croquet, or tennis. Boys hunted, fished, and swam, and girls sometimes joined in. Sylvia McCurdy and her sister, Irene, had two older brothers, and they fished with them, climbed trees, and generally ran wild when the family spent its usual six weeks of summer in the country. Others simply took holidays miles away from home—fishing trips to Scotland, walking tours of Wales or Ireland, or visits to relatives across Europe. Samuel Smith (b. 1836) went on tramps with his father into the hills, fishing and hiking for as long as ten days at a time.[20] Few British children of any class doubted the benefits of hours outdoors, and for better-off children, the countryside offered rare freedom from adult supervision.

ORGANIZED GAMES AND SPORTS

Victorians loved sports, particularly rugby, cricket, and football, and all classes took part. Working-class children played in the street with improvised equipment. They used empty salmon tins or blown-up sheep's bladders for footballs, and they marked goalposts with coats. For cricket, they chalked lines on the ground to stand in for wickets and used a lamppost as a cricket stump; any piece of wood worked for the bat. Games did not always proceed smoothly; periodically a cart and horse came through the middle of the playing field or a policeman came by. The police constables, Walter Southgate explained, "frowned upon cricket and football as dangerous to neighbours' window panes." Their fears were justified; more than one child remembered games broken up hastily when the ball went through a window.[21]

Well-off boys had up-to-date equipment and, instead of playing on the street, used their gardens or grounds; this was not without its dangers, as they too broke windows. Molly Hughes's four brothers broke so many windows playing cricket in their garden that she got to know the glazier. Despite these dangers, the importance of sports for building boys' characters meant that parents, schoolmasters, and even religious leaders encouraged boys to play as many sports as possible (more on this in chapter 5). Girls had fewer opportunities for sports, but by the end of the century, girls' schools had teams in field hockey, golf, tennis, and cricket (though girls played with a softer ball). In addition, many girls learned croquet and cycling. Indeed, this latter was a bit of a craze in the 1890s; boys and girls of all classes got bikes (the poorer children's were secondhand), and cycling clubs sprang up across the country—two thousand of them by 1900. Cycling allowed freedom to travel much greater distances than walking. For middle- and upper-class girls, in particular, the ability to escape chaperones was liberating.[22]

The most popular sports developed professional and amateur leagues and set rules in the nineteenth century. Professional sports matches attracted whole families, especially football, rugby, and cricket. An occasional boxing match was also popular, and Wimbledon formalized its tennis championships in 1877, but poor people preferred bare-knuckle fighting and did not patronize tennis matches. In contrast, attendance at cricket and football in the last half of the century, when more workers had Saturday afternoons free, was impressive. For example, the Cup Final in 1897 for professional football, held at the Crystal Palace, had attendance of sixty-five thousand people. In the 1890s, cricket matches averaged fourteen thousand viewers, despite the fact that many were played in the middle of the week. Though most attendees were adults, boys accompanied their fathers to matches, ensuring the success of the leagues.[23]

SPECTACLES AND HOLIDAYS

In addition to toys, games, and sports, the city streets offered an endless array of possible diversions. All kinds of performers, including jugglers, magicians, singers, and street patterers, attracted crowds or offered moments of levity. More formal venues for family fun also abounded. The major public entertainment for the working class in the first part of the century was the penny gaff, an inexpensive variety show put on in warehouses or tents. These shows tailored their programs for children from eight to sixteen years old; the normal audience was 150 to 200 people. According to Eric Hopkins, eighty to one hundred gaffs operated in London in 1838, doing three or four shows a night, and they were still numerous in 1870. The major acts were dancing and singing and mimed melodramas; they could not do traditional dramas or comedies (with spoken words) because they were not licensed theaters. After 1870, gaffs declined, and music halls filled the void. By 1868, Britain had 339 music halls, 39 of them in London. Music halls offered variety shows, and patrons could drink alcohol while they watched. They were extremely popular in the 1880s and 1890s, and they based their appeal on working-class tastes. The comedy was broad, the songs common and sometimes vulgar; both men and women worked in drag and sang parodies full of double entendres. Fewer children went to music halls, though; nonadults tended to be teenagers, primarily boys. Even with this more adult audience, middle-class observers worried that these entertainments were demoralizing to the spectators, but little evidence exists to confirm this fear.[24]

In contrast, well-off parents took their children to more elevated venues, such as to the National Gallery or the British Museum. Except for a few days a year, these museums charged for admission until late in the century, thereby limiting their clientele, though by the turn of the century, many had begun opening for free on Sundays. Pleasure gardens, though less popular than in the eighteenth century, still existed; because of the fee, they too had few poor patrons. People could also see panoramas (paintings with lights and moving panels, often depicting battles) and dioramas (living people on exhibit, usually from so-called exotic places like Africa). Parents valued these spectacles because of their educational content. Middle- and upper-class families also went to the theater, but primarily the audience was adults and perhaps adolescents. The one exception was the Christmas pantomime, which began its run the day after Christmas in many theaters. This was a musical variety show based on well-known stories; children from all classes enjoyed these programs, though they did not have quite the same educational content as a Shakespearean play.

Upper-class children had frequent holidays. As stated earlier, their families traveled regularly to the countryside to fish or hike; many also went abroad, mostly to Europe. Robert Graves's family, for instance, visited relatives in Germany regularly around the turn of the century. The middle classes also took family holidays. Because of cheaper rail fares, seaside resorts such as Ramsgate and Bexhill became popular. Families took rooms for a week or two, relaxed, and swam in the sea. Working-class children had far fewer opportunities, but they increased over the course of the century. In the 1830s to 1850s, large numbers of London workers took "hopping" holidays to surrounding counties, especially Kent. Employers paid their way to the countryside; in return for the trip, the families picked hops (flowers of the hop plant, used to make bitter beer), earning some money along the way. Obviously, this was not a real rest, but it did get the family out of the city; the tradition continued, in lower numbers, into the twentieth century. Some factory employers sponsored day outings into the countryside for their employees in the 1850s, often by train. After 1875, when seaside holidays became popular, working-class families took day excursions, and a number of resorts catered to them, including Llandudno, Scarborough, and Brighton. In the 1880s, mill workers in Lancashire took a week off and went to Blackpool, which led to a booming holiday business there; between 1883 and 1914, the number of annual visitors to Blackpool rose from one million to four million. Parents and children boarded in cheap lodging houses and brought their own food, making it affordable even for large families.[25]

Children in both country and city also enjoyed festivals throughout the calendar year. By the nineteenth century, many formerly rowdy events had become more sedate celebrations, suitable for children. Easter was a major holiday because of its religious significance; children remembered having extra food, though not necessarily sweets. May Day was a huge affair as well, especially in small villages or in close-knit neighborhoods. Katherine Warburton, who helped run a school for poor children in Soho in the 1860s, remembered May Day dancing, which the children practiced for a month. They had a procession, the boys carrying lit candles, and then they all danced around the maypole. In many villages, too, May Day was a major event, especially for the one girl chosen to be the May queen. Toward the end of the century, children also celebrated the anniversaries of Victoria taking the throne. Her fiftieth anniversary was in 1887, and her sixtieth in 1897, and even the smallest villages held fetes and parades, discussed more thoroughly in chapter 5. One child's description of the 1897 celebration summarized the kind of activities on offer: "A lady broke her leg, and my Mother won the thread-needle race, they also had the 'Greasy Pig' loose in the streets and those who could hold it so long were the winners." Rural communities had their own occasions. Walter Littler went to the Runcorn Wakes, in his village: "Here were all the usual coconut shies, shooting galleries and merry-go-rounds, and for a number of years there was even a small menagerie."[26]

Well-off children celebrated more holidays. Because they had more resources, they were more likely to give gifts and send cards. Molly Hughes adored Valentine's Day and sent anonymous cards to her family and friends in the 1870s; few working-class children even mention this holiday. Middle- and upper-class children also had more fuss made on their birthdays, receiving an unusual amount of attention. Eirene Botting (b. 1899) explained, "On 31 March [her birthday] I was queen of the house for an entire day; my father even forewent his tea-time pupil to attend my birthday party and cheerfully submitted to the indignity of wearing a paper hat. It was the one day in the year on which I could do no wrong and on which I could be sure of basking in a warm glow of approval."[27] All children, though, benefited from the increasing number of national holidays, called "bank holidays." After 1871, these included December 25 and 26, Good Friday, Easter Monday, the last Monday in May, and the first Monday in August. Many employers followed the

May Day was a major holiday, especially in the countryside. Students practiced for weeks for the dance around the maypole. This image from a Victorian book of poetry, called simply *May-Day*, is an idealized portrait of the celebrations from the early modern period (sixteenth and seventeenth centuries). From *Favourite English Poems: A Collection of the Most Celebrated Poems in the Language* (London: Sampson, Low, Son, & Co., 1863), 145.

government's example, which gave their employees six days off and at least three long weekends a year.

By far the biggest celebration of the year was Christmas. As long as Britain had been Christian, Christmas was an important holiday, but Victorians began many of the practices now associated with it—the cards, the tree, Father Christmas, and stockings. These traditions came from Germany, under the influence of Prince Albert, Queen Victoria's consort. Of course, Christmas remained a central religious holiday; many people went to a church service. In addition, the eating of an especially fine meal was also an old tradition; the most common meal was goose, and, if possible, a Christmas pudding, prepared days in advance and covered in brandy and then set afire. But strictly Victorian practices emerged as well. Alice Foley's poverty-stricken family had high tea on Christmas Eve, followed by games and her father reading *A Christmas Carol* by Charles Dickens (published first in 1843). Then the children hung up their stockings and called their requests for Father Christmas up the chimney. Early Christmas morning, they hurried down to find full stockings, usually some nuts and sweets, a piece of fruit, a cheap toy, and perhaps a small coin.[28] Having these special family times was so important that the children themselves might go out carol singing to earn a bit of money. One little girl and her brother did so on Christmas Eve when her father was off work because of illness; when they returned home, they explained to their annoyed mother where they had been:

> I chimed in, "Wait till you see what we have brought you," and tipped the lot in her lap. When she opened four envelopes out dropped a gold half sovereign and five shilling pieces in the others, besides the odd silver sixpences. I shall never forget the look on her face. . . . We were kissed and hustled off to bed, and I looked through the window and saw my Mother in her bonnet and shawl, with a carpet shopping bag, running down the main street. . . . What a Christmas Day we had! Plenty to eat, a six-penny toy in each of our stockings. . . . The best surprise of the day came when we all trooped into the parlour for tea, to see our Father sitting in his usual chair, a huge bunch of holly upside down, high up out of reach, with sugar pigs, mice, apples and oranges threaded with white cotton, and some paper trimmings made out of blue and brown sugar bags and flour paste. My Mother must have sat up all night preparing it all.[29]

In the middle and upper classes, the presents were grander and food richer, but the magic was the same. Christmas traditions varied, but most children decorated trees, received presents, and ate large meals; many families also pulled Christmas crackers (small paper tubes that, when pulled, popped open and contained party favors and a paper hat). Sylvia McCurdy did not hang stockings but instead received parcels in the mail on Christmas Day. The climax was the discovery of her parents' gifts in the dining room, often "one big present for all of us," such as a cooking stove or a printing press—note that both had educational purposes. Children also had far more time with their fathers on Christmas than on any day except their birthdays. In addition, in the upper classes, parents encouraged children to be charitable during the season; Boxing Day (December 26) got its name because better-off families traditionally delivered boxes of cast-off clothing and coins to the local poor the day after Christmas. Eileen Baillie's mother arranged an annual Christmas tea for the poor children of their parish; she collected toys for weeks so that each attendee would receive a present. Eileen had trouble matching her mother's charitable spirit: "Although I was intensely sorry for the ragged, hungry children of Poplar, I do not remember that it ever occurred to me to part with any of my playthings for their benefit, unless prompted to do so, somewhat grudgingly, by some pretty forceful hints from Nanny!"[30] Still, Eileen found Christmas magical, as her description shows:

> For us the real excitement began on Christmas Eve, after tea, when we had our Christmas Tree in the Tumty Room. Dressed in my best frock, I would wait in a delicious agony of suspense in the nursery until Nanny came to tell me that I could go downstairs. That moment when I descended the three steps into the Tumty Room seemed to me the most entrancing instant of the festival: perhaps of the whole year. The Tumty Room appeared to have become a darkened, magic cave in which the central object was the illuminated pyramid of the tree itself, glowing with colour, heavy with fascinating parcels, and flanked by a large and jolly Father Christmas. . . . Like most children I was far too deeply engrossed in what I myself had managed to acquire even to care from whom I had received it—it was the present and not the giver that mattered![31]

COMMERCIALIZATION AND CHILDREN'S INDUSTRIES

Gift giving at Christmas was only one example of the increase in goods for children. The growth of literacy in the working classes meant that large numbers of children read for pleasure; many working-class autobiographies include loving descriptions of favorite books and magazines. Hannah Mitchell (b. 1871) had very little schooling, but she loved reading. She bought a book of poetry from a traveling salesman and pored over it so much that her mother took it away from her, "threatening to burn it." Though some of the reading was educational, much was simply fun, particularly with the growth of cheap paperbacks late in the nineteenth century. Frederick Rogers (b. 1846), like many working-class boys, read stories about criminals and highwaymen, which he insisted did him no harm. He added, though, that he read an "entirely respectable novel" called *The Scalp Hunters* and had a desire to "scalp my little sister, which desire, however, I was much too fond of her to gratify." Serials and children's magazines also became popular. Walter Littler and his siblings received "the annual edition of 'Chatterbox'" every Christmas, which "was regarded as public property and read by all."[32] Poor children found ways to read a surprisingly variety of works, as Mrs. Scott, interviewed in 1931, recalled:

> [W]hile at home we had *Chambers' Miscellany* and *Chambers' Journals*. I used to sit for hours lost in these books, and Wednesday was a joyful day for it brought *The Family Circle* and *The Girls' [sic] Own Paper*. I used to creep downstairs to see if they were under the shop door, so that we could read them before we went to school. We went through the usual girls' books, *The Wide Wide World, Queechy, The Lamplighter*, and at our Sunday School we had a very good library, where the librarian used to let me roam through the shelves.[33]

Well-off youngsters had far more reading matter and parents who regularly encouraged the activity. Robert Graves remembers his family's library having thousands of volumes; not surprisingly, he confessed, "We read more books than most children do." Emily Lutyens read constantly in the 1880s, an activity that fed her active imagination. She concluded, "The happiest moments of my childhood were spent in an imaginary world which I created for myself," usually pretending to be characters from books. Victorian children read a great deal of "high" literature—for example, Sir Walter Scott, Shakespeare, and Charles Dickens—but they also read books written specifically for children, which almost always had moral lessons. Reading was also a family activity. Mary Marshall grew up in the 1850s and 1860s, and her father read to the family in the evenings from such works as *The Arabian Nights, Gulliver's Travels*, Homer's *Iliad* and *Odyssey*, and Shakespeare's plays. Both girls and boys loved reading, though boys preferred violent subjects. Francis Ommanney, for instance, greedily consumed the works of adventure story writer H. Rider Haggard and science-fiction author H. G. Wells.[34]

An impressive number of books and magazines geared specifically for children went on the market after 1860. In 1866, *The Boys of England*, a cheap periodical of adventure stories, premiered and was soon selling 150,000 copies a week, which rose to 250,000 by 1871. To counter these unedifying stories, the Religious Tract Society published the *Boy's Own Paper* in 1879. At a penny an issue, it was too expensive to be a mass publication, but a rivalry between improving literature and so-called penny dreadfuls developed in the 1880s and 1890s. *BOP* and the similar magazine *Chums* (1892) fought with those published by Harmsworth Press, including *The Marvel* (1893) and *The Union Jack* (1894), priced at a halfpenny. Though church leaders worried that the adventure stories were too lurid, in fact their content was fairly tame, if melodramatic. Girls had fewer periodicals specifically for them, though a companion to the *BOP, The Girl's Own Paper*, began publication in 1880. It featured more domestic stories and fewer adventures and was not as popular as the *BOP*, though perhaps this was the result of girls having less spending money. At any rate,

ORIGINAL JUVENILE LIBRARY.

A CATALOGUE

OF

NEW AND POPULAR WORKS,

PRINCIPALLY FOR THE YOUNG.

IN ELEGANT CLOTH BINDINGS.

SUITABLE FOR PRESENTS AND SCHOOL PRIZES.

PUBLISHED BY

GRIFFITH AND FARRAN,

(SUCCESSORS TO NEWBERY AND HARRIS),

CORNER OF ST. PAUL'S CHURCHYARD,
LONDON.

WERTHEIMER, LEA AND CO., CIRCUS PLACE, FINSBURY CIRCUS.

This advertisement for Griffith and Farran's catalogue of books "for the young" appeared at the back of Frances Freeling Broderip's *Tales of the Toys*. The sales of juvenile literature rose steadily during the Victorian period as literacy improved. Note that these books were in "elegant cloth bindings" and "suitable for presents and school prizes." Many poor children received their first real books as prizes at school. Broderip's book published in London by Griffith & Farrar, 1869.

girls probably read their brothers' magazines; literacy rose dramatically with compulsory education.[35]

In addition, by the 1890s, toy makers expanded and marketed their products more directly. The development of retail trade (symbolized by the growth of department stores) made goods more accessible to women and children and encouraged shopping for pleasure. Mothers and children went out to stores together and browsed, tempted by the clever displays and comfortable tearooms. Advertisements for hoops, tops, and games appeared in many Victorian periodicals, appealing to parents more than children, but still influential. Christmas displays of fancy dolls and beautiful dolls' clothing attracted girls; toy makers also sold many elaborate dollhouses, toy theaters, and jigsaw puzzles. Another sign of the growth of these industries was that manufacturers began making children's beach toys after 1870 (e.g., sand shovels and buckets), a reflection of the increase in seaside family holidays. The poor, of course, were not welcome in department stores; instead, they bought cheap toys from market stalls. But they were not immune from advertising, especially when companies began giving away free toys in return for coupons from their wares. For instance, in the 1880s, a tea company gave away wax dolls in return for so many coupons ("proofs of purchase," in modern terms). Soap companies were the most active because they rivaled one another. Various companies offered paper dolls, Punch and Judy shows, reproductions of famous paintings, and paper screens for dollhouses. By the 1890s, then, even poor children had entered the calculations of Victorian businesses.[36]

CONCLUSION

Working-class children's warm memories of happy occasions help to mitigate the view of these children's lives as completely bleak and miserable, punctuated only by struggle and hunger. Hardships certainly existed, but children also had moments of leisure. Indeed, the rarity of the pleasures may have heightened the children's enjoyment of holidays and games, lovely moments stolen from school or work. Well-off children had more time for pleasure and more opportunities to travel and socialize at parties. On the other hand, both boys and girls faced restrictions on their playmates; parents commonly forbade their children to associate with lower-class children or those of different religions, and they could rarely go out alone, at least not in cities.

Though entertaining, much of children's literature and activities were educational in this period. Games taught geography and history, and girls tended flower gardens in their free time and learned various accomplishments. Middle- and upper-class parents planned excursions to libraries and museums and urged improving literature on their children. Despite the growth of child-centered businesses, parents limited spending money to avoid any spoiling. Parents also taught lessons about charity, as they wanted their sons, and especially daughters, to think of others first. Thus, the beginnings of commercialization in children's books and toys did not necessarily lead to a child-centered society. In addition, the modern reader cannot help but be taken aback at the number of dangerous toys and games in children's lives and the lack of safety precautions. In some ways, then, Victorians were less protective of their children than in the present, accepting the risk of accident as an inevitable part of childhood.

By the end of the Victorian period, church and state authorities realized the importance of filling leisure hours with "healthy" activities, thus molding children into good citizens. Some organizations were of long standing, like Sunday schools, but others were more modern inventions, such as the Band of Hope or the Boy Scouts. These institutions gave a new focus to children's lives; though they might regiment girls and (particularly) boys, they also offered opportunities for sociability and travel. They were yet another strand to the Victorian interest in children's development.

5

"For God and Country": Building the Better Boy (and Girl)

British governments have always concerned themselves with shaping the population into obedient and useful subjects by issuing proclamations, enforcing laws, and regulating publications. The nineteenth century saw three developments that made this process even more crucial. First, Parliament expanded voting rights in 1832, 1867, and 1884, to include two-thirds of working-class men by the 1880s. Second, worries about degeneration, sparked by the ideas of social Darwinism, made well-off citizens more willing to invest money in the poor, as with compulsory schooling and restrictions on child labor. Third, the expansion of leisure time for the working classes posed a potential danger; Victorians firmly believed that the devil found work for idle hands. Thus, charity workers, church leaders, and government authorities tried to create organizations to build thrifty, self-reliant, temperate, and chaste subjects. National schools offered one way to inculcate these values in children, but this resource was limited, because the schools also had to teach basic skills and because so many children stayed the minimum time. As a result, churches and children's organizations filled the gap.

RELIGION IN CHILDREN'S LIVES

Churches had allied with the state in moralizing the poor for centuries. Britain's established churches, the Church of England in England and Wales and the Presbyterian Kirk in Scotland, both took part in training children, as did the dissenting Protestant chapels (largely Baptist, Methodist, and Congregationalist, but also some Unitarians and Quakers), and the minority religious groups such as Catholics and Jews. In the first half of the century, the influence of religion was overwhelming. Some rural working-class districts averaged 80 percent

attendance at the national church, though attendance in towns was less. If not
in Anglican churches, people went to dissenting chapels. On March 30, 1851,
60 percent of physically able Britons went to church; of these, 49 percent were
Dissenters, 47 percent Anglican, and 4 percent Catholic (Jewish religious services, held on Saturdays, went uncounted. Only around 30,000 Jews lived in
Britain in 1837, which increased to 157,000 by 1901, due to immigration from
Eastern Europe). Anglicans dominated in the southeast of England, while Dissenters were strongest in Wales and Catholics had a large presence in Lancashire.
Scotland was primarily Presbyterian, but with a sizable minority of Catholics
in industrial cities. About half of Britain's Jewish population lived in London,
largely clustered in the poor East End. Church attendance declined over time,
especially among the urban poor. By 1902, the percentage of the population
in church in London was only 20 percent; many working-class parishes averaged around 5.5 percent. Still, even where church attendance was low, people
held baptisms, marriages, and funerals in their local churches. In addition, new
religious groups formed, such as the Salvation Army, started by William and
Catherine Booth in 1865. The Salvation Army specifically targeted the poor
urban citizens and attracted followers through uniforms, singing, and informal services. Though their national attendance was not huge, they had local
influence; for instance, the Sheffield chapel had four thousand attendees in
1881.[1]
    The experiences of children in church depended on several factors. Rural
families attended more often than did urban ones, and early-nineteenth-
century families were more dutiful than late Victorians. Religion associated
with nationality perhaps led to more fervor, as with Scottish Presbyterians or
Irish Catholics, and denominations had some class differences. Though having
parishioners of all classes, the Anglican Church was the church of the establishment, made up of employers and landowners. As a result, more working
people attended other congregations; for example, about a third of churchgoers
in the mining town of Merthyr Tydfil in Wales went to Baptist chapels in
1851. The Catholic Church had long-standing elite families but also numerous
poor Irish immigrants in its fold. Similarly, Jewish synagogues were divided
between well-off, Anglicized members who had lived in Britain for generations,
and new, often Yiddish-speaking immigrants, who were wretchedly poor. More
important than time or class, though, was the attitude of a child's parents. Some
parents were deeply religious, while others were indifferent. A Methodist lay
preacher in the countryside or a convert to the Salvation Army in the slums had
more religious enthusiasm than a nominally Anglican urban worker. Because
of all these things, children's investment in religion varied widely.[2]
    Usually, children followed their parents' footsteps. Intensely religious par-
ents prioritized spiritual training for their children and wanted such concerns
to dominate family life. Nominally religious parents, in contrast, had religion
as a backdrop to life, always there but rarely intruding openly. An example
of the former was Marianne Farningham (b. 1834), daughter of a tradesman,

This early Victorian illustration depicts an Anglican church in a small town. Attendance at national churches was high in many such places before 1850, and the parish church was the center of social life. Much of this had changed by 1900, as attendance at all religious services dropped. "The Village Church," in Peter Frederick Robinson, *Village Architecture*, 4th ed. (London: Henry G. Bohn, 1837), plate #36.

who shared her parents' firm devotion to the Baptist denomination. She went to church all day on Sunday, including a prayer meeting at 7:00 A.M., Sunday school three times (9:00 A.M., 2:00 P.M., and 5:30 P.M.), and two worship services (3:00 P.M. and 6:00 P.M.). In addition, her father questioned his children about their Sunday school lessons and the sermon in the evening, to be sure they had listened. Though she later modified some of the patriarchal sternness of her faith, Farningham imbibed these strictures:

> We got on better than most, because our mother was our minister, and the lessons we had on Sunday evenings were those of love; but our home was conducted on strictly religious principles. Father always prayed for us individually. One special plea for me I remember because it was almost invariably uttered, "Bless dear Polly, and grant that she may find favour with Thee, and with the people with whom she may come in contact." I knew this was asked because I was so much more plain-looking and uninteresting than my brothers and sisters, and that my future prospect was a gloomy one, but I hoped it might prove truly an answered prayer.[3]

Children with fervent parents, like Marianne, went through conversion experiences when young. Revival meetings led to children "getting the call" or "being saved," though the effects of these meetings often wore off over time. One boy, born in 1816, literally wore sackcloth and ashes after his conversion, and spent all day Sundays (7:00 A.M. to 10:00 P.M.) in church services and meetings. Yet he later rejected this view of religion, leaving the church when he was twenty. Still, some children found satisfaction and peace in religious life and looked forward to Sundays; Farningham was a good example of that, and she grew up to write for the *Sunday School Times*. All the same, the majority of working-class children did not have fervent parents. They instead received most of their religious instruction from Sunday schools (discussed in the next section) and went to services only occasionally. These children simply accepted religion as an invariable part of their lives but without much emotional investment. Similarly, middle- and upper-class children went to church regularly, usually to the established church, but had a more relaxed approach to religion. One rector's daughter (b. 1900) went to church every Sunday, but she also attended dances, and the family's daily psalm reading was accompanied by hugs. Though faithful churchgoers, these families did not have the fervor or the introspection associated with Evangelicals.[4]

Catholic children's experiences could be more intense because they faced discrimination as a group, though some were only nominal members of the church. Catholic children's religious life often focused on central rituals, such as first communion, first confession, and confirmation. Alice Foley (b. 1891) remembered all three of these rites of passage as nerve wracking; at her first confession her mind went blank, and when she finally stammered out that she had eaten meat on Friday, she was appalled to learn that this was a mortal sin. Fortunately, her penance was simply to light a candle to the Virgin Mary. Tom Barclay received a great deal of attention on the day of his first communion (in the 1860s), including an especially good meal after the mass was over, and he remained strongly religious during his adolescent years. The importance of ritual for Catholic observance impressed memories on young minds, as could any attacks or discrimination by the majority. Even those children who did not go to church regularly saw themselves as different from the Protestant masses around them, which fostered group cohesion.[5]

All church services at the time were very long. Children enjoyed music, incense, or stained-glass windows if these were present, but the numerous rituals and rambling sermons tested their powers of concentration. The pews were not padded or comfortable, and churches had no climate control. In addition, the sermons were incomprehensible, and difficult concepts earned little explanation. God was a remote, distant patriarch; hell was very real but hard to conceptualize (how could a lake could be made of fire?). Children imagined heaven in materialistic terms—as a beautiful palace with plush furniture and lots of sweets—and often mispronounced the litanies. Molly Hughes, for instance, loved stories of Jesus, but she did not entirely understand the story of

Families with strong religious views often studied the Bible and prayed together in the mornings or evenings. In this image, a Scottish family gathers around candlelight to read Scripture. The father, the spiritual head of the household, leads. "Scene in a Scottish Cottage," in Robert Aris Willmott, *English Sacred Poetry* (London: Routledge, Warne, and Routledge, 1863), 213.

the cross. She thought it was "a pity" that Christ died telling a lie: "This is what I read: 'Jesus just tasted the vinegar, and said, "It is finished."' My idea was that he had been given this horrid stuff to drink, tasted it, and then out of politeness pretended that he had finished it up." The formal ceremonies offer little opportunity to correct such misunderstandings. Because of these factors, one of the overwhelming memories for children about church was being either bored or puzzled. Much of the misbehavior of children in church came from these circumstances rather than aversion to religion itself; youngsters fidgeted, fell asleep, or began playing games to pass the time. Molly explained her own boredom and discomfort vividly:

My back still aches in memory of those long services. Nothing was spared us—the whole of the "Dearly beloved," never an omission of the Litany, always the full ante-Communion Service, involving a sermon of un-believable length. The seats and kneeling-boards were constructed for

Church services in Victorian times were very long, and small children had
difficulty sitting through them. In this charming picture from 1863, a small
girl sleeps in her pew while the adults around her pray. In reality, pews were
often far too uncomfortable for children to sleep, even if parents allowed it.
"Places of Worship," in Robert Aris Willmott, *English Sacred Poetry* (London:
Routledge, Warne, and Routledge, 1863), 235.

grown-ups (and not too comfortable for them), and a child had the great-
est difficulty in keeping an upright kneeling position all through the
long intoned Litany.... Some energetic clergymen put in extra prayers
at the end, even the thanksgiving—always associated with my blackest
thoughts.[6]

The other major emotion religion evoked was fear. The Presbyterian Church
preached predestination, a difficult theological concept for adults, much less
children. Samuel Smith, born in 1836 in Scotland, wrote, "I can well remember
the dreary and hopeless feeling caused by the statement that our destiny was
fixed by the inscrutable decrees of God before the foundation of the world, and
that nothing we could do would alter the Divine purpose." In addition, preachers
in all denominations taught through fire-and-brimstone sermons. Both God

and the devil terrified children; Charles Cochran, growing up in the 1870s, remembered believing that "quite trivial offences natural to all children might draw down his [Satan's] appalling wrath.... God, I remember had 'an awful eye' which was constantly watching us children from somewhere in the nursery ceiling." Some children were wracked with guilt for minor transgressions and spent hours praying for forgiveness. Farningham became obsessed with hell: "Many a time when I have been walking up that road alone, with a weight of many sins upon my conscience, I have been afraid there would be an earthquake, which would swallow me up.... Once, in a very dry season, there was a slight fissure in the road, and until the merciful rain came and healed it I often slipped away from home to see if it had grown wider, for I quite expected to meet my doom there."[7]

Those children who took religion seriously, then, might have lived in a state of anxiety about the afterlife for years. Though this undoubtedly motivated them to good behavior, it also made them associate religion more with fear than with joy. In particular, more than one child, hearing a sermon on the unforgivable sin of blaspheming the Holy Spirit, dreaded the final judgment and eternal damnation, sure they had offended in the one way that could not be forgiven. Greville MacDonald, for instance, suffered for months from his own imperfect understanding of the doctrine:

> Thereafter the fear of blaspheming the Holy Ghost dominated my life. I do not think either father or mother ever talked to us of that dread Being; yet something may have been picked up in church to set the ghastly Fear stalking.... Anyhow, from that day onwards, I began to visualize, whenever I was in the dark, a white-sheeted, Holy Being always tempting me, compelling me, to blaspheme Him: and simply that I might perish everlastingly.... I never dared confess my sin, or ask help even from my mother; though either she or my father would have instantly exorcized the insane possession.... But the experience has left me with a strong conviction that young children should have religion found for them in fairy-tales, Saints' tales, and the simple Bible stories.[8]

Even when Sundays held no such torments, they were not always pleasant days. Many families forbade normal activities, including games, outdoor play, or light reading material. One could only read serious or improving works, such as John Bunyan's *Pilgrim's Progress* or John Foxe's *Foxe's Book of Martyrs*. Molly Hughes, growing up in the 1870s, could not draw or paint on Sundays or read most of her books. Her parents, though, made an exception for illuminated texts, so she and her brothers copied out the Scriptures and decorated them as a diversion. Not surprisingly, many children dreaded Sundays, considering them gloomy and dull. On the other hand, Sundays also came to be associated with family time by the end of the century. Especially in better-off homes, fathers spent time with their children and were more relaxed, and the Sunday meal was the biggest one of the week. Families might also visit with friends or kin nearby or take short outings in good weather. These happier memories helped mitigate the less pleasant accounts.[9]

Religion stretched out to other days than Sunday. Some families enforced a rule of family prayers, at either the morning or the evening meal. Nightly bedside prayers were common in the better-off classes, and many children also memorized Bible verses every week, another activity that caused anxiety. Such nightly prayers did not always teach children the meanings behind the words they memorized any more than did the long sermons and rituals of the church services. Alfred Graves, for example, related this story about his son Robert, the future poet:

> When Amy went upstairs one evening to hear the children's prayers Robert asked her: "Mother, if you were to die, would you leave me any money?" Without waiting for an answer he went on, "If it were as much as five pounds, I could buy a bicycle with it." "Oh, but Robby," she said, "you would surely rather have me than a bicycle?" "Well, you see," he explained, "I could ride to your grave on it."[10]

Moreover, children did not always greet family worship with respect; to get through the family prayers, Eric Bligh's father had to ignore his sons' misbehavior, including throwing pellets at each other (Eric grew up in the 1880s).[11] How much children absorbed of their parents' beliefs, then, varied. Many did not continue to attend churches when they got older, but they did send their children, and few questioned the existence of God until the catastrophic losses of World War I (1914–1918).

SUNDAY SCHOOLS AND THE BAND OF HOPE

More children received instruction from Sunday schools than from church services. Begun by Evangelicals in the eighteenth century, Sunday schools grew exponentially through the nineteenth century. Religious leaders founded Sunday schools because so many children worked during the week. Authorities feared that poor children would grow up ignorant of Scripture, so they offered classes on the one day the latter had off. In 1800, Britain had 1,800 Sunday schools, half of which were Anglican; the rest were Baptist, Methodist, and Catholic. Over the course of the nineteenth century, the number of Sunday schools increased by an average of two hundred a year, and attendance rose steadily. In 1833, more than 1.5 million children attended on any given Sunday; in 1851, the number had grown to 2.4 million; and in 1906, it was more than 6 million. Since the population of Britain was also rising during the century, the increase meant that an average of 15 percent of the British population attended Sunday school, with the peak of attendance in 1881 (19 percent). Obviously, children continued to come even after compulsory schooling, but they began

Well-off families often enforced nightly prayers for their children. Mothers were very concerned with the spiritual development of their children; in this picture, a mother encourages her daughter's evening prayer. Note the traditional posture of kneeling with hands clasped in front and eyes closed. "A Child in Prayer," in Robert Aris Willmott, *English Sacred Poetry* (London: Routledge, Warne, and Routledge, 1863), 386.

later (at school age) and stayed longer (four to five years). Even parents with no religious beliefs sent their children to Sunday school, if only to have a few hours of quiet.[12]

Sunday schools met in the morning and afternoon, and sometimes also in the early evening. As stated previously, Marianne Farningham attended three Baptist Sunday school services, at 9:00 A.M., 2:00 P.M., and 5:30 P.M., because her parents ran them. The majority of children went to one or two of these meetings. Every moment of the Sunday school lesson was planned out and included several spells of singing and prayer, Bible classes, reading lessons, and spelling. Children with good memories memorized large parts of the Bible, though those without good memories suffered great anxiety at the command recitations. Sometimes children also heard improving stories, but those were as frivolous as the lesson became. In short, the curriculum was heavily moralizing and limited in intellectual scope. A common teaching plan was a combination of religious training and simple skills like spelling or reading, as in this example, remembered in an oral history from 1970:

> We sat in rows, risen so we could all see and be seen. Our teacher, Miss Holmes, was a little elderly lady, a school-teacher who always dressed in black, severe but kind. Our Starcards were stamped, there was a hymn, a prayer, a Bible story, then taking up the pointer, she turned to the Alphabet Board which hung on the back of the door and pointed to A, and we answered[,] "A soft answer turneth away wrath but grievous words stir up anger". The pointer then moved to B, "Be kind one to another, tenderhearted, forgiving one another"; C, "Come ye children, hearken unto me, I will teach you the fear of the Lord"; D, "Depart from evil and do good, seek peace and pursue it"; E, "Enter not into the paths of the wicked and go not in the way of evil men". So each letter was repeated, with its pearl of Wisdom from the Word of God.[13]

Later in the century, schools included more subjects, like music or science, for those who stayed for longer than the usual four or five years, but many children only learned the basics.

For working children, Sunday school was often a bright spot in an otherwise dreary week. Charles Shaw, who went to work in the potteries at the age of seven in the 1830s, considered it the best part of his life. He insisted that Sunday school had saved him from drink and dissipation and gave him great joy. The sheer numbers of such schools meant that even very poor children could attend. Emma Smith (born in the 1890s), the abandoned illegitimate daughter of a servant, worked as a beggar for her guardians. She nevertheless went to a Methodist Sunday school every week and "drank in the story of the Saviour's love for children." An occasional child claimed not to have good-enough clothes to go to Sunday school, but these were the exceptions, especially late in the century when different denominations competed for children. Shaw, for instance, faced persecution from the other children at the Anglican Sunday school when he came out of the workhouse because of his pauper uniform. Still, he found a kind welcome at a Methodist Sunday school, where the master gave him and his brother new clothes and lent them books to catch up on their learning.[14]

Other children were unenthusiastic about attending, especially after sitting through the regular church service. Allan Jobson, who grew up in the late-Victorian period, protested at first, though his mother gave him no choice: "I remember dawdling over our railway bridge, weeping, but all to no purpose." His first visits were not auspicious, as the children herded into a large room and sang "Shall We Gather at the River." During the hymn, Allan "knew what

Sunday school teachers could have close relationships with the children they taught and worked with local religious authorities to reach as many as possible. In this picture, the Rev. Jabez Tunnicliff, a temperance advocate, visits one of his teachers in the latter's final days. In Frederic Smith, ed., *The Jubilee of the Band of Hope Movement: A Jubilee Volume* (London: United Kingdom Band of Hope Union, 1897), between 48 and 49.

it meant and had not the least desire to do any such thing." Later, though, he enjoyed it because he was fond of his teacher. Many teachers had a positive influence and developed friendships with the children, especially those in need. Louise Jermy's relationship with her Sunday school teacher, Miss Hanna, somewhat made up for her stepmother's cruelty; Emma Smith, shunned by most children because she sang on the streets for her guardians, loved Sunday school in part because "the teacher always seemed to make a special point of being kind to me."[15]

Sunday schools offered tangible benefits as well. Organizers served refreshments at the meetings themselves or gave children free breakfasts. Arthur Harding (b. 1886) claimed that everyone in his rough East End neighborhood went to the Sunday school twice on Sundays, morning and afternoon, so they could have free breakfasts at the mission the following week. He never missed, though he mostly enjoyed the pictures rather than the lessons. In 1875 in Liverpool, Samuel Smith promised a free roll or loaf of bread to all attendees at his evening Sunday school. So many people arrived on the first night, including many mothers with babies in their arms, that "the noise was like that of Pandemonium." Not surprisingly, given the poverty of the area, the evening school soon became an established part of the city; twenty-five years later, an average of a thousand children attended.[16]

By far the most popular aspect of Sunday school was the annual treat. Children had to attend regularly to go, which explains why so few were truant. Countless autobiographies recall these adventures in idyllic terms. For parents, the treat allowed a day of peace and quiet in otherwise crowded homes. For city children, a trip to the country was their one chance a year to play in green fields, pick flowers and berries, and climb trees. In addition, the Sunday school provided an afternoon meal, including cakes, rolls, and scones with jam and butter, and children could have all they wanted. The lengthy descriptions of these teas, recorded in luxurious detail, showed the deep satisfaction of a full stomach to children used to self-denial, but the entire day was dream-like for most participants:

> The Sunday School outing was the one event of the year which we all looked forward to. You were only allowed to go if you had attended regularly, and as we had never missed a single week we always went. Sometimes we would go to Redhill or Epsom Downs, or even to Epping Forest. It didn't matter to us where we were taken, because it was a day in the country.... There were trees to climb, frogs to catch and, best of all, tea at three o'clock.[17]

Middle-class children also went to Sunday school, but usually as helpers to their parents rather than attendees. Eric Bligh's father, a parish doctor, forced his sons to go with him to Sunday school, but he had never asked them to attend as pupils. (In part to help herd the many children, Eric always got to go to the treat, which he did enjoy.) Eric and his brothers did not agree with their father about the usefulness of Sunday school, and this led to family arguments:

> My father's children had all a rooted objection to the Sunday school, and I think rightly. Instead of Sunday being a day of welcome pleasures, of garden or indoor happiness, the whole house was in a turmoil of my father getting off to Sunday school, and of his children, now approaching their teens, being rounded up and forced there. Anything more detestable than being driven out of one's own home to spend Sunday afternoon with a lot of children of a different but no less admirable education, and of a different but no less useful class, I cannot imagine. My father never seemed to see this.[18]

Still, many others worked in Sunday schools voluntarily, and some young women, in particular, enjoyed teaching. For middle-class girls, Sunday schools were an opportunity to do good works and act as professionals without compromising their class status or marriageability. Because no established churches allowed women to preach, perform rituals, or act as deacons or elders, Sunday school was the one place they could lead in worship. Whether the upper classes took part voluntarily or not, middle- and upper-class reformers remained convinced that Sunday schools gave essential training to children who otherwise might have no idea of morality.

Second to Sunday schools in importance in religious-educational groups for children was the Band of Hope (or BOH), founded in 1847 by the leaders of a temperance society in Leeds. The BOH asked children to pledge never to drink alcohol. Any child who took the pledge became a member and attended weekly meetings; these lasted about an hour and consisted of prayers and singing and lessons about the evils of drink. The BOH also sometimes had entertaining programs, such as magic lantern shows, and it formed orchestras with members, who received free lessons on different instruments. Children also joined Band of Hope choirs and sang in public. An 1862 concert in London had a choir of a thousand singers; it was so popular that the mass choir concert became a yearly tradition. In 1886, three choirs combined to bring a total of fifteen thousand singers to the Crystal Palace.[19]

The Band of Hope offered not only social events but also prizes and awards for essays and recitations; in addition, the local band marched in parades on national holidays. Children remembered these as exciting events, and some held their first leadership positions in the group. Walter Southgate, growing up in one of the poorest parts of London in the 1890s, joined when he was ten years old and eventually became a captain. He loved wearing the blue sash, and his main job was keeping the younger children quiet. This was not difficult, because the biggest benefit of the Band of Hope was the annual treat; all one had to do was threaten to deny this to any member and he or she would obey immediately. The treat was Walter's favorite benefit as well:

> This annual treat, the only outing in the year when, as a child, I was able to see the open country, was given to us free by the church people to all the total abstainers under [twelve] years old. We had a long ride in four-horse brakes, a free tea of bread and strawberry jam and dollops of seedy fruit cakes. What we couldn't eat at the time we secreted in our pockets, which crumbled long before we got into the horse brakes to come home. Bad manners, of course, but what do half-starved kids care about etiquette?[20]

Whether these groups actually promoted temperance, though, is unclear. Most of the members broke their pledge after they grew up; the pub was simply too much a part of working-class life. This was especially true of the poorest classes, the ones most in need of the money spent on alcohol. One girl from Bristol

Band of Hope Recitations

IN HALFPENNY NUMBERS.

Each containing 8 pp., crown 8vo., with an attractive illustration on Front Page.

Recitations and Dialogues

FOR BANDS OF HOPE.

48 ILLUSTRATED NUMBERS, ONE HALFPENNY EACH,

containing

164 Recitations and 47 Dialogues.

☞ The Series may also be had in
TWO VOLUMES—

Volume I., containing Nos. 1 to 24.
Volume II., containing Nos. 25 to 48.

PRICES.

In cloth boards .. .. 1/0 (postage 2d.)
In superior style, gilt edges .. .. .. 1/6 (postage 2d.)

THE HALFPENNY ILLUSTRATED

TEMPERANCE RECITER

24 ILLUSTRATED NUMBERS, ONE HALFPENNY EACH,

containing

83 Recitations and 25 Dialogues.

THE SERIES MAY ALSO BE HAD IN ONE VOLUME.

PRICES.

In cloth boards .. .. 1/0 (postage 2d.)
In superior style, gilt edges .. .. .. 1/6 (postage 2d.)

25 per cent. Discount to Bands of Hope ordering direct.

UNITED KINGDOM BAND OF HOPE UNION,
60, Old Bailey, London, E.C.

Band of Hope meetings occurred once a week and involved a range of activities meant to warn of the evils of alcohol. This advertisement offers more than 200 "recitations and dialogues" for Band of Hope meetings. The central organization also sold inexpensive pledge cards, flags and banners, hymns, and award medals to local groups. From Frederic Smith, ed., *The Jubilee of the Band of Hope Movement: A Jubilee Volume* (London: United Kingdom Band of Hope Union, 1897), back matter.

joined the group and enjoyed the activities but admitted that the moment she got home, she went out to get beer for her mother and usually had a sip herself.[21]

Other religious-educational organizations gave older boys and girls safe spaces in the cities. The Young Men's Christian Association, founded by Sir George Williams in 1844, was one such group, offering sites for leisure and inexpensive housing. The YMCA started out associated with Dissenters but soon disregarded religious differences and invited people of all faiths (including Jewish youngsters). As early as 1851, the group boasted twenty-four branches and two thousand seven hundred members. A version for girls, the Young Women's Christian Association, began in 1855 in London. Emma Roberts had begun a hostel for young women coming to the capital, and her group merged with Mrs. Arthur Kinnaird's organization that helped returning nurses from the Crimean War (1854–1856). The YWCA spread quickly; it had a branch in Edinburgh by 1859. Both the YWCA and the YMCA targeted older children, usually those who had already begun work or lived outside their families and thus needed housing. On the other hand, this ecumenical approach set the organization apart from many other religious groups, and its success was evident, spreading across the empire and into other nations, including the United States.

The attempts of religious authorities to reform poor children garnered, at best, mixed results. Some children literally found salvation through Sunday schools, beginning lives of religious intensity; others received basic education and some of their happiest childhood memories. At a minimum, children enjoyed day holidays and their parents got much-needed quiet. Whether such groups actually indoctrinated the poor into habits of thrift, temperance, and self-reliance is doubtful. Even at their peaks, these groups missed some needy children; in addition, many attendees often came for the free food and treats, not the lessons. The majority lost interest in religion after they grew up, and precious few Band of Hope members remained teetotalers. Still, these groups filled children's leisure hours in a way Victorian authorities could approve, thus fulfilling the main goal for the middle and upper classes.

TRAINING IMPERIAL SOLDIERS

Britain's role as a world power and the ruler of a vast empire required fit subjects for both the army and the navy. Governments had needed armed forces and promoted British patriotism for centuries, but the Victorian period saw new urgency to the quest. After Charles Darwin published *On the Origin of Species* in 1859, social commentators applied Darwin's theory of natural selection to society. They argued that some societies and races were fitter than others and deserved to rule. Collectively known as social Darwinism, such theories were intellectually illegitimate but nevertheless popular. Unsurprisingly, British authorities assumed that the British race was superior, but the physical state of many poor children was a cause for alarm. Many commentators feared that such "degenerate stock" would ultimately bring down the empire. In addition, some of these writers specifically associated the idea of civilization with better treatment of all dependents, including women and children. In other words, the most evolved state was one that cared for its weakest members humanely. For instance, Herbert Spencer, the British sociologist who coined the term "social Darwinism," specifically linked the idea of progress in society with improved treatment of children in his book *Social Statics*, published in 1851:

> Concerning the extension of the law of equal freedom to children, we must therefore say, that equity commands it, and that expediency recommends it. We find the rights of children to be deducible from the same axiom, and by the same argument as the rights of adults; whilst denial of them involves us in perplexities out of which there seems to be no escape. The association between filial subservience and barbarism—the evident kinship of filial subservience to social and marital slavery—and the fact that filial subservience declines with the advance of civilization, suggest that such subservience is bad. The viciousness of a coercive treatment of children is further proved by its utter failure to accomplish the chief end of moral education—the culture of the sympathies.... It turns out, too, that the very need for a moral training of children is but temporary, and that, consequently, a true theory of the filial relationship must not presuppose like the command-and-obedience theory that such a need is permanent.[22]

When social Darwinist ideas combined with the urge to teach poor children religion, the result was a mixed bag of organizations meant to promote fitness in mind and body, especially for boys. A prominent early example of such groups was the Boys' Brigades, founded in Glasgow in 1883 by William Smith. Smith wanted to show that Christianity was manly and strong, and he signed up boys between the ages of twelve and seventeen. The Boys' Brigades adopted many of the traditions of the military, including uniforms, drills, and discipline. The movement soon spread across Britain; several English cities had troops by 1885, and in 1899, England and Wales had 470 companies totaling 19,715 boys. Brigades marched and drilled, and many boys claimed that the exercise improved their fitness. In addition, members learned to play musical instruments, mostly drums and fifes; in fact, Boys' Brigade bands were in demand at local events and marched in parades. By the 1890s, the brigades also sponsored camping trips during which the boys slept outside in tents. These groups offered many new experiences, but in practice, the situation was not always ideal. Walter Southgate had initial enthusiasm but was disappointed when his London troop did not have enough uniforms (a pillbox hat, a sash, and some equipment) for all boys. The angry boys at the initial meeting expressed their displeasure by marching about on their own and singing bawdy songs.[23]

The idea of military-style clubs for boys spread, with many variations of the theme. Walter Mallock Gee started the Church Lads' Brigade in Fulham in 1891.

This group stressed temperance and was associated closely with the Anglican Church; by 1897, every English and Welsh diocese had a troop. Those who did not want an Anglican indoctrination but still wanted to build boys' characters stepped in to build up their own groups. In 1895, Lionel Godsmid began the Jewish Lads' Brigade to promote good character and physical fitness in Jewish boys. By 1900, the brigades had one thousand members. One unspoken aim of the group was to Anglicize Eastern European Jewish immigrants, thereby proving their worth as new British subjects. Similarly, the Catholic Boys' Brigade began in 1896, mainly for sons of poor Irish Catholics, often dockworkers. They drilled, camped, and played sports as well as learned religious lessons. These clubs had attracted eight thousand boys in Britain and Ireland by 1906. A Congregational minister even began a less militaristic version in 1899, the Boys' Life Brigade, which stressed lifesaving over military skills. All these groups appealed more to the sons of skilled workers or to the lower-middle class than to those in the slums, but they offered social events and exercise to those who could join.[24]

Unsurprisingly, girls did not have many imperial-military clubs. Instead, their clubs focused on protecting them from vice. For example, the Girls' Friendly Society (GFS), founded by the Anglican Church in 1874, filled young working women's leisure time with religious and improving activities, to steer them away from sexual falls. The heart of the GFS was the relationship between upper-class associates and lower-class members. Both categories of young women had to be unmarried and of virtuous character; founders hoped that the cross-class relationships would ease class tensions and promote godly living. By 1885, the GFS had 821 branches with 39,926 associates and 197,493 members in England and Wales; the group was highly popular with servants (57 percent of the employed members in 1891 and still 49 percent in 1906), but it did try to reach out to factory workers and shop clerks with limited success. Most non-domestic workers disliked the condescension of the associates and considered the group an outpost of the Conservative Party. (Though apolitical, the group argued for godly submission from its members, which clashed with the more assertive working-class politics of the 1880s and 1890s.) In the early 1880s, the organizers added a third type of member, a candidate, to appeal to younger girls. This section was supposedly the girls' equivalent to the Boys' Brigades, and the number of candidates rose to 81,374 by 1914. The group offered several benefits: social activities, holidays, a job registry, and popular reading material, including *Our Letter*, the newsletter for younger girls, which had a circulation of sixty-nine thousand in 1905. The experience of candidates, however, did not match those of Boys' Brigades in physical activities or military emphasis; girls' main roles were to be good mothers, producing future godly soldiers for the empire.[25]

The GFS clearly met a need for safe social spaces for young workers; it also showed a growing trend of attempts to reach across class divides. Similar impulses led to the opening of boys' clubs in larger towns in the 1870s and

Sporting clubs sprang up all over Britain in the nineteenth century. Some were attempts to cross class lines to promote fitness, while others fed into the growing professional leagues. The Amateur Athletics Association held regional championships in a number of sports, including pole-vaulting. "Pole Vaulting on a Mattress at Bradford," in Caspar W. Whitney, *A Sporting Pilgrimage* (New York: Harper and Brothers, 1894), 295.

1880s. In London, public schools sponsored these, such as the Mallard Street Club, founded by Eton in 1880, and the Notting Dale mission, started by Harrow in 1883. These clubs had games, playing fields, and libraries, and one in Portsmouth, run by Winchester College, even had a gymnasium. Boys of different classes mingled there, usually upper-middle-class boys mixing with those of the skilled working class. Ironically, the class differences mattered most when local hooligans, boys from the poorest neighborhoods who resented the intrusion, attacked the centers. The Portsmouth mission members, for instance, had to defend themselves from local toughs who broke the equipment and harassed them. The better-off boys and their teachers fought off these attacks, but relations remained strained and showed the limitations of class mixing.[26]

Though they were fewer, girls' clubs also started in the late nineteenth century. For example, Maude Stanley, a district visitor in Soho, founded the Soho Club for Girls in 1880, which gave teenaged girl workers a place to go in the evenings and offered classes in accomplishments like drawing, music, and French. As with the boys, this club catered to better-off working-class girls, as it charged fees. To lodge in the club, a young woman had to pay between three and seven shillings a week or a shilling a night, and meals were extra. In 1889, the club had 230 members aged thirteen to twenty-one. Some members were lower-middle class (e.g., clerks, shop assistants), but others were servants or factory workers. Stanley published a book called *Clubs for Working Girls* in 1890, in which she argued that clubs should teach discipline and cleanliness, first for the girls' character development but also so that they could influence their future families. Again, these clubs appealed to girls to help raise future sons of empire, but not to rule it themselves:

> If we raise the work girl, if we can make her conscious of her own great responsibilities both towards God and man, if we can show her that there are other objects in her life besides that of her gaining her daily bread or getting as much amusement as possible out of her days, we shall then give her an influence over her sweetheart, her husband and her sons which will sensibly improve and raise her generation to be something higher than mere hewers of wood and drawers of water.[27]

Though its beginning was slightly past the Victorian era, the culmination of all these efforts was the Boy Scouts, the brainchild of Robert Baden-Powell, a British war hero. In 1907, he invited twenty boys, some working class and some from public schools, to camp out for a few days, learning woodcraft and other outdoor skills. The camp was a success, and Baden-Powell wrote a handbook in 1908 called *Scouting for Boys*. The idea was so popular that a general movement took off almost at once. Aimed at boys between the ages of eleven and fifteen, the troops emphasized resourcefulness, patriotism, and chivalry, as well as teaching skills like following animal tracks, giving first aid, and tying knots. All scouts took oaths to support their country, help others, and obey scouting rules, and they had the motto "Be prepared." Scouting built comradeship and loyalty, in theory overcoming superficial class differences by stressing British nationalism and fitness to rule a large empire.

Boys' memories of being in the scouts were generally positive; they loved being outside, wearing a uniform, and acting as leaders. Edward Ezard joined as soon as a troop formed near his home, and he devoured *Scouting for Boys*. He could not afford a full uniform, but he could get by with a hat and stave, which was fairly common in his troop. (Eventually, better-off parents outfitted the entire group.) Ezard learned to march in fours to the beat of a drum, signal, tie knots, make campfires, and provide first aid. He also served as a patrol leader for a time, and he particularly looked forward to the outings to the woods, where he could build fires and follow animal tracks. In addition, he learned botany, boating, and hiking. Ezard quit when he was fourteen, after disagreements with the scouting leader, but the troop had dominated his social life during his early adolescence.[28]

At a large rally of Boy Scouts in 1909 at the Crystal Palace, a few girls appeared, wearing approximations of the uniform and asking to be included.

Baden-Powell did not think boys would join troops with girls, but he did not want to discourage the latter. Thus, he and his sister Agnes founded a girls' version of the organization in 1910, called the Girl Guides (a name changed to Girl Scouts in the United States). Despite the fact that Agnes Baden-Powell issued a book called *How Girls Can Help Build the Empire*, girls did not have the same experience as boys. Instead of outdoor activities, girls' early programs emphasized home economics, with lessons in cooking, needlework, laundry, and child care. Few Edwardian working-class girls record joining the group, perhaps because poor girls had too many responsibilities at home, or perhaps because the activities were not as attractive. Edna Wheway (b. 1903), who grew up in an orphanage, became a captain of the troop that her children's home sponsored. Edna generally enjoyed herself, but she later detected both class and gender biases in the Girl Guides. The better-off girls, though kind, were much better educated than those from the home and also had less difficulty buying the uniforms and equipment. If Edna had not had a sponsor, she could not have participated. In addition, her experience contrasted with many Edwardian boys, as she earned badges in domestic tasks rather than camping or drilling.[29]

BUILDING EMPIRE THROUGH SPORTS

Though focusing most of their efforts on the working class, Victorians also believed in building up manly character in more affluent males who might grow soft from book learning or comfortable surroundings. One main method was athletics. Organized sports at public schools, especially cricket and football (soccer), were glorified as character-building experiences. The major events of the year at most schools were sporting contests with rival schools, and the leaders of the teams were the undisputed heroes of their houses. Headmasters believed that exercise and games stopped boys from developing "unhealthy" habits, which, in this period, primarily meant masturbation. The emphasis on sports also came from the movement for muscular Christianity, a way to make the morality of the Christian faith manly and tough. Sports ensured that British boys competed successfully on the world stage and encouraged a sense of fair play. One should play hard but never break the rules, and courage in the face of adversity (called "showing pluck") was particularly admired. Winning was good but not the point; competing well, showing team spirit, and keeping one's honor were the real victories (these values were in contrast to those of German and American athletes, who played to win). Thus, gentlemen did not compete for money, leaving some of the best players out of the growing professional leagues; instead, they played for honor.

The connection to the military in game playing was purposeful; many headmasters saw the game field as a precursor to the battlefield, and the games themselves as battles to be fought and, if not won, at least defended to the last. Educational reformers were convinced that the character built on a cricket pitch or football field made for brave, resourceful, and honorable military officers.

Playing sports was a central part of building imperial soldiers and officers. Competitive team sports—cricket, rugby, and football—were the most useful. The basic playing rules and regulations were well known by the late nineteenth century and provided early leadership roles for upper-class boys. "Putting the Ball in Play from Side Lines in Rugby Union," in Caspar W. Whitney, *A Sporting Pilgrimage* (New York: Harper and Brothers, 1894), 195.

Sir Henry Newbolt's 1890s poem "The Schoolfellow" made the connection between school games and warfare explicit:

Our game was his but yesteryear;
We wished him back; we could not know
The self-same hour we missed him here
He led the line that broke the foe.

Blood-red behind our guarded posts
Sank as of old and dying day;
The battle ceased; the mingled host
Weary and cheery went their way.

"To-morrow well may bring," we said,
"As fair a fight, as clear a sun."
Dear Lad, before the world was sped,
For evermore thy goal was won.[30]

As this poem demonstrates, upper-class boys gained leadership abilities from games. In this way, public school training was different from that aimed at working-class boys. The upper classes learned both to obey and to command, while the lower classes primarily learned to obey.

Though some girls' schools offered organized sports, the emphasis on character building was not as strong. Girls' clothing was restrictive, and upper-class parents feared that women athletes would "unsex" themselves by learning rough games. As a result, girls played noncontact sports (e.g., tennis, cycling, archery) in the safe confines of private clubs or their parents' homes. But the late-Victorian stress on sports did not entirely miss girls. A growing number of girls' schools developed teams and rivalries, especially in field hockey and cricket, though not with the same fervor as their brothers. The connection between sports and military prowess was not an issue with girls, but their schools stressed their need to be mothers of the empire, rearing fit subjects and ensuring future British prosperity.

PROMOTING PATRIOTISM: NATIONAL CELEBRATIONS

Large celebrations, like the Queen's Golden and Diamond jubilees in 1887 and 1897, were venues where all Britons—male or female, rich or poor—could come together and celebrate national triumphs. Whole towns turned out for parades and fairs that emphasized British feats of arms and worldwide empire. Many children remembered receiving presents (often cups with pictures of the royal family) and good food. Communities sponsored races and games and hired jugglers and clowns; others ended the day with concerts by local choirs or bands. These occasions helped shape children's view of the rightness of British rule. Empire Day, May 24, was similar, though largely confined to the latter part of Victoria's reign. At the turn of the century, London schools sponsored special activities for Empire Day, including the distribution of Union Jack flags and drills by the boy students. More elaborate processions had a succession of children in costume, representing various parts of the empire, or dramatic tableaux on patriotic topics, such as famous victories by British troops. The day ended with everyone singing patriotic songs, including such lyrics as, "What is the meaning of Empire? / Why does the cannon roar? / Why does the cry 'God Save the King' / Echo from shore to shore?"[31] Unsurprisingly, given this indoctrination, children rarely questioned the rightness of their country's causes.

The Boer War (1899–1902) brought out fiercer patriotism, with children roped in to help raise funds and support the war effort. The war was between the British, who wanted to control all of South Africa, and the Boers, descendants of Dutch settlers, who preferred to remain outside of British control. The African inhabitants were caught between these two groups of well-armed Europeans. The war went poorly for the British in the early stages; the Boers besieged major cities, like Mafeking, and the British suffered heavy losses. Children helped raise money by selling programs or tickets to concerts and enthusiastically paraded in victory marches or recruiting drives. On the darker side, many of them, especially adolescent boys, were not friendly to those who supported the Boers. One boy in Salford joined a gang of boys who broke every windowpane in the local vicarage when the vicar put up a Boer flag.[32] On the other hand, children happily joined in the explosion of celebrations that occurred when good news came from the front. Historians argue about how much the general population of Britain cared about the empire, but support for the British military rarely wavered, as Walter Southgate remembered:

> Naturally we children were all for the celebrations. We played games like "English versus Boers," wore celluloid buttons on our lapels portraying our favourite generals.... It only required the relief of Ladysmith or Mafeking to set the whole populace dancing, singing, waving flags, getting drunk and finishing off the celebrations with bonfires and fireworks.... We children enjoyed it immensely especially as the fire brigade was called out to save the cottages from going up in flames too.[33]

CONCLUSION

To some extent, socialization of children into support for Christian morality and fervent patriotism was successful. Children joined religious and imperial groups enthusiastically. Most followed the basic rules of decency and had respect for (or at least fear of) the law, and few doubted the need for British rule. Most working-class people firmly disapproved of atheists or pro-Boers. An occasional socialist or anarchist drummed up support for pacifism, but such positions had a limited appeal. Laborers preferred to express their grievances through unions or, increasingly, the ballot box, and working-class leaders, including socialists, expressed great pride in the empire. The middle and upper classes staunchly supported the importance of religion and patriotism. Even those who no longer believed in a personal religion attended church to set a good example, and these families sent their sons to India, Burma, and South Africa as administrators or army officers. Many children grew up without the slightest doubt that their privileges—of nationality, class, and gender—were natural and inevitable.

Nevertheless, these groups also show the limitations of organizations and preaching, especially for promoting religious fervor. Children too young to understand theology came to associate church with boredom or terror; after they grew up, they sent their children to Sunday school but did not attend services themselves. This was also true for the upper and middle classes; the Graves family prayers and church attendance did not stop Robert Graves from discarding religion after World War I, along with his beliefs in patriotism and class and gender superiority.[34] The reaction against these tenets in the 1920s, in fact, led to the picture many people have of Victorians today—prudish, hypocritical, and earnest to a fault. This is an unfair and incomplete generalization, but it is not surprising given the moralistic and Evangelical tone to most children's organizations.

In addition, these groups quite often left out large numbers of children. Girls did not have the same opportunities as boys. Sunday schools and the Band of Hope targeted all poor children, but those with respectable or skilled parents gained the most; those who lived in the worst slums or with criminal parents remained outside the pale. Indeed, whole groups of children did not fit into the norm, including orphans, paupers, illegitimate children, and juvenile criminals. These so-called lost boys and girls posed problems for Victorians who assumed that children grew up in two-parent households, and they were an even bigger challenge to a nation determined to shape the next generation into a law-abiding, productive citizenry.

6

Lost Boys and Girls

The experiences of orphans, paupers, and criminal children show the difficulties of any child without a functioning family, no matter how poor. Children growing up in institutions had huge disadvantages, including lifelong stigmas and endless sermonizing about their need to be grateful for the charity they had received. In these as in so many instances, class was a crucial dynamic. Any factor that made a child stand out from the norm was problematic, but economic resources mitigated some of the difficulties. A poor child without family support had a most difficult road ahead.

ORPHANS AND WORKHOUSE INMATES

Well-off children might live outside the family for a number of reasons, but their class position gave them advantages. For instance, when such children lost their parents at young ages, wider kin offered them alternative homes. As stated in chapter 1, the Troubridge siblings (four sisters and two brothers) suffered the deaths of both their parents in one six-week period in 1867. Both their maternal grandfather and their paternal grandmother offered to care for them in the wake of the tragedy (they chose the former). At times as well, parents lived abroad but did not want to take their children with them. For example, children of British imperial officials often lived with wider kin or even strangers, because the British assumed that the climate of India or Burma was unhealthy and the education there inferior. Famously, Rudyard Kipling's parents, stationed in India, left him and his younger sister in the care of strangers when they were six and three years old, respectively. The Holloways turned out to be abusive, yet Rudyard stayed with them for six years until his parents sent him to boarding school.[1]

Poor orphans, on the other hand, had fewer options. If they could afford it, relatives or neighbors took them in. In 1883, George Sims, a middle-class investigator of the poor, highlighted the charity the poor showed to one another in his book *How the Poor Live*. One example was a woman who temporarily adopted two children of a neighbor who had gone to prison for assault. The woman already had four of her own, but "she washed them and dressed them and did for them what she could, and she intended to keep them if she was able till the mother came out." Other records bear out this generalization. For example, Anna Davin studied London school files in the late nineteenth century; the documents revealed that orphans lived with a variety of family members, including cousins, siblings, and grandparents, most of whom were badly off themselves.[2]

Despite these heroic efforts, some children had no choice but to apply for state aid. The basis for public assistance to the poor was the 1834 Poor Law Amendment Act. This law authorized the formation of poor-law unions across the country and the erection of workhouses, according to the policy of "less eligibility." The latter meant that conditions inside the workhouse should be less eligible (i.e., less attractive) than even the lowest-paying job, to discourage lazy paupers. In addition, the poor-law commissioners limited outdoor relief (or out relief), small weekly grants of money or food to allow the families to stay in their homes. In theory, after 1834, if a family asked for help, all its members had to enter the workhouse. These regulations were a break with the past. Workhouses had existed before 1834 but often with fairly relaxed regimes, and the pre-Victorian poor had also received much out relief. In short, the Victorian rules showed new toughness on the "undeserving" poor. Once a family entered the institution, the authorities separated husbands from wives and parents from children as well as segregated the sexes. The food was, at best, unappetizing and without variety. Families saw one another rarely; in some unions, the visiting time was one day a week for one hour. Victorians stigmatized anyone who had been in the workhouse, and hiding the fact was close to impossible, as the following inspector's report from 1861 made clear:

> The girls are generally not unbecomingly dressed, but unnecessarily disfigured by cropping their hair, a practice which marks them out as workhouse girls when they are placed in service. Some Boards of Guardians have been considerate enough to allow their hair to grow to an ordinary length before they place them in situations. The boys, besides being hideously cropped, are disfigured and degraded by a dress which seems as if it had been specifically designed to humble them and impress on their mind ... that they are paupers. The material of which it is composed has the further demerit of an intolerable and unwholesome smell until it has several times been washed.[3]

Unless the head of the family could find someone to offer work, the family could not leave, and finding a job from inside the workhouse was difficult.

The workhouse was the most feared institution for the poor in the nineteenth century. This image, from 1837, is of the new workhouses built in the wake of the Poor Law Amendment Act of 1834. The architect tried to make it look less forbidding, but this made little difference to the children forced into the union. "Prospective View of Workhouse," in Peter Frederick Robinson, *Village Architecture*, 4th ed. (London: Henry G. Bohn, 1837), plate #20.

Most workhouses did not implement all of these policies because of lack of funds or local resistance. Nevertheless, workhouses have an evil reputation; Charles Dickens's *Oliver Twist*, published in 1837, has been hugely influential, and an occasional scandal fanned the flames. For instance, in 1855, the Bakewell workhouse authorities actually enforced all the rules of feeding and work, and the children's health deteriorated disastrously, to the point that the workhouse inspector insisted on changes. Still, one can easily overstate the horribleness of these regimes. During business depressions, when unemployment soared, workhouses could not hold all those who needed relief, so out relief continued. In addition, within the institutions, authorities provided food, clothing, and shelter, as well as some education, to the children. The conditions were unnecessarily harsh, but most workhouses changed their policies as regards children almost immediately. For one thing, children were supposed to be rigidly separated from adults so they would not "learn pauperism," but most workhouses were too small to do this. For another, children younger than seven received less harsh treatment than did those between the ages of seven and fifteen; many unions allowed young children to stay with their mothers. Curiously, too, the workhouse regime insisted that all people younger than sixteen were children and treated them as such; in the outside world, in contrast, many teenagers worked full time.[4]

Most important, four-fifths of the children on some kind of relief were outside the workhouse between 1834 and 1909, ranging from two hundred thousand to three hundred thousand most years. Considering the small amounts of relief, these children may well have been hungrier and more ragged than their counterparts inside the institution. Most unions gave only a shilling or a shilling and sixpence a week for each child, sometimes supplemented by a loaf of bread. Nor would unions pay school fees, though Parliament passed legislation allowing them to do so in 1855. In 1856, more than 200,000 children were on out relief but fewer than 4,000 of them went to school; by 1869, this had gone up to 22,033 but was still not a tenth of the children on relief. Schooling for children on poor relief was not mandatory until 1873. In addition, out relief could be removed at any time. Will Crooks's family went on out relief after his father lost his arm; they received two to three shillings and a loaf of bread a week. After some time, with little warning, the poor-law guardians called Will's mother to a hearing and said the payments would stop, but that they would give indoor relief to the children. Mrs. Crooks tried to struggle on alone but could not make ends meet, so the five youngest children went to the workhouse.[5]

In short, the workhouse was the place of last resort. Pure poverty, especially when fathers were unemployed, brought whole families there, but others came for different reasons. Orphans made up a large part of the population, as did many half orphans whose widowed mothers could not support them. Some children's parents deserted them, voluntarily or not; for instance, fathers and mothers could go mad or to prison, leaving their children to the parish. Moreover, in 1889 and 1899, Parliament passed laws allowing unions to take children away from irresponsible or dangerous parents. By 1902, around eight thousand children had been adopted this way. A summary of the various reasons a child might be in the workhouse can be seen in a report from 1837 on the workhouses in Norfolk and Suffolk. According to the report, the workhouses had 1,906 children between the ages of two and sixteen. Of these, 443 were illegitimate, 382 were orphans, 279 had been abandoned by their fathers, 54 had been abandoned by both parents, 171 had fathers in prison, 116 were the children of adults who needed relief, 144 were children of widows too poor to live outside, 36 were the children of widowers, and 122 were from large families who could not support all their children.[6]

Obviously, then, a number of unfortunate circumstances could force children into state care. Poor families with sons or daughters with mental or physical disabilities, for instance, had limited options. The poor-law authorities might give them a small amount of money per week or offer a place in an asylum or home for the blind or deaf or "feeble minded" (where such homes existed). Others, though, went to the workhouse. If they were not uncontrollable, they simply lived in the regular children's wards; if violent, they had to go to asylums.

Still, over time, a diminishing number of these children lived in workhouses. In Scotland and Wales, for example, most Victorian children diagnosed with learning disabilities or mental illnesses were boarded out or lived with their families. In addition, some institutions for educable "idiots" opened between 1840 and 1870, hoping to train such children for work by the time they were fifteen, though these had limited places.[7] Putting children in workhouses because they were disabled seems cruel, but alternatives to workhouses were not always better. Some council schools had separate facilities for such children, but these often left them open to ridicule, as Ethel Mannin remembered:

> There was at this school, as with many other council schools, I believe, a department for mentally deficient children. It was known as "the silly school." The teachers themselves referred to it as such.... A child who had a clubfoot or a deformed back would be sent to this department, irrespective of its mental condition. The preposterousness of this did not seem to occur to anyone.... They were in all respects completely segregated, and as such were of intense interest to the rest of us, and with the terrible cruelty of children we had no compunction whatever about taunting a child with having to go to "the silly school." For myself I was always terrified of these abnormal children.[8]

One of the largest groups of workhouse children were those who were illegitimate. In England, illegitimate children were legally parentless, and not even the subsequent marriage of their parents could change this (in Scotland, in contrast, the marriage of the parents legitimated the children if the parents could legally have been married at the time of the children's births). For upper-class children, these provisions were humiliating but could be overcome by carefully worded trusts and wills. For the poor, illegitimacy often meant dire poverty. The 1834 Poor Law Amendment Act held only the mother of the illegitimate child responsible for his or her maintenance, while the fathers got off scot-free. Though Parliament revised the law in 1844 and 1872, so more mothers could sue the fathers for support, many could not get enough money to take care of children on their own. Thus, these mothers gave birth in the workhouse, the least expensive place to have a child, and their children remained there until adolescence. Evangelicals regarded such children as products of sin; in addition, social Darwinists branded such "bad blood" as potentially dangerous to Britain's national health. Even those taken in by kin (the majority) could not escape ridicule, so those who were both illegitimate and workhouse "brats" faced much discrimination.

How long children remained in the workhouse varied as much as their reasons for being there. Deserted children or orphans might stay until they were apprenticed, anywhere from age fourteen to sixteen, boys to a trade or the military and girls to domestic service. Many children, though, stayed for shorter periods. Sometimes relatives claimed them and received outdoor relief for doing

Early in the nineteenth century, children with disabilities went to the
workhouse or faced discrimination in regular schools. Later, more homes
for children with special challenges opened. This image shows a teacher
helping a mute girl to speak. "Teaching the Dumb to Speak," in George
C. T. Bartley, *The Schools for the People* (London: Bell & Daldy, 1871),
between 398 and 399.

so. At times, a stranger requested a workhouse child as a servant or worker,
though unions investigated such requests carefully. Later on, too, workhouses
paid orphanages to take orphaned children, thinking it best to remove them
from the influence of pauperism. Finally, some children went in and out of the
workhouse, depending on the family's fluctuating income or on the willingness
of relatives to continue to care for them. Known as "in-and-outs," these cases

were the most difficult, as they disrupted the institution's routine. Again, the 1837 report gives an idea of the variety: 193 child inmates stayed less than two weeks, 223 between two and four weeks, 548 from one to three months, 307 for three months, 275 for six months to a year, and 474 for more than a year.[9]

Over time, the emphasis on giving children an education in the workhouse grew. In the 1840s and 1850s, workhouse children attended school at most for three hours a day and then worked for five or six hours, interspersed with meals and church services. Many early workhouses had schools inside the union, though not led by trained schoolmasters, so the education was poor. For instance, in 1868, one inspector reported that he examined workhouse children who had no knowledge of the Bible or basic math, and others who appeared to read well turned out to be reciting memorized passages; the inspector discovered the deception because some of the children held the book upside down as they read. In 1848, Parliament passed an act allowing unions to band together to build schools for the children; these were called "barrack" or "district" schools and could have as many as one thousand students. The barracks atmosphere was not ideal for teaching, and contagious diseases, like the eye disease ophthalmia, spread easily. Still, most of these institutions had professional teachers, so some basic learning took place. Other workhouses sent the children to the local schools; unfortunately, their haircuts and uniforms made them stand out. George Hewins (b. 1879) was outraged when he saw classmates ridicule two schoolchildren for wearing shirts with giant red letters that read STRATFORD-ON-AVON WORKHOUSE. Hewins complained to his wife, but she defended it. He concluded, "She was wrong, the Guardians was wrong, and all of us, letting it happen. Why was you punished for being poor?" Unfortunately, the situation he described was the rule, not the exception.[10]

Inside the workhouse, better-off unions hired professional teachers to improve the level of education. The school day lengthened over time too, though this was somewhat illusory. Half the hours spent on education were actually industrial training. Boys learned some sort of trade or worked at agriculture, while the girls did laundry, cooked, cleaned, or worked in a dairy. Poor-law officials insisted that the children had to have employable skills, which left less time for academic study. Workhouse boys and girls also often went to Sunday school at least two Sundays in the month and had church services every Sunday morning, sometimes at the workhouse and sometimes at the local church. Schooling came to an end at the age of apprenticeship, from fourteen to sixteen. After that, boys did the work of the men, often mindless and unpleasant labor, such as picking oakum (taking apart the fabric of old ropes). Girls' training continued to be almost exclusively domestic.[11]

Children's memories of growing up in the workhouses were uniformly negative. Charles Shaw entered the workhouse in 1842, when employers blacklisted his painter father for leading a strike. The food was vile and the sleeping quarters crowded. The sanitary arrangement in the boys' quarters consisted of a tub at the end of the room, which two boys carried down the stairs in the morning,

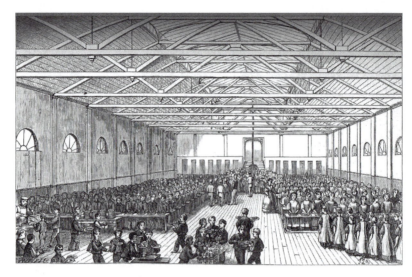

District schools helped workhouses combine their resources to provide education to child inmates. The size of such schools, however, was immense, which limited their effectiveness. This image shows the large dining room at the Hanwell District School, ca. 1871. "Dinner at Hanwell District School," in George C. T. Bartley, *The Schools for the People* (London: Bell & Daldy, 1871), between 204 and 205.

often spilling it. During the day, Charles had lessons from the workhouse administrators, and punishments were severe for any infraction. All inmates went to church services every Sunday, followed by a "special" dinner of bread, thin cheese, and water. The one bright spot was the hour he visited his parents, on Sunday afternoon. Though Charles escaped the workhouse when he was ten, his indignation about the treatment remained decades later, as in his description of his frightening initiation in the regime:

> It was all so unusual and strange, and so unhomelike. We finally landed in a cellar, clean and bare, and as grim as I have since seen in prison cells. . . . We might have committed some unnameable crime, or carried some dreaded infection. . . . We youngsters were roughly disrobed, roughly and coldly washed, and roughly attired in rough clothes, our under garments being all covered up by a rough linen pinafore. Then we parted amid bitter cries, the young ones being taken one way and the parents (separated too) taken as well to different regions in that merciful establishment which the statesmanship of England had provided for those who were driven there by its gross selfishness and unspeakable crassness.[12]

Over time, conditions slowly improved in workhouses. At first, some guardians meted out punishments such as caning, roping, and locking children in dark rooms for hours, despite contrary orders from the government. The majority, though, followed the rules, especially after workhouses opened to inspections in the 1860s. In addition, reformers publicized the need for less corporal punishment, better schooling, and more outside exercise, as with H. S. Tremenheere's reaction to a workhouse school in East London in 1843:

> The School had existed some years, and I found that the children (about 1,000 boys and girls) had never been allowed to go beyond the play-ground! With great difficulty I got the Guardians to consent to their being taken out for a walk twice a week. They declared they would be perfectly unmanageable. I anticipated that they would be so at first, for though surrounded by fields and woods they had never been in one. Consequently, their delight was such when they found themselves on grass and under trees and in green lanes, that they burst all bounds, screaming with delight at finding and picking the flowers. A remonstrance was addressed to me upon the subject but I induced the Poor Law Commissioners to issue a peremptory order that it should be continued. After a few weeks all went well, and the Guardians were reconciled.[13]

Moreover, by the late-Victorian period, more working-class men ran for local office and insisted on better treatment for inmates. Will Crooks had the great satisfaction of becoming a poor-law guardian in Poplar in the 1890s, and he saw to it that the conditions improved, including better food, elimination of uniforms, and proper schooling for the in-and-outs. After the first twenty years of operation, then, the workhouse was usually dreary because of the lack of love and the social stigma rather than starvation or beatings. Emma Smith, for instance, who went in and out of the workhouse in the 1890s, survived the regime but hated the stigma; her schoolmates called her "Old Union maid" because of her cropped hair. She concluded, "Children can suffer untold humiliations through such things." Many working-class autobiographies echoed this sentiment, waxing indignant over the purposeful shaming of the luckless children.[14]

ALTERNATIVES TO THE WORKHOUSE

By midcentury, many Victorians concluded that the workhouse was not a good place to bring up children, especially because institutionalized children might be unable to function in the outside world. Thus, at the end of the century, some workhouses tried to bring up children in cottage homes, which approximated family living. First opened in 1889, the cottages held twenty to thirty boys or girls, still a large number, but did have a mother or father figure in charge. On the other hand, they were all grouped together in the same villa, and so were similar to barrack schools in education. Another alternative was the scattered home system, where children lived in regular houses separated throughout a town or area. The first area to use this method was Sheffield in 1893; within three years, Sheffield had nine scattered homes with a total of ninety-seven beds. The advantage with this method was that the children went to the local school and gained knowledge of the world beyond the institution.[15]

In addition, unions worked with private charities to get other children out of the workhouse. A variety of homes took specific types of children—for example, those who were hearing or sight impaired, or those of specific religions like Methodism, Catholicism, or Judaism. Around ten thousand pauper children lived in these places by the end of the century. Most important, in 1868, Parliament passed a law allowing the unions to board out children to foster homes. This process had been common in Scotland for some time but was new in England, and slow to catch on, as a result of fears of abandoning less eligibility and concern for the children's safety. Still, eventually more and more unions followed the practice, paying a standard rate, often three to five shillings a week, to those willing to foster a pauper child. Dorothy Hatcher, an illegitimate child in the early twentieth century, was born in the workhouse but fostered out to a woman she called "Auntie Bea" when she was four years old. By 1906, 8,781 children were boarded out in families.[16]

These foster homes were, by necessity, temporary, as children had to leave when they were fourteen. Nor did they have assurance that they would not be sent back should their circumstances change. For instance, Hatcher returned to the workhouse when her foster mother took in a relative's child. Adjusting to a regular family life also took some doing; children accustomed to institutional control did not have social skills necessary to deal with regular schoolchildren. Dorothy Hatcher explained that

> I never really fitted in with the children at Smallhythe school. I had spent four years of life going from pillar to post and it took a long, long time for me to adjust; in fact it has taken the best part of my life. Auntie had quite a time placating angry mothers who complained I had kicked their child. I did this because all the children in the workhouse kicked out at anyone who upset them.[17]

Still, these alternatives were preferable to the workhouse regime, which was structured around adults. By the turn of the century, then, most pauper children lived outside the workhouse, in schools, cottage or scattered homes, orphanages, or with foster parents. Only children younger than three and a core group of children (mainly in-and-outs) could not be accommodated elsewhere. In 1906, 15,000 to 20,000 children were in workhouses but far more were outside the walls: 12,393 in district schools, 14,590 in cottage and scattered homes, 11,368 in special institutions, and a whopping 179,870 on outdoor relief.[18]

Wherever they lived, state children had little choice about their futures. Boys had to accept any trade the workhouse found for them, and girls all became servants or laundry workers. Boys, in particular, could be apprenticed

" Undertaking of Foster-Parent.

"Boarding-out of Child in a Home beyond the limits of the Union [or Separate Parish] to which such child is chargeable.

.................Union [or Separate Parish].
.................Boarding-out Committee.
.................Name of Child.
.................Religious Creed of Child.
.................Name of Foster-Parent.

"I, *A.B.*, of   , do hereby engage with the Guardians of the above-named Union [or Parish], in consideration of my receiving the sum of   per week, to bring up *C.D.*, aged   years on the   day of   last, as one of my own children, and to provide h   with proper food, lodging, and washing, and to endeavour to train h   in habits of truthfulness, obedience, personal cleanliness, and industry, as well as in suitable domestic and out-door work, so far as may be consistent with the law; to take care that the child shall attend duly at church [or chapel*], and shall attend school according to the provisions of the law for the time being; that I will provide for the proper repair and renewal of the child's clothing, and that, in case of the child's illness, I will forthwith report such illness to the Guardians of the above-named Union [or Parish], and to the above-named Boarding-out Committee; and that I will at all times permit the child to be visited and the house to be inspected by any member of the Boarding-out Committee, and by any person specially appointed for that purpose by the Guardians or by the Local Government Board. I do also hereby engage, upon the demand of a person duly authorised in writing by the Boarding-out Committee or by the Guardians, to give up possession of the child. †

" Dated this   day of   , 18   .
.........................*Signature (in full) of Foster-Parent.*
.... *Address of Foster-Parent.*
.... *Witness to the Signature of the Foster-Parent.*
....*Address of Witness.*

" *N.B.*—1. Communications to the Guardians to be addressed........................
2. Communications to the Boarding-out Committee to be addressed
...................................."

* Insert "church," "chapel," or according to the religious creed to which the child belongs.
† Any other matter which may be agreed upon may here be added.

(F) Form of Receipt of a Child by Foster-Parents.

" Union [or Separate Parish].

"I, *A.B.*, of   , hereby acknowledge that I have this day received *C.D.*, aged   years, from the Guardians of the poor of the above-named Union [or Parish], on the terms and conditions contained in the annexed under-taking; and that I have also received for the use of the said *C.D.* the articles of clothing set out in the list appended hereto.

" Dated this   day of   , 18   .
"Signature and Address..
"Signature and Address of Witness....................................
" List of Clothing.   Here set out the Articles in detail."

(G) Form of Schoolmaster's Report.*

" Report for the quarter ending....................

"(1) Name of child. (2) Age. (3) Name and Address of Foster-Parent. (4) Days absent from school during the quarter. (5) Alleged causes of absence. (6) Observations as to appearance, conduct, and progress of child. (7) Books and stationery suppled during the quarter. (8) School fees and cost of books and stationery.

"Signature.................... Address........................ Date..............
" N.B.—This report may be arranged in any other manner which may be deemed more convenient, provided that all the particulars above mentioned be included in it."

* See also form used by the Burton-on-Trent Board of Guardians, *ante*, p. 412.

Poor-law unions began boarding out pauper children to families in the late-Victorian years. Foster parents had to agree to provide a certain level of care, as the requirements of this form indicate. Note that the parents must agree to send the child to school every day and to church (or chapel, for Dissenters) every week. "Form of Undertaking by Foster-Parents," in W. Chance, *Children under the Poor Law* (London: Swan Sonenschein, & Co., 1897), 415.

while fairly young, often in agriculture, but also in crafts like shoemaking
or tailoring, which might already have too many workers. Disproportionate
numbers also went to the military. In 1895, 773 boys left the London poor-law
schools; of these, 185 went to the military (the rest worked in shoemaking,
tailoring, bakeries, or service). London girls had even fewer prospects; in 1895,
459 of 464 became servants. Because the workhouse had housed and fed them,
the authorities were not sympathetic if the children left their positions. Dorothy
Hatcher went to visit friends on a day off from her first job, as a kitchen maid,
and the employers immediately reported her as "absconded" to the union. The
guardians did not ask why she left but blamed her for running away. They
eventually found her another job, but threatened that if she left again she
"would be kept in the Union for the rest of [her] life." Hatcher resented this
treatment, complaining, "I was to them a chattel to be disposed as they thought
fit."[19] Even with all these alterations for the better in the late-Victorian period,
children still suffered from the stigma of pauperism. Unfortunately, this did
not change until the abolition of workhouses in the twentieth century.

CRIMINAL CHILDREN

The other major children of the state were those in jails and prisons. The
Victorian criminal justice system went through several reforms, but only later
ones addressed the needs of minors. In the early nineteenth century, the British
Parliament revised the criminal codes substantially. Most important, the government reduced the number of capital crimes from two hundred in 1800 to only
eleven in 1841 and carried out the remaining death sentences rarely, commut-
ing the majority to prison terms or transportation. Trials took place either in
local magistrates' courts (summary courts) or at the higher level (assize courts,
overseen by common-law judges), depending on the magnitude of the crime.
The crime rate during the Victorian period declined overall, and 90 percent of
trials were for property crimes rather than violent ones. In the early Victorian
period, though, the courts remained determined to stamp out juvenile crime;
they assumed that children older than age seven knew right from wrong and so
were responsible for their actions. As a result, courts treated child defendants
much as they did adult ones.

Victorians argued that they had a reason to fear youthful criminals. Especially
during bad economic times, children swarmed the streets, begging, thieving, and
"sleeping rough," and any of these behaviors could result in an arrest. In 1837,
over 2,000 children between the ages of seven and sixteen—1,962 boys and 334
girls—went to jail. In 1853, sixteen thousand children were in prisons, about
11 percent of the total prison population, mostly for trivial offenses. Before the
1850s, children received the same punishments as adults if found guilty. For
lesser offenses, they went to jail for periods of one week to three months, often
over and over. For example, one boy in 1858, at the age of eleven, had been
convicted fourteen times for crimes since the age of eight, mainly for stealing

food; his longest sentence was for three months. After the Juvenile Offenders Acts of 1847 and 1850, all crimes committed by children younger than sixteen could be heard in summary courts, and magistrates could order boys to be whipped or flogged rather than imprisoned. This meant being hit between fourteen and twenty-four times with a birch rod or whip, an extremely painful ordeal. For more serious offenses, children as young as nine were transported to the colonies or went to prison; an occasional child was also sentenced to hang, though these sentences were almost always commuted to prison sentences or transportation.[20]

Children in prison were heavily male, a ratio of six to one in 1837, seven to one in 1865, eight to one in 1875 and 1890, and twenty-two to one in 1900.[21] Their crimes were those of poverty—stealing, vagrancy, or begging. Far more adolescents, aged thirteen through seventeen, were convicted than younger children. Sometimes children were arrested simply for being homeless, though these children often ended up in the workhouse or industrial schools (discussed later) rather than prison. The high rate of recidivism was unsurprising, then, as the main cause of juvenile crime was poverty, and the Victorian criminal justice system did little to address it. Indeed, early in the century, the treatment of child criminals promoted recidivism rather than discouraging it. Boys and girls were not separated from adult criminals in jails while awaiting trial, so they had mentors of the entirely wrong sort.

The early Victorian view of prison was to punish, not to reform, so the conditions of prisons and houses of correction were dire. Life inside prison varied by the type of institution, however. The first prison solely for children was Parkhurst Prison, opened in 1838, which took only boys, mostly those awaiting transportation. After a probationary period, boys twelve and younger went to the junior ward, where they went to school for two hours and worked the rest of the day, and older ones went to the general ward, where they worked either at industrial training or on an adjoining farm. Misbehavior brought one to the refractory ward, which meant solitary confinement and reduced food, with whipping for more serious cases. Those who did well still were transported, but they received a conditional pardon upon arrival in Australia. Similarly, Tothill Fields Prison, rebuilt and opened in 1836, took only prisoners under the age of seventeen after 1850. The prison averaged 270 boys in the 1850s and maintained a strict schedule. The prisoners got up at 6:30, at which time they cleaned their cells and themselves. They began work at 7:00, then had a break for breakfast and chapel at 9:15. They had exercise and some schooling from 10:15 to 2:00, when they had lunch. They worked another two hours from 3:00 to 5:00, had dinner at 5:30, and were locked up in their cells again at 6:00 P.M. Children with long sentences got enough time for education and often made real progress. The work, though, was mind numbing, including picking oakum, repairing prison clothing and shoes, and making sacks.[22]

Especially in the 1830s and 1840s, the majority of child offenders went to mixed-age institutions. In such places, the first week of any prison sentence meant a diet of only bread and water, and any further weeks involved hard manual labor. The houses of correction (called "Bridewells" after Bridewell Hospital, an early example of the institution) were slightly less harsh, as they had some reforming roles, but they were hardly pleasant. In the 1840s, the British began experimenting with modern penitentiaries, in the hope of making the inmates penitent about their sins. These institutions had separate cells and enforced solitary confinement. This turned out to be too expensive, so many penitentiaries instead promoted the silent system, which forbade any talking between inmates but did have them work together and sometimes share accommodation. Such a system was completely wrong for children, who had great difficulty remaining silent and being restricted to cells. As a result, some prisons altered the rules for the younger inmates, allowing them to work in the garden, for example, rather than picking oakum. However, the strict regime of chapel, work, and school left little time for frivolity.[23]

When sent to such mixed-age prisons, children were not excused from hard labor. This term generally meant the treadmill, a large wheel with steps that turned a cylinder. Adults and children had to walk on the steps for up to six hours at a time. Other prisons required stone crushing or turning the crank, which simply meant performing revolutions with a crank. Some prisons required a number of turns before inmates could have breakfast, and others required ten thousand cranks before the end of the workday (6:00 P.M.) or the prisoner received no food. Anyone who refused to do the labor was punished with the loss of food, confinement to a dark cell, or a straitjacket. In fact, any insubordination received harsh treatment, including "impertinence at school," "having a very dirty cell," and "disorderly conduct." One boy, driven to distraction by punishments for refusing to turn the crank, hanged himself in his cell in 1853. His death caused a minor scandal but led to no consequences for the prison authorities. Still, typical punishments for any insubordination were a diet of bread and water or solitary confinement, though an occasional flogging or application of handcuffs and foot irons also occurred.[24]

As bad as these mixed-age prisons were, the floating prisons were worse. Called "the hulks," they were made from old warships that were no longer serviceable. As early as the 1820s, the authorities tried to have separate ships for boys, but there were too many juvenile offenders to do so. Rather than a strict discipline, the hulks were chaotic, as they were vastly overcrowded and had notoriously poor diets—outbreaks of scurvy, tuberculosis, and scrofula were common. Without effective oversight, the boys bullied one another mercilessly. Most of the labor was making clothes, which the prisoners did for as many as nine hours a day. Escape from the hulks was impossible; boys either completed their sentences or stayed on the hulks until they were transported, usually not before the age of fourteen. Though the conditions were terrible, the ships were not entirely scrapped as prisons until the 1850s, despite the opening of Parkhurst in 1838. After serving time on the hulks, boys went to British colonies in the South Pacific (currently Australia, New Zealand, and Tasmania).

Though transportation for children was suspended in 1846, this was temporary; the practice did not entirely stop until 1868. The overwhelming majority of offenders sent out of England—more than 90 percent—were boys. When they arrived in the colonies, they either went to the juvenile prison at Point Puer, in today's Tasmania, or they were immediately indentured to employers for seven years.[25]

ALTERNATIVES TO PRISON

Considering these conditions, many mid-Victorians questioned the suitability of prison for children and argued for more preventative actions. To help with the latter issue, Parliament passed a law establishing industrial schools in 1857. The law granted authorities the power to send any child younger than fourteen who was a beggar or who seemed likely to turn to crime to these places. In 1880, Parliament added any children in immoral surroundings, such as brothels, to the list of those who could be taken into protective custody. Many of these schools were overseen by religious or private foundations, such as the Church of England's Waifs and Strays Society. The relationship of working-class families to these institutions was complex. Parents who had abandoned or neglected their children usually continued to do so; though they were supposed to contribute to the cost, few did. On the other hand, the occasional parent used these schools to rein in problem children. Alice Linton's oldest brother, Arthur, hated school and began sleeping in the streets at ten years old to avoid going. His mother, afraid he would end up in prison, convinced the police to arrest him so that he could go to an industrial school. Arthur did very well in this more disciplined environment because he loved playing in the band and participating in sports; thus, his mother's gamble paid off. The majority of industrial schools were more like orphanages than prisons, though the requirement for work (e.g., cutting firewood or making matchboxes) meant that the education was limited.[26]

Several philanthropic organizations lobbied Parliament to offer alternatives to prison for children who had already committed crimes as well as those who were at risk. The leader was Mary Carpenter, who studied the backgrounds of child criminals and determined that they deserved pity, not condemnation. In 1851, she published a book arguing for reformatories rather than prisons, and she opened one herself in Bristol in 1854, a home for girls. Her guiding principle was that criminal children should receive education and discipline based on love rather than punishment:

> The principles already laid down will make it evident that love must be the ruling feature of the treatment of these children; this must not be a weak sentimental feeling, but a wise love which shall *evidently* have as its object the true welfare of the child.... Let him once be made to *feel* that all the discipline to which he is subjected emanates from a spirit of

love, and even the most severe will not alienate him from the teacher who enforces it, but rather bind him to him.[27]

Parliament passed the Youthful Offenders Act in 1854 (consolidated with other measures in 1866), which mandated that jails have separate facilities for prisoners younger than sixteen and that anyone sixteen or younger convicted of a crime with a penalty of fourteen days in prison would go to a reformatory after serving his or her time. (The length of the sentence changed to ten days in 1866; the requirement about the mandatory prison stay was made optional in 1891 and entirely abolished in 1899.) By 1858, England boasted more than fifty reformatories, and by 1907, the number of children in them averaged between 5,500 and 6,500. The juvenile population of prisons was often twice this in the 1850s, so Victorians had made progress in getting children out of jail, though not, perhaps, in stopping criminal or risky behavior. If one added in the population of industrial schools, the totals were higher; in 1882, England and Wales had ninety-nine industrial schools, holding 12,901 children, all of whom might have been in custody in the 1850s. Still, at least these boys and girls no longer turned cranks or walked on treadmills.[28]

Reformatories were not prisons, but the discipline was strict. In addition, the schools were always short of funds, and students' work made up the difference. As in workhouses, reformatories excused this use of child labor by insisting that they were giving industrial training. In the 1860s, for example, the Bridge Park Farm School reduced school hours so the boys could spend more time cutting firewood. Boys woke up at 5:15 A.M. and went to school from 6:00 A.M. to 7:15 A.M. They ate breakfast and had a short religious service, then began work at 8:00 A.M. Except for a lunch break, they worked until 4:45 P.M., then had one more hour of lessons, another church service, and a brief period of play before bed. The Mount Vernon Green Reformatory Home for girls was similar. The girls had a few hours of school but spent far more time on domestic work— cooking, cleaning, and knitting. Older girls worked in the laundry, which was the equivalent of hard labor. In part because of this limited education, reformatory children had few career options. From 1895 to 1897, for instance, 14,701 boys left reformatories. Of these, 1,620 went to the army, 412 to the Royal Navy, and 911 to the merchant marine; the majority of girls went to domestic service. Reformatories emphasized moral improvement, subservience, and hard work; they were superior to prisons but were not holiday homes. Religious groups ran many of them, and they stressed repentance and discipline.[29]

Reformers also worked to get more flexibility in sentencing children. In 1879, the Summary Jurisdiction Act allowed magistrates and judges to admonish children instead of sending them to an institution, and the 1887 First Offenders Act added in the alternative of probation for lesser offenses, those with less than two years' imprisonment as punishment. All the same, an entirely separate system for juveniles, being pioneered in the 1890s by some cities in the United States and in Australia, did not come to Britain until 1908. Though reformers pushed

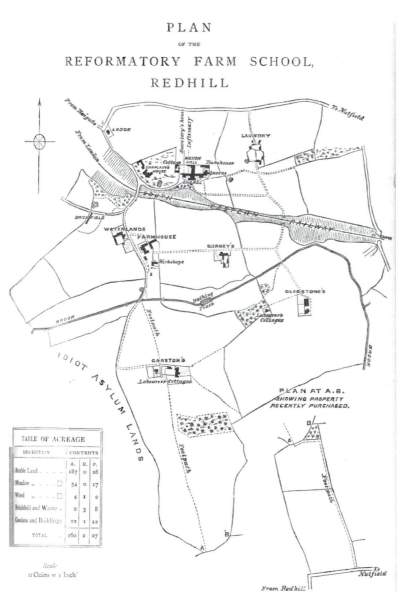

PLAN
OF THE
REFORMATORY FARM SCHOOL,
REDHILL

TABLE OF ACREAGE

DESCRIPTION	CONTENTS		
	A.	R.	P.
Arable Land	187	0	28
Meadow „ . . . ☐	54	0	17
Wood „ . . . ☐	4	1	2
Brickfield and Waste .	2	3	8
Gardens and Buildings	12	1	12
TOTAL .	260	2	27

Scale
12 Chains = 1 Inch

One alternative to prison for criminal children was a reformatory. This image shows an early blueprint for such an institution at Redhill. The plans include extensive farmland, a laundry, various workshops, and an "idiot asylum." Most reformatories were much smaller establishments and catered to specific needs. From George C. T. Bartley, *The Schools for the People* (London: Bell & Daldy, 1871), between 152 and 153.

for the change, their efforts were hindered by the Victorian fear of rewarding crime. The growing number of people who considered child criminals pitiable were counterbalanced by those who still feared victimization. Especially late in the century, respectable people felt threatened by hooligans, gangs of young, disaffected youths roaming the large cities all night, stealing and bashing where they could. These concerns were a typical Victorian panic, one that eventually subsided, though many Victorians continued to believe that adolescent males were a particular public safety concern.[30]

PROBLEM GIRLS

Clearly, the Victorian preoccupation with child crime was primarily directed at boys—for example, the Artful Dodger. Because criminal boys outnumbered girls by large margins, this was understandable. The one exception was the fear of vice, that is, prostitution. Many Victorian authorities argued that girls whose parents deserted or abused them, or girls who had been the victims of sexual molestation, were especially at risk for going on the streets. Once there, they could only make a living by begging, crime, or prostitution. Girls could also become pregnant, adding another illegitimate child to the population, or they could spread venereal disease. (A Parliamentary Select Committee in 1852 heard horror stories of twelve-year-olds with such illnesses, due to child prostitution.) Victorians assumed that any sexual knowledge ruined a girl, whether she initiated the contact or not.[31]

Moreover, girls who committed any crimes offered a real dilemma, as women's sections of prisons were small, and separating the girls from older convicts—often prostitutes—was difficult. Girls did not go on hulks, and far fewer were transported than boys; nor did most magistrates feel comfortable flogging them. Thus, most ended up in women's prisons, subject to the same regime as adult prisoners. Only larger institutions had separate facilities for girls, and these were overcrowded. In 1851, the Liverpool Borough Gaol had fifty-four girls but only twelve cells for them. The Westminster House of Correction also had a separate section in the 1850s; it had an average of 250 girls younger than seventeen between 1851 and 1855. Girls' regime in prisons consisted of long hours of work, laundering, picking oakum, knitting, and straw plaiting for hats. Rather than whipping, girls who misbehaved primarily were put into straitjackets or dark cells. Many went directly back to the streets upon their release; unable to get a recommendation from former masters, they had little hope of finding honest employment.[32]

To help remedy this situation, private organizations, like the Ladies Association for the Care of Friendless Girls, the Society for the Rescue of Young Women and Children, and the Salvation Army, took in at-risk girls and trained them for domestic service (more on these institutions in chapter 7). Others tried to reclaim the characters of first offenders. Mary Carpenter's reformatory for girls, mentioned previously, was one attempt at reclamation. Another,

Aaron's Court in Bristol, opened in 1856, specifically for Catholic girls; four others formed later the same year. The six together could take around 250 girls. Reformatories took girls who had committed a variety of crimes, including arson and theft, and tried to redirect them through hard work and religious instruction. Many places had laundries and used the free labor to make a profit; Hampstead Reformatory claimed to earn six hundred pounds per year from theirs. Laundry work was truly physical labor in an age with no electrical appliances, and the hot water and slippery floors led to burns and falls, but reformatories claimed the work gave their inmates training for an honest living. (Commercial laundries were more likely than private employers to hire girls with dubious pasts, as laundries kept all employees together and under direct supervision.) Girls convicted of serious crimes served their entire sentences in reformatories. First offenders of minor crimes, in contrast, might go to mission homes or refuges, such as the Dean Bank Refuge, in Scotland, where the regime was less strict.[33]

Most of these institutions concentrated on moral development, impressing on the inmates the need to repent their sins. This was the result of the authorities' fear, amounting almost to obsession, that girls would become prostitutes and spread their moral and physical "contagion" widely. Emma Smith, whose male guardian had molested her, ended up in a Catholic institution that helped "fallen" girls. At twelve, she was the youngest girl there. Despite being the victim, the authorities at the institution assumed that she had been ruined and had the same sexual knowledge as a prostitute, when, in fact, she was quite ignorant. Nevertheless, she shared their negative opinion; before her first communion (at age thirteen), she felt guilty about her sexual "sin" but was too ashamed to confess to the priest. She did not pluck up the courage to admit what had happened until she was sixteen.[34]

In part because of child prostitution, some girls did have extensive sexual knowledge by the time they were arrested or rescued. These girls posed a dilemma. Even organizations that did not blame such girls for their situations saw them as dangerous to innocent children. Many homes for criminal girls had limited space and did not want to use their beds for potentially "contagious" inmates; most refused to take them at all. Finally, in 1901, the Salvation Army set up a home in North London specifically for victims of sexual assault; several others, operated by the Church of England, opened between 1908 and 1914.[35] In short, at-risk, sexually victimized, or criminal girls had limited options throughout the nineteenth century, though things improved somewhat in the years before World War I.

GROWING UP IN INSTITUTIONS

Though gender differences were strong, the main influence that consigned children to institutional care was class. Upper-class boys got up to high jinks or "sowed wild oats," while lower-class boys were hooligans and threats to society. Poverty was the root cause of most children's crimes, and it led many children to the workhouse. Though the children were not responsible for their poverty, Victorians assumed they were the products of failures and had to be drilled on morality to avoid continuing the cycle of pauperism. Industrial schools and reformatories were preferable to prisons, but they too operated on the assumption that poor children needed only the rudiments of education and job training, with a strong emphasis on obedience and humility. The vast majority of institutionalized children were caught up in mechanisms they could not control and were blamed for sins they had not committed.

How did children react to being labeled a "pauper," "fallen girl," or "hooligan"? What results came from growing up in institutions rather than in families? First, all such children had a stigma, something that induced feelings of inferiority. Children dreaded being different, for it marked them out for teasing and cruelty. Poor children, in particular, had few ways to feel superior in life, but one way was to ridicule the pauper, the illegitimate, or the disabled child. Second, these children lacked the personal love that families both give and receive. Institutional life was bleak and dull. Eventually, the Victorian authorities recognized this fact and moved to foster and cottage homes, but these were not the same as having parents. As a result, a third outcome was that many children experienced depressions when they grew older; a number of illegitimate children, for example, attempted suicide or went to asylums as adults. More than one child complained of feeling worthless or that he or she had no right to exist. Unfortunately, their problems simply reinforced many social Darwinist beliefs that pauper or illegitimate children were defective and unfit; Victorians did not understand psychological concepts like self-fulfilling prophecies or inferiority complexes. Fourth, many children felt helpless in the face of state control. Pauper children had no choice about their futures; the state chose where they lived, where they went to school, and when and where they were employed. Such lack of control led to passivity in some cases but rebellion in others. The main problem for pauper and criminal children, in fact, was the total lack of interest in them as individuals, people with their own minds and hopes.

How much of the message of obedience and humility the children imbibed is also unclear. Certainly, the institutions made many pauper or criminal children ashamed of being different. But autobiographies also record growing senses of self-worth later in life and the conviction that no child should have to suffer for things that were not his or her fault. And the effect of prison and transportation on children was even more mixed. Victorians may have discouraged some children from further crimes, but recidivism remained a major problem. Arthur Harding, born in 1886 to a poor family in the Nichol slum of London, was arrested for the first time at age fourteen for being an obstruction in the streets. He went to prison for a year at sixteen for stealing a cart. Despite attempts to save him by private charities and the state, he became a regular part of the criminal world as a thief and pickpocket. All the punishment and reform in

Will Crooks (second from right) went to the workhouse with four of his siblings when his father could not support the family. Will's experience in the workhouse was so negative that he rebelled against the idea that poor people should be treated like criminals and later reformed the regime. His reaction showed that the Victorians' attempt to instill upper-class values in poor children sometimes backfired. From George Haw, *From Workhouse to Westminster: The Life Story of Will Crooks, M. P.* (London: Cassell & Company, 1907), between 18 and 19.

the world could not overcome his environment—his neighborhood, drunken father, and dire poverty.[36]

Obviously, some children's lives were better for the intervention of the state. Children whose parents were drunken or violent benefited from being removed to the workhouse or to industrial schools. Examples abound of authorities intervening to stop parental abuse, and the state care may well have saved children's lives. For instance, the Lambeth police arrested Mary Ann Payne for neglect of her three children in March 1854, because she habitually locked them up in her lodgings "for days and nights together, while she herself was at the publichouse [sic] wallowing in drunkenness and dissipation." Payne received four months in prison at hard labor while her children went to the workhouse. The workhouse was no playground, but at least the children had some freedom of movement, a warm bed, and a steady diet. Similarly, George Fenton beat and starved his five-year-old daughter in 1866; the Clerkenwell Police Court found him guilty of neglect and sent him to jail for three months. When found, the little girl was "covered with weals and bruises from head to foot." The workhouse may have seemed a paradise in comparison.[37]

As these examples make clear, Victorian state institutions could boast that some children were happier in the workhouse or even in prison after starving on the streets or enduring neglectful, drunken, or violent parents. Quite often newspapers reported that children gained weight and became healthy after they moved from parental to state care. Saving a child from a hopeless future was the point, even if Victorian methods were not always enlightened. And, over time, conditions improved. In fact, the treatment of lost children became a dominant concern for child savers and for Parliament at the end of the nineteenth century. This was all part of the Victorian expansion of childhood, the subject of the final chapter.

7

The Victorian Expansion of Childhood

Previous chapters in this book have noted numerous legal and social changes that increased the number of years that children could remain children. In the home, at least in the middle classes, family size declined, so parents spent more time with each individual child. Outside the home, the state legislated work hours and conditions for children while increasing the years of compulsory schooling. Leisure time for children expanded; numerous companies produced products marketed directly to them, and religious and patriotic groups recruited them. Finally, reformers insisted on alternatives to the workhouses or prisons for troubled children. In other words, on average, childhood lasted longer in 1890 than it did in 1830.

Why did so much of this change happen in the Victorian period? Attitudes toward children and childhood did change, though historians can easily overstate this; most parents in previous centuries loved their children and wanted the best for them. All the same, in the eighteenth and nineteenth centuries, the ideal of domesticity sharpened and increased the importance of parenting, especially mothering, in rearing children. Though this began in the middle classes, it soon spread up and down the social scale. The romantic movement's view of the child as inherently innocent also influenced the Victorians; it existed in tension with the longer-held view of Evangelicals that children needed to be disciplined and their wills broken to find salvation. These approaches were contradictory, but both urged parents to a close and intense relationship with their children. Political changes also influenced the expansion of childhood. As enfranchisement spread, so did concerns about the education of future voters. In addition, the growing anxiety about Britain's national power meant that child rearing become public policy, because the worldwide empire and mass armies of the late-Victorian period demanded an increasing number of healthy recruits. Finally, the economic changes of the period, especially urbanization, made hiding poverty difficult. Anyone walking through a large city saw vagrant, dirty children begging on the streets or sleeping in parks. Especially during the severe economic downturn of the 1840s, and again in the late-Victorian depression (1875–1893), the numbers swelled alarmingly, perhaps to as many as thirty thousand in London in 1848.[1] As a result of these factors, the nineteenth century saw an explosion of child-saving organizations and reforms.

CHILDREN AND CHARITY: HELPING THE DESERVING

The most long-standing way to help poor children was through charity, but Victorians did not believe in indiscriminate giving. Instead, they divided possible recipients into deserving and undeserving categories. Major charitable groups argued that only the deserving should receive private help; everyone else should go to the workhouse. Thus, any family whose poverty was the result of drunkenness or crime was excluded, as were unwed mothers, prostitutes, or couples who cohabited without marriage. The children who received help from these bodies, then, tended to be orphans, children of widows, or those whose parents were disabled. The main proponent of this view was the Charity Organization Society (COS), founded in 1869. The COS was an umbrella organization over religious and secular private charities, and it acted as a unified voice in lobbying Parliament. The COS tided over respectable families during crises but otherwise urged self-help; direct monetary gifts, then, were small and of short duration. Not all charities followed this strictness, but most groups did at least try to reform families before dispensing aid, to avoid wasting resources. Poor children, then, received help, but in return they listened to sermons or followed middle-class ideas of moral behavior.

For example, beginning in the eighteenth century, a number of middle-class do-gooders entered working-class homes to dispense advice and aid. The earliest, beginning in the eighteenth century, were district visitors, who went into poor homes and urged the families to stop drinking or gambling while handing out limited amounts of food, clothing, or fuel. In 1857, Ellen Ranyard organized the Ranyard Bible Mission, which tended to the poor in the St. Giles area of London. Ranyard trained Evangelical working-class women to go into homes and sell Bibles but also to help cook and clean. By 1860, she employed 137 so-called Biblewomen. The popularity of her home led Ranyard to expand into nursing. In 1868, district nurses began visiting homes and offering medical treatments and health advice. Such services spread to the countryside by 1889, funded by donations from Queen Victoria's Jubilee Institute (these women were known as the "Queen's nurses"). Similarly, health visitors, who stressed sanitation, began work in 1861, though they primarily distributed pamphlets with unrealistic advice for working-class homes.[2]

Other charities for the deserving centered on institutions. These organizations were legion in the Victorian period; London alone had seven hundred charitable groups. A donor could choose from a bewildering variety of causes, including fever hospitals (for children with infectious diseases), free libraries, mental asylums, or homes for sight- or hearing-impaired children. Those that targeted poor or abandoned children had particular resonance; few Victorians could resist pleas to help "poor orphans." Private orphanages ranged from large-scale institutions to small places with questionable credentials; such institutions mushroomed after the New Poor Law in 1834. The best orphanages kept children clean and fed, but all had the disadvantages inherent in institutional life, including lack of family life, strict discipline, ugly uniforms, and cropped hair (to prevent lice). One boy remembered going to an orphanage in 1897 when his widowed mother could no longer support him; as he walked on the playground, swarming with boys, he remembered deep dismay: "my heart sank into my boots, I wished the earth would open and swallow me up." In addition, like so many institutions, these places trained children only for manual labor and domestic service. The previous writer, for example, eventually apprenticed to a shoemaker at the age of fourteen. Edna Wheway, whose widowed mother put her in an orphanage when she was three (in 1906), had enough to eat and received schooling, but life in the orphanage was strict. She knew her siblings probably ate less and had shabbier clothes, but she nevertheless missed being part of a family. In addition, though she earned a scholarship for secondary school, she had no money to pay for her keep, so she left school at the age of fourteen for a life in domestic service.[3] She summed up her experience of being different by emphasizing her difficult interactions with so-called normal children:

> We had to wear a uniform to school which meant that we could always be recognised... we felt that they set us apart from other school girls who teased us. We could be seen from a long distance processing along the roads and the other girls would chant: "Here come the Home girls," which upset us. Sometimes boys joined in and chucked things at us: we dared not retaliate unless a bold girl stuck her tongue out. It never seemed to occur to grown ups that our identifying clothes could possibly cause children mental distress. I know that there were many excellent and practical reasons for having uniforms but children do not always use logic for things they like or dislike.[4]

Though open to criticism, charitable homes undoubtedly helped abandoned and unwanted children. Emma Smith, an illegitimate Cornish girl, had a brief stint in a Salvation Army home and remembered it as one of the best times in her childhood. She was clean, had decent clothing and enough to eat, and went to school every day. She also made friends and enjoyed the church services; for the first time in her life, she received Christmas presents and celebrated holidays. She did not feel stigmatized either, as this institution did not require uniforms. Unfortunately, the directors of the home soon expelled her, saying that she had been naughty. Emma could not remember having done anything wrong, but she later speculated that she had inadvertently sung an obscene song; she would not have known any better. But she never forgot the brief period of a "real" childhood, and it came not from a family home but from a charity made specifically for unwanted children, one that was sensitive enough to minimize the differences between its charges and other children:

> Clean and tidily dressed, my awful sense of inferiority was lifted, and though I certainly felt out of it all where lessons were concerned, my teacher was patient and helpful. Besides, I had the other home children to go to school with and to mix with at playtime. We were not dressed in any sort of home uniform, so that we were not obviously home children.[5]

In the stories of Edna and Emma, one can see both the good and the bad of charity to deserving children. The recipients had to be obedient and humble, and any behavior that indicated otherwise disqualified them. Those with uniforms and cropped hair could never forget that they were charity cases, and they could look forward only to domestic service or, in the case of boys, manual labor or the military. On the other hand, the health and education of many children improved, and institutions often served those who were not strictly orphans. Edna was the daughter of a widow, and Emma's mother and stepfather refused to keep her because she was illegitimate, but both girls found places. Some charities stretched the definition of deserving to include many children, though only as long as the latter conformed to good behavior.

HOMELESS CHILDREN AND FOUNDLINGS

By the early Victorian period, swarms of street children, called "street arabs," congregated in cities, begging or thieving to survive. As with district visiting, efforts to save these children began in the eighteenth century. For instance, the Marine Society, founded in 1756, trained poor, "distressed" boys for the navy or the merchant marine and was still operating in the 1830s. The Philanthropic Society, founded in 1788, took both criminal children and the children of criminals, training them for work over two years. Other pre-Victorian groups had wider purposes, such as the London City Mission (founded 1835), which helped children living in the streets find positions or places in institutional homes. Another early rescue attempt was the Children's Friend Society, founded by Captain Brenton in the 1820s, which sent homeless children to the colonies. All of these societies were small with tiny budgets, and thus they could only help a minuscule number of children; the Philanthropic Society had rooms for only 160 children, while the Children's Friend Society sent only 278 boys and 37 girls out of Britain between 1830 and 1834.[6]

Though these beginnings were humble, the second half of the century saw a boom in groups created to help homeless children, including fifty in London

Middle-class charities tried to get children off the streets. This image shows philanthropists offering a safe playroom to poor children. The room is unusually well stocked with toys and a piano; most charities would offer more basic accommodations. From Dorothy Stanley, *London Street Arabs* (London: Cassell & Co., 1890).

alone by 1878. Many were funded and run by religious denominations, both established religions and new ones like the Salvation Army. Changes in the laws aided them; the beginnings of compulsory schooling took most children off the streets, thus making children who lived "rough" more conspicuous.[7] These societies dealt far more with undeserving poor, and so they expressed class bigotries differently than did more traditional charities. Rather than hold the children responsible, child rescuers blamed the parents and pointed out the disadvantages of parental control of children. Consequently, these child savers worked to lessen parental custody rights and even moved tentatively toward a theory of children's rights.

Among the bewildering array of reform and rescue groups, a few stand out as notable examples of both the good and the bad in Victorian rescue work. Dr. Thomas Barnardo became immersed in child saving when he taught at a ragged school in East London in 1867. He opened his first refuge in 1870 and built its reputation with two unusual policies: his refuge accepted all children and stayed open all night. He argued that time was of the essence in saving a child. Any investigation into the children's backgrounds, then, came after they were admitted. In fact, Barnardo did not wait for children to come to him; he and his assistants prowled the streets of London at night, urging street children to come into the home. Barnardo had a refuge for boys in London and one for girls in Essex; by 1900, eight thousand children lived in his homes and one thousand babies in his Waif's Association. The homes trained children the same way that other charities did—the boys for a trade and the girls for domestic service. Barnardo also had a scheme to send children to various colonies, where (in theory) they could find work more easily; by 1901, as many as 5,500 children had left the country for Canada, Australia, and South Africa. According to the society, it had rescued 17,122 children by 1890 and given clothing and food to many more.[8]

Barnardo's tactics were controversial from the beginning. He had little respect for parental rights and boasted about kidnapping children from harmful environments. He was also firmly Protestant and proselytized the children, to the ire of Roman Catholics. In addition, his propaganda was often deceptive; one would think, looking at his literature, that all the children he took in were destitute nomads, but in fact many were half orphans or had respectable, if poor, families. Barnardo justified his tactics by the need for fund-raising, and his portraits did bring in money, but parents resented their depiction as drunks, louts, or abusers. Finally, Barnardo made little effort to ensure that the children he sent out of the country had decent places to live and work. Families did not adopt these children; the latter were, instead, unpaid workers, often in mines or on farms. They lost touch with their families in Britain and did not much improve their standard of living, at least in the short run.[9] Barnardo's work, then, encapsulated both the negatives and the positives of rescue societies; he helped many children, but his religious and class prejudices indelibly marked his approach.

In Barnardo's defense, most of the rescue groups in this period had similar limitations. For example, his was only one of many emigration schemes. Poor-law unions from across Britain sent out children (mostly boys), some as young as six years old, between 1869 and 1874 with little concern about what happened to them. In 1874, one board sent an inspector to Canada who discovered that many of the children were simply unpaid laborers, with minimal schooling or leisure, which led to a temporary suspension in emigration. Unfortunately, economic stress led to renewed shipments after 1883. In addition, many private groups also participated, including a Catholic charity devoted to emigration, led by Father Thomas Seddon. Seddon did not send girls older than nine years old and wanted thorough follow-up inspections for all. Though he got his wish, these inspections did not really help, as they only occurred once a year, and children were too afraid of retaliation to complain. In short, some child emigrants were better off, but others suffered abuse. Also, the numbers of immigrants to the empire, even at the height of the movement, were limited. In 1890, 101,593 children left England, but four-fifths of these went to the United States, far more than to any of the imperial destinations.[10]

Another prominent rescue organization was the Church of England Waifs and Strays Society (CEWSS, and later the Children's Society), which began work in 1881. Similarly to Barnardo, the group began in London and hunted out strays on the streets at night. Once it had rescued children, the CEWSS took them into one of its many homes (thirty-five by 1890), which served 1,600 children. The CEWSS arranged emigration for some of them or sent them to affiliated homes; in addition, between 20 percent and 30 percent went to foster parents. A few were unofficially adopted, either by their foster parents or others (adoption was not legal in England until 1926). The society expanded in the years before World War I. In 1905, for instance, it had ninety-three homes in England and Wales with 3,410 children in care: 2,406 were in the homes, 249 in affiliated institutions, and 745 with foster parents. Like almost all institutions, the CEWSS homes required distinctive uniforms, cropped hair, and strict discipline; some even required silence at meals or during walks to and from school. But the organization fed, clothed, and housed many deserted children, including "unrespectable" ones. They also kept records on their charges and performed follow-up inspections to see how they were progressing in their lives.[11] Because of this caution, the CEWSS files are an unusually good source on the lives of unwanted children. The following is a typical case summary, covering the life of a servant between 1886 and 1927:

> A. was illegitimate. Her father was drowned shortly after her birth, her mother stated that they would have married had he lived. After the death of A's father her mother married and had further children.... Her step-father was cruel to A. and beat her severely, this ill treatment may have contributed to her restricted growth.... A's temperament was quiet and patient. Her education was neglected although she had spent some time in school. On 21 September 1886 she was sent briefly to Connaught House Home for Girls, Winchester and then to Mrs[.] Fitzgerald's Orphanage at Elm Grove, Wimbledon. In December 1888 she was placed in service in Tooting and remained with the same family for over forty years.[12]

As this example shows, illegitimate children offered particular difficulties. Unmarried mothers faced real challenges both before and after giving birth to their babies. Some went to workhouses, but others gave birth alone. Ignorant and frightened, new mothers might desert or harm their babies. Even if they tried to keep the child, they had no money to support it; few employers, for instance, would hire a servant with a baby of any kind, much less an illegitimate one. Not surprisingly, the death rate for illegitimate infants (those younger than one year old) was twice that of legitimates. For example, in the 1880s, Glasgow's infant morality was 27.5 percent for illegitimate children and 13.7 percent for legitimate children; the figures for Manchester were 39 percent and 17 percent, respectively. To deal with this long-standing problem, Captain Thomas Coram had raised funds to build the London Foundling Hospital (LFH) in 1739. Originally, the LFH accepted all babies without question, but by the Victorian period, it had strict rules of admission. The babies had to be younger than one year old, and their mothers had to have "fallen" only once; in addition, the mother needed to have employment waiting for her should her child be accepted. Unsurprisingly, the hospital rejected far more babies than it took. The children who were accepted and survived infancy grew up in the institution, and most never saw their mothers again. After schooling, they went out as apprentices by the age of fourteen or fifteen. Like workhouse children, they had the twin stigmas of illegitimacy and poverty, though some overcame these difficulties. John Brownlow, for instance, grew up in the LFH and went on to make a career as the secretary of the hospital; he wrote an account of Coram's work in 1858. The LFH removed one group of London children from life on the streets, but only a tiny minority.[13] Few private charities could solve expensive national problems like child poverty and abandonment.

VIOLENCE AND NEGLECT

Simple poverty led many children to seek help, but others had more severe difficulties. Children whose parents were alcoholics, for example, often ended up in care. Drunkenness was a serious problem during the Victorian era. The pub was the central place in working-class social life, and drink took large parts of working-class pay. In 1880, the British spent 122 million pounds on alcohol, and the per capita spending rose almost 2 pounds (from 2 pounds, fourteen shillings and sixpence in 1855 to 4 pounds, seven shillings and three pence in 1875). A temperance advocate in 1882 estimated that drinking contributed to 40,500 direct deaths a year, as well as another 80,000 subsidiary deaths of the drinkers' dependents. Drunken fathers spent money that should have gone for food or came home surly and violent, causing serious problems for their families. In 1885 in Stockton, Margaret Dover sent her two sons, John Henry and William Scott, to beg in the streets. When the police arrested them for vagrancy, she explained that her partner was unemployed and their seven children were hungry. The police superintendent identified the real problem, explaining that "the man was drinking all Saturday night and Sunday." The magistrates dismissed the case on Dover's assurance that she would not let the boys beg again, but this hardly solved her problem. Drunken mothers, too, broke up homes; husbands returned from work to find their children dirty and unfed and the wife gone to the pub. William Bell and Elizabeth Morrison had two children, one who was two years old and one three months. By 1895, Elizabeth had been arrested for drunkenness nineteen times; she went to jail for the twentieth time in May 1895, and the magistrates sent both children, described as dirty and unhealthy, away from the parents. Even without blatant cruelty, alcohol abuse contributed to the hunger and raggedness of many children.[14]

In addition, children were vulnerable to violence. Because of the assumption that parents had the right to discipline children, much abuse went unpunished. Neighbors intervened in cases of life-threatening behavior, but the courts often did not follow through by giving appropriate sentences. Stepchildren or illegitimate children were in particular danger; in her study of Victorian Kent, a county in Southeastern England, Carolyn Conley found that 67 percent of the child

A portrait of Thomas Coram, the founder of the London Foundling Hospital. Despite its good intentions, the hospital could take no more than a tiny fraction of unwanted infants. "Captain Thomas Coram," in *The History and Design of the Foundling Hospital* (London: W. and H. S. Warr, 1858), by title page.

homicides were of either stepchildren or illegitimate children. A typical example was the 1853 case of George Vickers, who abused his stepdaughter, Harriet Herbert, after marrying her mother, Ann. Harriet was illegitimate, and both parents resented her presence. At six years old, she did most of the housework and still received constant beatings. The neighbors reported the incidents to the police, and George and Ann were both convicted of assault. Vickers was sentenced to a month in prison at hard labor and Ann to three months, sentences that showed that mothers were punished more than fathers, but both got off lightly. In Kent, 68 percent of those who killed children received eighteen months or less in prison, while only 21 percent were hanged, compared to 55 percent who were hanged for killing adult males. In addition, Harriet probably went to the workhouse while her parents were incarcerated only to be returned to their "care" when they were released. The poor-law authorities often refused to support children if they had able-bodied parents, no matter how cruel, and few alternatives to the workhouse existed in 1853. Later in the century, children like Harriet might go to industrial schools, but these places were limited even in 1900.[15]

Children were also victims of sexual abuse. Agricultural gangs were notoriously dangerous for adolescent girls, who risked rape from fellow workers or the gang master; similarly, servants had difficulties fending off unwanted advances from employers. Philander Kerry, of Suffolk, suffered a rape by her employer at the age of fifteen in 1854; though a court eventually found him guilty of assault, his only punishment was a ten-pound fine. Even when the attacker was a stranger, courts assumed that girls as young as eight might have "provoked" the attack. As a result, convictions were rare and sentences light. In Kent, for instance, the courts heard thirty-nine trials of sexual assaults on girls younger than twelve between 1859 and 1880. Of these, judges dismissed nine and reduced the charges to aggravated assaults in the rest. The maximum punishment, then, was six months, and only ten people received this; the rest served six weeks or less. However, these figures compared favorably with those of adolescent girls. Victorians assumed that girls older than twelve (changed to thirteen in 1875) could consent to sexual relations. In Kent between 1859 and 1880, only 52 percent of charges of rape of girls between the ages of twelve and sixteen were convicted, and 70 percent of these received eighteen months or less in prison.[16]

Sexual abuse also occurred in the home; incest was not as common as many middle-class observers assumed, but it was not unknown. Because incest was not a criminal offense in Victorian England, historians can only guess at its prevalence, but an occasional sensational case came to light. For example, Thomas Chekeley's wife went to an insane asylum in 1873, and he soon began a sexual relationship with his fourteen-year-old stepdaughter, Ann. (Many cases of incest came about when an adolescent daughter had to fill her mother's shoes.) When Ann had a child in 1875, Thomas strangled the baby, boiled the body, and buried it in an ash heap. The crime came to light when Ann became ill and had to see a doctor. Thomas was convicted of manslaughter and given a life sentence for the death of the baby, but his abuse of his stepdaughter was ignored. A man having sex with his fourteen-year-old stepdaughter was not illegal; in fact, Ann was sentenced to eighteen months in prison for concealing the birth of the child. Judges assumed that a long-term relationship implied the girl's consent, despite the vast power difference between the two. Incest did not become a criminal offense until 1908 in England. (In contrast, Scotland referred incest to criminal courts as early as 1567, and such trials were not unknown in the Victorian period. For example, the High Court of Justiciary held forty-five incest trials between 1867 and 1892.) Finally, another type of sexual abuse involved child prostitution, which was a growing problem by the 1880s, in part because of the erroneous belief that sex with a virgin cured venereal disease. Parents occasionally sold girls to brothels to make money; at other times, abandoned girls or young servants fell victim to procurers. In either case, the girls were virtual sex slaves and had little chance for escape.[17]

Though earlier periods had also seen condemnation of child abuse, sexual or otherwise, the Victorians were the first to make systematic efforts to combat it. The most important group in this fight was the Society for the Prevention of Cruelty to Children, organized in Liverpool in 1883. The group soon gained a national reputation, and a London branch began in 1884, which became the national organization in 1889, renamed the National Society for the Prevention of Cruelty to Children, or NSPCC. Run by well-off men and women, the NSPCC both lobbied Parliament for legal changes to help children and inspected claims of abuse. In so doing, the officers had to balance the defense of brutalized or neglected children with the desire to keep families together. They also had to separate cases of deliberate neglect with those families who were simply poverty stricken. The NSPCC's inspectors responded to allegations of cruelty with home visits, and, if necessary, criminal charges, though they removed only a minority of children. Parents resented the interference, but their neighbors often gave the NSPCC tips about cruel treatment. As with charity, the poor used middle-class institutions as one way to cope with problem families.[18]

The NSPCC had its successes. Parents who woefully neglected or abused their children received a visit from the "cruelty man"; if he was not satisfied, the society followed up with more inspections or legal action. Historian George Behlmer has found that local NSPCC branches interpreted abuse differently, but all publicized the problem of child abuse to a horrified public. The societies printed stories of parents who locked children in boxes while they went drinking or who beat children for minor offenses. The society avoided explicit discussions of sexual abuse but acknowledged such cases with fairly obvious euphemisms. Certainly such stories indicated the need for intervention and legal reform.[19] However, the majority of the cases in the NSPCC were for neglect rather than abuse, and here the society and its clientele differed. Many of the inspectors were obsessed with dirt and vermin, but working-class homes were notoriously difficult to keep clean or free of nits. In addition, many children had poor vision, dental problems, or skin rashes; these were minor complaints compared to the need for food and clothing. Mothers would not use their limited funds for one child's glasses when the family had little to eat. The inspectors, though, were likely to see dirt, vermin, or running sores as neglect, and they overemphasized this in some of their cases.

For example, in 1902, at the Central Criminal Court in London, the NSPCC brought a case of neglect against Eleanor Hannah Frost. Frost lived with Antony Greener, who was tried with her, and the two between them had nine children. A neighbor complained twice about Frost's treatment of Edith, her partner's child, sparking the NSPCC's intervention. The first time the inspector visited, Frost showed him a different child to get him to go away. The second time, after Edith's death, Frost admitted the deception but pointed out that Edith had consumption. In addition, Frost insisted that she had done all she could for her stepdaughter, sending for a doctor and feeding the girl the same food as the rest of the family. According to medical testimony, Edith died of tuberculosis, not neglect. Nevertheless, the NSPCC brought the case to court, as the inspector, Charles Ross, reported that the "bed and bedding where she slept were filthily dirty, and covered with vermin." Almost all working-class homes had nits and bugs, and Frost had nine children to feed and dress, but the NSPCC and the courts expected her to keep up high standards. Frost received four months in jail at hard labor; her partner, deemed less culpable because he was away working most of the day, was sentenced to one month.[20] Ambiguous cases like this did not mean that the NSPCC was useless or always unfair. On the contrary, it was a well-respected and effective pressure group;

Child savers often used pathetic images of children to stir up Victorian sentiments. George Smith's image of a ragged girl, begging for her "pittance" of a wage, is one example of this technique. "A Brick-Carrying Girl Craving Her Pittance," in George Smith, *The Cry of the Children from the Brick-Yards of England* (London: Houghton & Co., 1879), between 32 and 33.

its efforts were partly responsible for many helpful legislative changes, such as restrictions on street selling by children. In addition, the NSPCC willingly acted as prosecutor in cases of violent parents, offering an escape avenue for brutalized children. But the effects of their cases were often mixed for poor parents.

Moreover, rescue groups rarely included well-off children in their aims; though abuse occurred in middle- and upper-class homes, affluent families hid it more effectively. The NSPCC did investigate children's treatment in institutions, some of which were middle- and upper-class schools, but this netted only a handful of cases. Once in a great while, a case of middle-class abuse was so egregious that the society insisted on prosecuting. For example, Robert King, who worked in the offices of the North East Railway Company, chained up his fifteen-year-old son in his back garden and beat him with walking stick for fifteen minutes; the boy had dared to pursue his own choice of career over that of his father. The NSPCC prosecuted King, despite misgivings of some of its supporters, because the case was both public and unusually brutal; at the trial, the court found King guilty and fined him five pounds. Such cases occasionally led elite supporters to withdraw from membership, as when a curate's wife was arrested for assaulting her teenaged servant and the local bishop protested. As a result, the NSPCC prosecuted few upper- and middle-class families. Instead, its main relationship with middle-class children was to get them involved in rescue work by joining the League of Pity. The league required five-shilling membership dues, and members were asked to solicit funds from others to help support the cause, so the class stratification was clear.[21] In addition to these class concerns, a child's sex also helped shape child-saving activities. Despite their dismissal of rape charges, Victorians worried most about girls when it came to issues of sexuality.

SEXUAL ABUSE AND RESCUE

As stated in chapter 6, many child advocates assumed that girls who had been molested, raped, or lived in brothels had become "fallen." Thus, the child savers' attitude toward such girls was one of pity mixed with condemnation; they were both victims and potential spreaders of moral and physical diseases. Few refuges existed to help them until late in the century, but some private child savers concentrated on reclaiming them (in contrast, no refuges at all existed to help sexually abused boys). An early example was the London Society for the Protection of Young Females, founded in 1835. Typical of early groups, the society did not accommodate the girls themselves but instead sent them to live in asylums for prostitutes, hardly an ideal solution. In 1838, then, the society built its own asylum for girls younger than fifteen, to train them to be servants. This organization was unusual in taking in young girls, though eventually two additional homes opened for them in the 1860s.

A number of different philanthropists eventually involved themselves in working for the redemption of sexually exploited girls in the late-Victorian period. One prominent figure was Agnes Cotton, heiress to a banking fortune, who used her inheritance to set up a refuge in North London. In the 1880s, the CEWSS, some Anglican sisterhoods, and the Jewish Association for the Protection of Girls and Women also built homes that targeted "sexually knowing" girls. The policy in all these homes was to separate girls from older women, and, for that matter, older from younger girls, basing treatments on degrees of sexual experience. Despite this expansion, the refuges were still too few, so many girls ended up in prostitute refuges. By the turn of the century, though, attitudes toward fallen girls became more nurturing. As stated in chapter 6, the Salvation Army set up a home for victims of sexual assault in 1901 in North London, and the Home Office also formed industrial schools for them between 1908 and 1914. All these refuges were dedicated to producing devout, industrious servants from problem girls, so they leaned heavily on religious teaching and job training. Agnes Cotton's home, for instance, had a schedule of four hours of school followed by domestic work for the rest of the day. Cotton also allowed the use of corporal punishment to control wayward charges. Cotton's approach was not ubiquitous; many of the refuges instead tried to build motherly feeling between the matrons and the children, as they believed a mother's love was the most powerful weapon in reaching a child. Girls' experiences of reclamation, then, varied widely, but the emphasis on domestic training was universal.[22]

The late-Victorian anxiety about prostitution was a major reason for the proliferation of these refuges, and some groups made preventing the social "evil" their stated goal. The Ladies Association for the Care of Friendless Girls, founded in the mid-1880s, formed branches all over Britain and had reached 106 by 1885. One of its primary aims was to prevent prostitution before it started, so the directors rescued girls from risky environments. The directors wanted the children to break with their homes, so they required parents to sign over parental authority and agree to limited visits, the most generous being once every two weeks. Not surprisingly, these homes stressed religious and moral training even more than usual, and job training was purely domestic—cleaning, cooking, and child care. Fortunately, because the girls were "untainted," they could work in private homes rather than commercial laundries, and thus at least had some choice in employment. Again, discipline was strict, though the national branch discouraged caning.[23]

Historians who have studied these private refuges express doubts about their effectiveness. Few of the girls went on the streets, but only a minority made successful servants. Upon leaving the Salvation Army home in the early twentieth century, for instance, most girls lived with relatives, found other work (e.g., in factories), or quit service in fewer than two years. In addition, discipline problems were ever present; some girls went back to their parents, and others acted out despite punishments. An example highlighted by historian Louise Jackson was a girl named Lily, who came to Agnes Cotton's institution in Leytonstone in 1895 at the age of eleven. She was apparently a victim of sexual abuse and had begun committing petty crimes and resisting her parents' authority. Cotton accepted her and tried strict discipline, but the treatment failed utterly. After a year, Cotton sent Lily back to her father and stepmother, claiming the girl's "evident delight in evil associates—bad talk, bad ways, is sad to behold."[24] Not all girls could adapt to such a different environment; even the most willing girls found the transition wrenching. Emma Smith had difficulty conforming to the quietness and self-abnegation required by the Catholic refuge that accepted her when she was twelve, though she was glad to be there. She described the harsh penalties for slight offenses with resentment that lasted for her lifetime:

> This sister even locked me in a little cell alone the whole of one night for some trivial offence. I was only thirteen at the time; it does not soften the memory when I recall that I was taken ill in the night. I think my crime had been that I had bumped into her sacred person when running round a corner of a long passage. I had burst into uncontrollable laughter at the time; I had been rushing like a mad thing, when I should have been walking sedately and, as I drew near to her, I should have respectfully curtsied.[25]

Less tractable girls than Smith had an even harder time becoming docile servants after having lived rough or endured drunken or abusive environments. Thus, both the preventative and the rescue homes for girls gave limited help to any girl who did not accept middle-class expectations.

LEGISLATIVE CHILD SAVERS

Child-saving activities reached a critical mass in the 1880s with the founding of the NSPCC. The same was true of attempts to change the laws to protect children, which occurred throughout the century but peaked in the 1880s and 1890s. The laws highlighted in previous chapters show this pattern; for instance, compulsory education began in 1880 and free schooling in 1891. This section focuses on three changes that exemplified the many laws passed to protect children between 1870 and 1914: the Infant Life Protection Act of 1872, the Criminal Law Amendment Act of 1885, and the Prevention of Cruelty to and Protection of Children Act of 1889. All three embodied the limitations but also the successes of the child-saving movement. The more substantial changes of the Edwardian period (1901–1910), discussed at the end of this chapter, came from these Victorian beginnings.

The Infant Life Protection Act centered on the problem of infanticide and baby farming. Many Victorians sympathized with unmarried mothers who deserted or harmed newborn babies, assuming they were temporarily insane or driven to distraction by shame. In contrast, the public condemned those who killed for profit, the so-called baby farmers who "adopted" or "fostered" infants for a price. Women with illegitimate children paid either a lump sum or a weekly fee to such women; the mother assumed the child would be adopted or that the buyer would rear the child herself. Often the child died within a year. Some deaths were due to dry-nursing, as infants who could not breast-feed were in great danger of infection. But others died because of deliberate cruelty or neglect; in particular, women who took lump payments had little incentive to nurture infants.

Though the scope of the problem is impossible to know, the practice came to notice in the 1860s; medical and legal journals warned of a flourishing business in such adoptions. But the catalyst for legal change was a series of well-publicized criminal trials, culminating in that of Margaret Waters in 1870. Waters and her sister, Sarah Ellis, adopted many infants who died in droves. Waters was arrested, convicted, and hanged for murder, and the trial provoked sensational newspaper headlines. Parliament held hearings on the matter in 1871 and eventually passed the Infant Life Protection Act the following year. The new law ordered all those who accepted more than one child "for hire or reward" to register with the state. In theory, this allowed the authorities to monitor the babies' care or to trace deceased infants. All the same, inspectors were few and the number of children covered was small, so the act had limited force. Parliament was reluctant to do more because so many working-class families relied on neighbors to mind their children. In addition, poor-law authorities and charity homes allowed families to adopt babies for a standard fee and fought any attempt to restrict this. Thus, the only further legislation, in 1897, increased monitoring of all children under five in nursing care. At the base, of course, the problem was poor women's poverty (true of both the mothers and the baby farmers) and the shame of illegitimacy. None of the proposed solutions to the problem of infanticide, then, had much chance of reducing child mortality.[26]

The Criminal Law Amendment Act of 1885 was also a gendered law that related to a Victorian sensation, but its passage was due to the editor of the *Pall Mall Gazette*. W. T. Stead was a crusader for various causes and, under the influence of Benjamin Waugh, the leader of the NSPCC for many years, Stead exposed the (supposedly) growing trade of working-class girls into prostitution. In July 1885, he published the article "The Maiden Tribute of Modern Babylon," which contained horrifying stories of parents selling their children to madames, procurers either buying young girls or tricking them into entering brothels, and "white slavery" rings—groups that sold girls into prostitution abroad. Most sensationally, Stead himself bought a thirteen-year-old girl whose alcoholic mother had sold her for a pound to a procuress (Stead paid five pounds, so the profit margin was impressive). The reaction to the piece was swift; some people condemned Stead, while others argued that he had done a public service. Stead eventually served jail time for taking a girl from her mother without permission, but the story ensured his journalistic success.

The main legal result of Stead's actions was the Criminal Law Amendment Act of 1885. Members of Parliament had proposed similar acts in every session since 1881, but none had passed the House of Commons. In the wake of the controversy, though, both houses approved the bill. The act raised the age of consent (the age at which a girl could consent to sexual relations) from thirteen to sixteen years old. Sexual assaults against girls younger than thirteen were

Benjamin Waugh was a founder and longtime president
of the NSPCC. He encouraged W. T. Stead to expose
the scandal of child prostitution to pressure Parliament
to pass legislation to protect young girls from sexual exploitation. This portrait, "The Champion of the Child,"
is from Rosa Waugh, *The Life of Benjamin Waugh* (London: T. Fisher Unwin, 1913), frontispiece.

felonies; those on girls from age thirteen to sixteen were misdemeanors. In
addition, anyone selling girls younger than eighteen to brothels out of the
country could be prosecuted, and taking a girl younger than eighteen from her
parents' home for "immoral" purposes was also illegal. Obviously, this law had
limitations. The provisions were difficult to enforce, especially as many sexual
crimes occurred within the home, and the law severely limited girls' freedom of
action. In addition, it entirely ignored sexually exploited boys. The controversy
did, however, at least spotlight the problems of sexually abused children.

   The NSPCC was determined to push the issue of protection further, especially
making the prosecution of erring parents easier. Thus, only four years after the
Criminal Law Amendment Act, Parliament tackled the thorny issue of parental
and children's rights. Legally, children had little standing in the nineteenth
century; fathers "owned" their legitimate children. This control was modified

during Victoria's reign, but primarily to give mothers more custody rights rather than children rights of their own. Of course, with the restrictions on child labor and compulsory schooling, the state already interfered with parents' freedoms. Other examples existed, too, such as compulsory smallpox vaccinations of children, begun in 1840–1841. Still, fathers and mothers retained great authority. They had not only the right but also the duty to discipline their children, and they could also take their children's wages (indeed, many families only survived by pooling family earnings). Thus, any bill to give children rights had to strike a balance between parents and their dependents.

The bill that emerged into law in 1889, the Prevention of Cruelty and Protection of Children Act, formally made violence and neglect of girls younger than sixteen and boys younger than fourteen a crime. Any guardian whose child was "ill-treated, neglected, abandoned, or exposed," if convicted, faced fines or imprisonment; the maximum sentence was two years. To help convictions, wives were allowed to testify against husbands, and the authorities could also remove children to a safe place until the trial. It also permitted the authorities to take away custodial rights from convicted parents. In short, in this bill, the British state recognized that children and their parents sometimes had different interests and that children needed a separate legal identity. Further acts followed in 1891 and 1894. The first broadened the definition of cruelty and raised the ages covered by the acts; the second allowed nonparental relatives to claim children who would otherwise go to industrial schools.[27] Enforcement of these acts was difficult, and the NSPCC rather than the police instigated many of the cases brought under it—but it was a beginning.

The culmination of all these trends came in the Edwardian period, both on the issues of poverty-stricken children and those who were victims of deliberate cruelty. First, legislators began to recognize that private charity was not adequate to eradicate child poverty. The Liberal government that came into power in 1906 passed many early attempts at family welfare, including limited programs for unemployment and health insurance. In addition, one of its first acts (in 1906) was a law allowing local governments to provide free meals to school children; in 1907, it passed legislation that required medical inspections in school, though parents still had to pay for any treatments deemed necessary. In 1908, Parliament finally dealt with incest as a crime in England. The Punishment of Incest Act criminalized sexual acts between men and their granddaughters, daughters, sisters, or mothers, with punishments of three to seven years in prison. Consent was no longer an issue; the sexual act itself was enough for conviction. This act offered new legal protections, though it neglected boys as victims of incest, showing the typical preoccupation with sexuality and girls.

Second, the Liberal government built on the 1889 act by passing the Children Act of 1908, which consolidated and expanded the separate laws on prevention of cruelty. Inspectors checked up on children who had been treated cruelly for longer periods and also inspected those in care or foster homes. Authorities had

Child hunger became a major issue in British politics in the early twentieth century. This picture, from 1905, shows children lining up to receive the food about to be thrown away by a local businessman. The Liberal government that came to power one year later passed laws to help such children. "Feeding on Garbage," in Robert Harborough Sherard, *The Child-Slaves of Britain* (London: Hurst and Blackett, 1905), between 14 and 15.

more power to remove children from abusive homes, even arranging emigration if necessary. In addition, the act prohibited children younger than fourteen from being in brothels, gambling, smoking in public, or buying tobacco. Finally, the act created a juvenile court system for defendants younger than sixteen, with separate facilities, less formal proceedings, and a complete prohibition of prison sentences. By 1908, then, the British state had tackled most of the major issues involving child welfare and safety, even if much remained to be done. As Anna Davin put it, after 1908, "children's separate identity and needs were fully recognized."[28]

As with most pieces of legislation, these changes had both good and bad consequences. Different treatment for young offenders and incest victims were long overdue legal reforms, and children whose guardians were violent or indifferent gained more legal protection. Nevertheless, some of the laws put an inordinate burden on working-class mothers, because they demanded higher levels of cleanliness and health without any enhanced income to pay for it. One example was health inspectors who insisted that mothers buy glasses for their nearsighted children, an expense that most could ill afford. School inspectors also checked the clothing, shoes, and hair of each child. Many working-class autobiographies record mothers combing out hair carefully, trying to make sure the schools did not send their children home because of lice or nits. Others made each child in turn wear the only decent pair of boots until all had passed inspection. These higher expectations were the Edwardian equivalent of today's unfunded mandates. The only way to achieve real improvement in health and cleanliness was to give substantial financial support, which did not occur until after World War II.[29]

Despite these problems, the Victorian and Edwardian achievements on child welfare were impressive. By the end of the nineteenth century, virtually all children went to school for a period of years and worked fewer hours. Numerous agencies existed to rescue abandoned children, and the courts and private charities worked to protect them from cruelty and poverty. Much more work remained to be done, and the child savers could be both oppressive and patronizing, but children had far less chance of slipping through the cracks in the 1890s than in the 1830s. Unsurprisingly, the intervention of the state into personal life was a mixed blessing, and the state continued to treat children as passive objects rather than as actors in their own right. Still, by 1900, many Britons had accepted the idea that children were valuable to the nation and that cruelty to children was the sign of an uncivilized nation.

How did the children feel about being made the objects of such solicitude? Those with miserable home lives welcomed life in institutions as vast improvements. But most children did not live in such extreme situations and, consequently, were ambivalent. State and charitable interventions helped make their lives more comfortable, but this was accompanied by the anxiety of inspections and especially home visits. Many disliked seeing their mothers harassed and strained by the demands. Others were terrified that they would be sent home with lice or embarrassed by being given their meal tickets in front of others. Children also feared being taken from their homes; some parents drilled their children on the answers to give to inspectors in case of visits (e.g., parents told their children to say they had eaten breakfast whenever asked). Depending on the attitude of the official, families could be grateful for any help, resentful of the subservience demanded in return, or both. Eventually, many parents incorporated these programs into their normal strategies for coping with poverty, and the children followed suit.[30]

How much the actual attitude to childhood changed during the course of the century is subject to debate. After all, parents in previous centuries loved their children and considered childhood a separate period of development. Legal protection of children was not unknown; for instance, laws existed to shield apprentices from abuse during the early modern period. Yet the amount of resources devoted to children and the volume of private and state initiatives for children in the Victorian period was a quantum leap from previous times. The argument that children were national resources and needed economic support was commonplace by 1900. Marianne Farningham, for instance, did not doubt that the changes had been profound by the time she wrote her autobiography in 1907, declaring in its conclusion, "I am thankful to have watched a wonderful growth of respect for the child. Children are among the chief assets of the nation, and now that they are regarded in this light a good deal will be done for them. It is time." Farningham's opinion was in the vast majority at the turn of the century.[31] When Victoria died, gender and class still heavily influenced childhoods. Moreover, children's experiences differed markedly from the contemporary, child-centered lives of modern times. However, childhood in 1900 was also very different from childhood in 1800, and there was no going back. Indeed, the state went forward, as the many Edwardian legal changes made clear. Thus, the Victorian years marked a crucial transition period in the modern expansion of childhood.

CONCLUSION

Evidence from the proceeding chapters supports both the good and the bad myths about children's lives in the nineteenth century. In some ways, childhood in this period was indeed difficult, harsh, and all too brief. Poor children went to work at young ages, had inadequate clothing and nutrition, and received substandard teaching when they did attend school. They also endured corporal punishment from parents, neighbors, teachers, and employers, and their prospects in life were highly limited. Moreover, some parents were drunken and violent, and the state did little to protect children from abuse until late in the century. If poverty stricken, disabled, or illegitimate, a child might not even live in a family, but instead in that most dreaded of Victorian institutions, the workhouse. Though better off financially, boys and girls of the upper classes also faced firm controls from the adults in their lives. Parents and guardians restricted their contacts with others, chose their schools, and rarely let them venture out freely. Girls, in particular, were closely monitored. For fear of spoiling their children, middle- and upper-class parents also tried to train them in fortitude and thrift, discouraging complaints and giving out small allowances. Many of the stereotypical sayings associated with Victorians' child rearing come from well-off families, including one of the most ubiquitous: "Children should be seen and not heard." Indeed, generational tensions at the end of the century highlighted the restiveness of late Victorians against the seeming prudery and hypocrisy of their parents.

Yet the evidence also shows support for the rosier myth of the Victorian past, that of strong family values and a simpler life. Despite their poverty, many working-class children grew up with loving parents and siblings as well as chums from schools or the street. Poor families pulled together to make the best of things, tied through bonds of obligation and love. Mothers and fathers sacrificed to make a better life for their children, who reciprocated when they were old enough to work. In bad times, in fact, the family's kin and neighbors did their best to keep everyone in the family fed, sheltered, and out of state care. In the upper classes, the ideal of domesticity urged fathers to be heavily involved with their children, and mothers to be nurses, teachers, and spiritual guides to sons and daughters. Children recorded loving relationships with both parents and with one another, as well as great sorrow at any deaths. After all, sayings associated with Victorianism show the good side of close family life as well: "Be it ever so humble, there's no place like home."

Of course, even given these facts, the myths cannot adequately describe all Victorian childhoods. The major reason was that both the good and the bad often existed within the same family, school, or workplace, or differed between sexes, classes, nationalities, and generations. In this and many other ways, the Victorian view of childhood was full of contradictions. The century that had the most public exploitation of child labor was also the one that saw numerous laws restricting children's work. Victorians had sharp class stratifications, but precisely because of those divisions they reached across the divide with organizations, religious groups, and charities. These attempts were not always successful, but they did offer tentative beginnings in cross-class cooperation. In addition, domesticity preached strict gender differences, but the middle nineteenth century also saw the birth of the feminist movement, which expanded the world of possibilities for girls and young women. Victorians worried about spoiling children with too many material goods at the same time that retail and child-centered businesses flourished with the establishment of department stores, mass audiences for children's literature, and elaborate celebrations at Christmas. The list of contradictory impulses could go on and on; it is little wonder that childhood in this period seems both so distant and so close to the twenty-first century.

In some specific ways, the Victorian experience of childhood is deeply foreign to today's sensibilities. For one thing, though seemingly sheltered and chaperoned, nineteenth-century children had few protections. Poor children went into the workplace at young ages, subject to industrial accidents, cruelty from masters, and workplace diseases. They also ate adulterated food and went out in inclement weather with inadequate clothing and shoes. As a result, as stated in chapter 1, child mortality was appallingly high in poor districts up to World War I, a rate that would simply be unacceptable in contemporary Britain. Though less likely to catch infectious diseases or eat bread adulterated with sawdust, well-off children also faced dangers unknown to the twenty-first-century Western world. Few parents or authorities considered regulating toys or games, for instance, and they accepted the possibility of accidents as inevitable as children competed in sports without protective gear, climbed trees without supervision, or learned to ride horses and hunt. Oddly, in this way, contemporary children actually have less freedom; infants ride in car seats, children wear helmets when cycling, and governments restrict food, drugs, and toys until they have met certain quality standards. Protecting children, then, has shifted to more government intervention and less reliance on siblings and chaperones. Child health is much better but boys and girls have less freedom of action, and parents have lost some of their control as well.

Another major difference is the lack of a child-centered approach to the family. Parents loved their children, but they did not all express this care the same way. Thus, family dynamics differed. In the upper classes, parents might not see their children except at designated times of the day, and boys left home as early as seven years old, coming home only on school holidays until they were grown. Elite children also knew that the schedule and decisions for the household centered on the needs of the adults in the family, not the children. In the middle classes, affection was overt, but the insistence that children do as they were told did not waver. Middle-class mothers and fathers believed that to rear healthy, happy children they must emphasize obedience, duty, unselfishness, and fortitude. Children had many moments of fun and whimsy, but they did not determine the major decisions of the household or have unlimited material goods. In the working class, the affection was even more muted, as the need for bare subsistence overrode all other considerations. Mothers and fathers worked for their children, sometimes heroically, but they did not have quality time with them. Instead, they expected the children to look after one another and understand the need to contribute to the family purse as soon as possible. In contrast to today's families, a Victorian parent would not allow children to decide what to eat for meals or where the family would go on vacation. Nor would a Victorian parent spend a large proportion of his or her income to amuse children. Victorian parents cared about their children, but they did not cater to them, and they had little or no knowledge of the psychology of childhood.

In addition, religion played a great role in the socialization of children in the nineteenth century, and religious leaders did not temper their messages to appeal to young listeners. Scottish Presbyterians continued to preach predestination, and Anglican services ignored children's mangling of the liturgy and puzzlement at theological concepts. Moreover, the religious emphasis on original sin had significant implications for child rearing. Parents who believed that their children were naturally depraved stressed the importance of repentance and humility. Even those with more relaxed approaches to spirituality watched their children's religious development carefully, anxious that they come to a right understanding. All the same, by the end of the century, working-class parents were only nominally religious, and the younger generation in the well-off classes was falling away. To some extent, national enthusiasm and patriotism became alternative unifying ideals to religion. In this way, religious issues had both similarities and differences with the centuries that followed.

Indeed, the similarities between the Victorian era and contemporary times were as great as the differences. Victorians pioneered many movements and ideas that became commonplace in the twentieth and twenty-first centuries. Most obviously, the nineteenth century saw the standardization of years of schooling as a regular part of childhood, including national board schools, compulsory attendance, and the abolition of school fees. Victorians passed numerous laws restricting child labor, eventually pushing small children entirely out of the workplace and making part-time work usual for adolescents. They also founded many of the major interest groups that worked for children's rights—the National Society for the Prevention of Cruelty to Children, the Children's Society, and Barnardo's Homes, just to name a few, as well as some of the most famous children's organizations, like the Band of Hope. Their approach was paternalistic and sometimes too cavalier with respect to the effects on children, but they did make commonplace the argument that children mattered, for themselves and for the good of the state. During the Edwardian period, Parliament passed a children's act that finally recognized children as having legal standing on their own, not as appendages of their parents or guardians. The continued efforts to help at-risk children, lasting to the present day, came out of these beginnings.

Though Victorians struggled against indulging children, they still lived in an age of commercial expansion. Thus, entire industries for children mushroomed and children's literature abounded. Many beloved children's books (and Disney films) were published in the 1800s—*The Jungle Book*, *Alice's Adventures in Wonderland*, and *Treasure Island*, to name only a few. Children's toys and games, often with educational purposes, sold well, and retailers began appealing to parents and children through advertising and promotions. The expansion of the market for children's goods into many areas, including beachwear and toys, reflected another similarity to life today, the family vacation. The paid vacation spread down to the working class by the late-Victorian period, with trips to the country or to the seaside becoming an annual event. The most prominent holiday, Christmas, remains the major festival today, and many of its customs began in mid-Victorian England. Again, the amount of leisure and play differed greatly from that of today's children, and Victorian children had considerably less spending money, but the trend toward more commercialization was clear. "Making time for the family" came to mean having a regular schedule for leisure as a group, primarily on weekends, but also on the growing number of days off work. In short, imagination and play were never obliterated even in the poorest and most deprived child's life; if they could do nothing else, boys and girls could pretend, dream, and fantasize.

Most important, thoughts about childhood subtly changed over the course of the century. Late-Victorian memoirs and autobiographies differed from those early in the period and show a growing realization of the central importance of early experiences. In general, autobiographical works written between 1800 and 1870 were more factual, retelling the basic events in a life—first memory, first school, and first job—with minimal comment. These books, in fact, often glossed over the younger years quickly to reach the more important adult stage. The ones that did give details about childhood did so for specific reasons, for instance, showing how the writer got from a poverty-stricken childhood to success in business or politics (the rags-to-riches tale). Others used childhood to support an agenda, as when authors justified their work in trade unionism by exposing the long hours and poor conditions of children in industry, or when they focused on childhood to encourage religious conversions and spiritual growth. Though fascinating in their own ways, these autobiographies are not particularly introspective; their remarks about childhood in general tend to be commonplace rather than personal.

In contrast, late-Victorian memoirs were more interested in childhood for its own sake rather than as a precursor to a later triumph or as a propaganda tool. They are richer and more detailed about relationships with family, schoolmates, and the wider society. In addition, far more of the later authors were women or workers, a sign in itself of the change of the times and one reason for the broadening of topics of discussion. By the end of the century, one need not have been successful later in life, have worked for political causes, or have desired to proselytize to tell one's life story. Of course, many of these works did include political or religious causes, but they nevertheless show a growing recognition of childhood as an important developmental stage with emotional consequences for later life. They, then, prefigure the twentieth-century childhood autobiography, influenced by the rise of professional psychology. One should not overstate this; the Victorians remained amazingly insensitive to some traumas in childhood, treating abuse victims with little sensitivity, for instance. But over time, their personal writings show subtle recognitions of the importance of the internal life of the child and its possible future ramifications.

Victorian childhoods, then, both prefigured modern interests and defied them. Readers may object to such a seemingly inconclusive conclusion, but making overall statements about the Victorian child does violence to the historical record. Just as today, children's lives varied by generation, gender, class, race, and nationality. And just like today, most children survived, grew up, and became parents themselves, continuing the process of socializing the next generation. Twenty-first-century parents may congratulate themselves on their more enlightened methods of child rearing or mourn the loss of a more innocent age, and both would, to some extent, be correct. In this way, the Victorians' successes and failures in child care became a measure for the generations that followed.

NOTES

CHAPTER 1

1. Claudia Nelson, *Family Ties in Victorian England* (London: Praeger, 2007).

2. Eric Hopkins, *Childhood Transformed: Working-Class Children in Nineteenth-Century England* (Manchester: Manchester University Press, 1994), 101, 268; Ellen Ross, *Love and Toil: Motherhood in Outcast London, 1870–1918* (Oxford: Oxford University Press, 1993), 92–97.

3. Hopkins, *Childhood Transformed*, 101, 123; Ross, *Love and Toil*, 181–182.

4. A. S. Jaspar, *A Hoxton Childhood* (London: Centerprise Publications, 1969), 11.

5. Thomas Okey, *A Basketful of Memories: An Autobiographical Sketch* (London: J. M. Dent & Sons, 1930), 15; George Ratcliffe, *Sixty Years of It: Being the Story of My Life and Public Career* (London: A. Brown & Sons, 1935[?]), 7.

6. Kathleen Woodward, *Jipping Street* (1923; Reprint, London: Virago, 1983), 19–20.

7. Raphael Samuel, ed., *East End Underworld: Chapters in the Life of Arthur Harding* (London: Routledge and Kegan Paul, 1981), 28; Grace Foakes, *Between High Walls: A London Childhood* (London: Shepheard-Walwyn, 1972), 6, 33.

8. Foakes, *Between High Walls*, 20.

9. Jaspar, *Hoxton Childhood*, 38.

10. Hannah Mitchell, *The Hard Way Up: The Autobiography of Hannah Mitchell, Suffragette and Rebel*, ed. Geoffrey Mitchell (London: Faber and Faber, 1968), 40.

11. Foakes, *Between High Walls*, 11; George Acorn, *One of the Multitude* (London: William Heinemann, 1911), 35–36.

12. Samuel, *East End Underworld*, 30.

13. Alice Linton, *Not Expecting Miracles* (London: Centerprise Trust, 1982), 10; Emma Smith, *A Cornish Waif's Story: An Autobiography* (London: Popular Book Club, 1956), 15.

14. Mitchell, *Hard Way Up*, 42–43.

15. Acorn, *One of the Multitude*, 278–291.

16. Hopkins, *Childhood Transformed*, 102.

17. Walter Littler, *A Victorian Childhood: Recollections and Reflections* (Belbroughton, Worcestershire: Marion Seymour, 1997), 21–26; Foakes, *Between High Walls*, 11.

18. Alice Foley, *A Bolton Childhood* (Manchester: North Western District of the Workers' Educational Association, 1973), 38.

19. Allan Jobson, *The Creeping Hours of Time* (London: Robert Hale, 1977), 68.

20. Philip Magnus, *Gladstone: A Biography* (London: John Murray, 1954), 125; Alfred Perceval Graves, *To Return to All That: An Autobiography* (London: Jonathan Cape, 1930), 243.

21. H. A. L. Fisher, *An Unfinished Autobiography* (London: Oxford University Press, 1940), 16.

22. Sylvia McCurdy, *Sylvia: A Victorian Childhood* (Lavenham, Suffolk: Eastland Press, 1972), 25–27; Eileen Baillie, *The Shabby Paradise: The Autobiography of a Decade* (London: Hutchinson & Co., 1958), 94; Eric Bligh, *Tooting Corner* (London: Secker & Warburg, 1946), 84.

23. William Manchester, *Visions of Glory, 1874–1932*, vol. 1, *The Last Lion: Winston Spencer Churchill* (New York: Dell, 1983), 116–117; Baillie, *Shabby Paradise*, 142–152; quotes from 152 and 143.

24. Graves, *To Return to All That*, 26–27, 20.

25. Agnes Hunt, *Reminiscences* (Shrewsbury: Wilding & Sons, 1935), 9.

26. Molly Hughes, *A London Child of the 1870s* (Oxford: Oxford University Press, 1934), 31–32; Laura Troubridge, *Life among the Troubridges: Journals of a Young Victorian, 1873–1884* (London: Tite Street Press, 1999), 15.

27. G. B. Grundy, *Fifty-Five Years at Oxford: An Unconventional Autobiography* (London: Methuen & Co., 1945), 14.

28. Hunt, *Reminiscences*, 11–12; Mary Carbery, *Happy World: The Story of a Victorian Childhood* (London: Longmans, Green, and Co., 1941), 92.

29. Edgar Jones, ed., *The Memoirs of Edwin Waterhouse: A Founder of Price Waterhouse* (London: B. T. Batsford, 1988), 57; Hunt, *Reminiscences*, 10; Francis Downes Ommanney, *The House in the Park* (London: Longmans, Green, and Co., 1944), 28; Mary Paley Marshall, *What I Remember* (Cambridge: Cambridge University Press, 1947), 1.

30. Hughes, *London Child of the 1870s*, 8–12; Maud Ballington Booth, *A Rector's Daughter in Victorian England: Memories of Childhood and Girlhood* (Metairie, La.: Volunteers of America, 1994), 3–8; Baillie, *Shabby Paradise*, 54.

31. Ommanney, *House in the Park*, 50.

32. McCurdy, *Sylvia*, 10; Hughes, *London Child of the 1870s*, 7.

33. Carbery, *Happy World*, 51, 134–135; Lady Emily Lutyens, *A Blessed Girl: Memoirs of a Victorian Girlhood Chronicled in an Exchange of Letters, 1887–1896* (New York: J. B. Lippincott Company, 1954), 283.

34. Greville MacDonald, *Reminiscences of a Specialist* (London: George Allen & Unwin, 1932), 28.

35. Troubridge, *Life among the Troubridges*, 22–24, 108; Leah Manning, *A Life for Education: An Autobiography* (London: Victor Gallancz, 1970), 11–12.

36. Bligh, *Tooting Corner*, 70; McCurdy, *Sylvia*, 9, 23; Booth, *Rector's Daughter*, 6–7; Graves, *To Return to All That*, 11.

37. Edmund Gosse, *Father and Son* (1907; Reprint, London: Penguin, 1989), 249.

38. John Tosh, *A Man's Place: Masculinity and the Middle-Class Home in Victorian England* (New Haven, CT: Yale University Press, 1999), 190–193.

CHAPTER 2

1. Charles Shaw, *When I Was a Child by an Old Potter* (London: Methuen & Co., 1903), 1–11; Tom Barclay, *Memoirs and Medleys: The Autobiography of a Bottle Washer* (1923; Reprint, Coalville, Leicestershire: Coalville Publishing Company, 1995), 14–23; Marianne Farningham, *A Working Woman's Life: An Autobiography* (London: James Clarke & Co., n.d.), 18, 26–28, 44.

2. Hopkins, *Childhood Transformed*, 138–139; Pamela Horn, *The Victorian Town Child* (Stroud, Gloucestershire: Sutton Publishing, 1997), 72–73.

3. Hopkins, *Childhood Transformed*, 139; J. H. Davies, *The Life and Opinion of Robert Roberts, a Wandering Scholar, as Told by Himself* (Cardiff: William Lewis, 1923), 106.

4. Davies, *Life and Opinion*, 256–257.

5. Hopkins, *Childhood Transformed*, 136–138; 233–238.

6. Ratcliffe, *Sixty Years of It*, 4.

7. Acorn, *One of the Multitude*, 1; Walter Southgate, *That's the Way It Was: A Working-Class Autobiography, 1890–1950* (Oxted, Surrey: New Clarion Press, 1982), 20–21.

8. Horn, *Victorian Town Child*, 76.

9. John Burnett, ed., *Destiny Obscure: Autobiographies of Childhood, Education and Family from the 1820s to the 1920s* (London: Routledge, 1994), 151; R. D. Anderson, *Education and Opportunity in Victorian Scotland* (Oxford: Clarendon Press, 1983), 104–105; Ethel Mannin, *Confessions and Impressions* (London: Hutchinson & Co., 1936), 30; Foley, *Bolton Childhood*, 33.

10. Littler, *A Victorian Childhood*, 32.

11. Anna Davin, *Growing Up Poor: Home, School and Street in London, 1870–1914* (London: Rivers Oram Press, 1996), 114–115; Horn, *Victorian Town Child*, 78.

12. John Kerr, *Memories Grave and Gay: Forty Years of School Inspection* (London: William Blackwood and Sons, 1902), 330; Mannin, *Confessions and Impressions*, 30.

13. Katherine Warburton, *Old Soho Days and Other Memories* (London: A. R. Mowbray & Co., 1906), 27–28.

14. Burnett, *Destiny Obscure*, 82–83, 74; Smith, *Cornish Waif's Story*, 25; Ratcliffe, *Sixty Years of It*, 5.

15. Burnett, *Destiny Obscure*, 195; Littler, *Victorian Childhood*, 35.

16. Albert Henry Lieck, *Narrow Waters: The First Volume of the Life and Thoughts of a Common Man* (London: William Hodge and Company, 1935), 11.

17. Burnett, *Destiny Obscure*, 201; Davin, *Growing Up Poor*, 124–131; Thomas Gautrey, *"Lux Mihi Laus": School Board Memories* (London: Link House Publications, 1937?), 154–155.

18. Davin, *Growing Up Poor*, 143–147; Jane McDermid, *Schooling of Working-Class Girls in Scotland* (London: Routledge, 2005), 91–94.

19. Burnett, *Destiny Obscure*, 159, 175–180; Anderson, *Education and Opportunity*, 152–153; McDermid, *Schooling of Working-Class Girls*, 114–142.

20. Linton, *Not Expecting Miracles*, 14; Foley, *Bolton Childhood*, 32.

21. Burnett, *Destiny Obscure*, 88.

22. Mannin, *Confessions and Impressions*, 35.

23. Burnett, *Destiny Obscure*, 203–205; Littler, *Victorian Childhood*, 33–34; Frederick Rogers, *Labour, Life and Literature: Some Memories of Sixty Years* (1913; Reprint, Brighton, Sussex: Harvester Press, 1973), 49; Horn, *Victorian Town Child*, 165.

24. G. B. Grundy, *Fifty-Five Years at Oxford: An Unconventional Autobiography* (London: Methuen & Co., 1945), 21–29; Horn, *Victorian Town Child*, 32.

25. Horn, *Victorian Town Child*, 36–37.

26. Grundy, *Fifty-Five Years at Oxford*, 24; Graves, *To Return to All That*, 35.

27. Ethel Smyth, ed., *Little Innocents: Childhood Reminiscences* (London: Cobden-Sanderson, 1932), 83; Robert Graves, *Good-bye to All That* (1929; Reprint, New York: Doubleday, 1985), 37–42, 49–51.

28. MacDonald, *Reminiscences of a Specialist*, 33; Ommanney, *House in the Park*, 42.

29. Fisher, *An Unfinished Autobiography*, 34–36, quote at 34.

30. Hughes, *London Child of the 1870s*, 41–44; Baillie, *Shabby Paradise*, 100–101; Marshall, *What I Remember*, 6.

31. Smyth, *Little Innocents*, 81; Sheila Fletcher, *Victorian Girls: Lord Lyttelton's Daughters* (London: Phoenix, 1997), 61.

32. Horn, *Victorian Town Child*, 39; Troubridge, *Life among the Troubridges*, 29–33; Marshall, *What I Remember*, 6–7.

33. McCurdy, *Sylvia*, 21, 69–70, quote at 69.

34. Carbery, *Happy World*, 190–193; Smyth, *Little Innocents*, 81.

35. Smyth, *Little Innocents*, 72.

36. Marshall, *What I Remember*, 7; Manning, *Life for Education*, 25; Hughes, *London Child of the 1870s*, 58.

37. Horn, *Victorian Town Child*, 43; Molly Hughes, *A London Girl of the 1880s* (1946; Reprint, Oxford: Oxford University Press, 1978), 35–37, quote at 35.

38. Marshall, *What I Remember*, 10–15; Manning, *Life for Education*, 28–42; 86, 164.

CHAPTER 3

1. George Mockford, *Wilderness Journeyings and Gracious Deliverances: The Autobiography of George Mockford* (Oxford: J. C. Pembrey, 1901), 2–3.

2. Hopkins, *Childhood Transformed*, 14–17.

3. Margaret Llewellyn Davies, ed., *Life as We Have Known It by Co-operative Working Women* (1931; Reprint, New York: W. W. Norton, 1975), 109–112.

4. Burnett, *Destiny Obscure*, 304.

5. John Burnett, ed., *Useful Toil: Autobiographies of Working People from the 1820s to the 1920s* (New York: Penguin, 1984), 64; Thomas Jordan, *Victorian Childhood: Themes and Variations* (Albany: State University of New York Press, 1987), 119.

6. Hopkins, *Childhood Transformed*, 22–32, quote at 28; Burnett, *Destiny Obscure*, 189.

7. Hopkins, *Childhood Transformed*, 22–32, 63–65.

8. Louise Jermy, *Memories of a Working Woman* (Norwich: Goose & Son, 1934), 42–49, 69–76.

9. Horn, *Victorian Town Child*, 104; Burnett, *Useful Toil*, 67–75; Davies, *Life as We Have Known It*, 85–89.

10. Burnett, *Useful Toil*, 5–51; Davin, *Growing Up Poor*, 171, 192–194.

11. Jermy, *Memories of a Working Woman*, 28–29.

12. Davin, *Growing Up Poor*, 72.

13. Henry Mayhew, *London Labour and the London Poor*, 4 vols. (1861–1862; Reprint, New York: Dover, 1968), 1:151–152, 136–137; 2:222–223, 505–506.

14. Mayhew, *London Labour*, 3:166, 171–172; Horn, *Victorian Town Child*, 121; Smith, *Cornish Waif's Story*, 34–58.

15. Kerr, *Memories Grave and Gay*, 314–315.

16. Horn, *Victorian Town Child*, 122.

17. Davies, *Life as We Have Known It*, 20–25.

18. Burnett, *Useful Toil*, 215–217, quote at 216–217.

19. Burnett, *Useful Toil*, 154–162; Jermy, *Memories of a Working Woman*, 72–74.

20. Jordan, *Victorian Childhood*, 35–37; Horn, *Victorian Town Child*, 107.

21. Shaw, *When I Was a Child*, 8–18, quote at 14.

22. Barclay, *Memoirs and Medleys*, 14; Jordan, *Victorian Childhood*, 35–37, 111–122.

23. Hopkins, *Childhood Transformed*, 46–49.

24. Ibid., 51–61.

25. William Wright, *From Chimney-Boy to Councillor: The Story of My Life* (Medstead, Hampshire: Azania Press, 1931[?]), 13–14; George Elson, *The Last of the Climbing Boys* (London: John Lang, 1900), 39–66, 206–251, quote at 46.

26. Horn, *Victorian Town Child*, 114–116.

27. Ibid., 108–117.

28. Ibid., 107–112.

29. Burnett, *Useful Toil*, 69.

30. Horn, *Victorian Town Child*, 102; Burnett, *Destiny Obscure*, 89–90.

31. Southgate, *That's the Way It Was*, 51; Burnett, *Useful Toil*, 89–99.

32. Jobson, *Creeping Hours of Time*, 101–102 (for quotes), 112.

33. Foley, *Bolton Childhood*, 49–51; Foakes, *Between High Walls*, 71–77.

34. Woodward, *Jipping Street*, 57–63; Samuel, *East End Underworld*, 42–50.

35. Mitchell, *Hard Way Up*, 52–57.

36. Burnett, *Destiny Obscure*, 90; Woodward, *Jipping Street*, 92.

37. John Wilson, *Memories of a Labour Leader: The Autobiography of John Wilson, J. P., M. P.* (1910; Reprint, Firle, Sussex: Caliban Books, 1980), 71–82, 221–278, Mitchell, *Hard Way Up*, 114–170.

CHAPTER 4

1. Jermy, *Memories of a Working Woman*, 5; Southgate, *That's the Way It Was*, 37.

2. Carbery, *Happy World*, 23; MacDonald, *Reminiscences of a Specialist*, 16–17.

3. Booth, *A Rector's Daughter*, 3; McCurdy, *Sylvia*, 21–22.

4. Samuel, *East End Underworld*, 30, 37; John Paton, *Proletarian Pilgrimage: An Autobiography* (London: George Routledge & Sons, 1935), 35.

5. Horn, *Victorian Town Child*, 161; Burnett, *Destiny Obscure*, 98.

6. Troubridge, *Life among the Troubridges*, 13; Baillie, *Shabby Paradise*, 136–137.

7. McCurdy, *Sylvia*, 54.

8. Jaspar, *Hoxton Childhood*, 94.

9. Smyth, *Little Innocents*, 33; Ommanney, *House in the Park*, 29–30.

10. Catherine Cookson, *Our Kate* (London: Corgi, 1997), 150; Southgate, *That's the Way It Was*, 36.

11. Horn, *Victorian Town Child*, 155; Baillie, *Shabby Paradise*, 19.

12. Bligh, *Tooting Corner*, 113.

13. Ellen Chase, *Tenant Friends in Old Deptford* (London: Williams & Norgate, 1929), 70.

14. Jobson, *Creeping Hours of Time*, 31; W. Pett Ridge, *A Story Teller: Forty Years in London* (London: Hodder and Stoughton, 1923), 198.

15. Edward Ezard, *Battersea Boy* (London: William Kimber, 1979), 76; Foakes, *Between High Walls*, 41.

16. Ratcliffe, *Sixty Years of It*, 11.

17. Littler, *Victorian Childhood*, 141; Paton, *Proletarian Pilgrimage*, 36.

18. Littler, *Victorian Childhood*, 57.

19. C. Richard Toye, *Sandy: The True Story of a Boy and his Friends Growing Up in Cornwall in the Late 1800s* (Milverton, Somerset: Great Western Books, 2003), 80–89, 104; J. D. Hicks, ed., *A Victorian Boyhood in the Wolds: The Recollections of J. R. Mortimer* (Hull: East Yorkshire Local History Society, 1978), 10–13, 19–22; Ezard, *Battersea Boy*, 55–65, quote at 60.

20. McCurdy, *Sylvia*, 18–20; Samuel Smith, *My Life-Work* (London: Hodder and Stoughton, 1902), 10.

21. Southgate, *That's the Way It Was*, 25.

22. Hughes, *London Child in the 1870s*, 14; Hopkins, *Childhood Transformed*, 304.

23. Hopkins, *Childhood Transformed*, 302.

24. Ibid., 294–295, 301.

25. Graves, *Good-bye to All That*, 22–28, 33–35; Hopkins, *Childhood Transformed*, 304–305.

26. Warburton, *Soho Days*, 12; Pat Barr, ed., *I Remember: An Arrangement for Many Voices* (London: MacMillan, 1970), 123–124; Littler, *Victorian Childhood*, 151; Hopkins, *Childhood Transformed*, 302.

27. Hughes, *London Child in the 1870s*, 21; Susan Chitty, ed., *As Once in May: The Early Autobiography of Antonia White and Other Writings* (London: Virago, 1983), 324–325.

28. Foley, *Bolton Childhood*, 27.

29. Barr, *I Remember*, 142.

30. McCurdy, *Sylvia*, 27; Baillie, *Shabby Paradise*, 110–111.

31. Baillie, *Shabby Paradise*, 166–167.

32. Mitchell, *Hard Way Up*, 51; Rogers, *Labour, Life and Literature*, 10–11; Littler, *Victorian Childhood*, 118.

33. Davies, *Life as We Have Known It*, 84.

34. Graves, *Good-bye to All That*, 29–30; Lutyens, *A Blessed Girl*, 9; Marshall, *What I Remember*, 6; Ommanney, *House in the Park*, 112.

35. Hopkins, *Childhood Transformed*, 305–306.

36. Horn, *Victorian Town Child*, 163.

CHAPTER 5

1. Hopkins, *Childhood Transformed*, 147–150, 297–299; Jordan, *Victorian Childhood*, 301–303.

2. Hopkins, *Childhood Transformed*, 148, 298–300.

3. Farningham, *Working Woman's Life*, 14–17, 32–34, quote at 34.

4. Burnett, *Destiny Obscure*, 20–23.

5. Foley, *Bolton Childhood*, 35; Barclay, *Memoirs and Medleys*, 36–38.

6. Hughes, *London Child of the 1870s*, 53 (first quote), 68–69 (second quote).

7. Smith, *My Life-Work*, 6; Smyth, *Little Innocents*, 75–76; Farningham, *Working Woman's Life*, 29.

8. MacDonald, *Reminiscences of a Specialist*, 24–25.

9. Hughes, *London Child of the 1870s*, 71; Burnett, *Destiny Obscure*, 25.

10. Graves, *To Return to All That*, 275–276.

11. Bligh, *Tooting Corner*, 160–162, 196–197.

12. Burnett, *Destiny Obscure*, 136, 25; Jordan, *Victorian Childhood*, 161–167.

13. Jordan, *Victorian Childhood*, 166–167; Barr, *I Remember*, 33 (for quote).

14. Shaw, *When I Was a Child*, 6–8, 137–140; Smith, *Cornish Waif's Story*, 50–51.

15. Jobson, *Creeping Hours of Time*, 88; Jermy, *Memories of a Working Woman*, 55–67; Smith, *Cornish Waif's Story*, 51.

16. Samuel, *East End Underworld*, 25–26; Smith, *My Life-Work*, 105–107, quote at 105.

17. Foakes, *Between High Walls*, 33–34.

18. Bligh, *Tooting Corner*, 208.

19. Horn, *Victorian Town Child*, 172.

20. Southgate, *That's the Way It Was*, 26.

21. Horn, *Victorian Town Child*, 172.

22. Herbert Spencer, *Social Statics*, (1851; Reprint, New York: Augustus M. Kelley, 1969), 191–192.

23. Horn, *Victorian Town Child*, 176–177; Southgate, *That's the Way It Was*, 39.

24. Horn, *Victorian Town Child*, 178.

25. Brian Harrison, "For Church, Queen and Family: The Girls' Friendly Society, 1874–1920," *Past and Present* 61 (1973): 107–138.

26. Horn, *Victorian Town Child*, 179.

27. Maude Stanley, *Clubs for Working Girls* (London: MacMillan, 1890), 4–5.

28. Ezard, *Battersea Boy*, 82–95.

29. Edna Wheway, *Edna's Story: Memories of Life in a Children's Home and in Service, in Dorset and London*, ed. Gillian Hall (Wimborne, Dorset: World and Action, 1984), 40–41.

30. Sir Henry Newbolt, "The Schoolfellow," (1910; Reprinted e-text http:infomotions.com/etexts/Gutenberg/dirs/1/3/9/0/13900/13900.

31. Davin, *Growing Up Poor*, 200–203, quote at 203.

32. Burnett, *Destiny Obscure*, 89.

33. Southgate, *That's the Way It Was*, 32.

34. Graves, *Good-bye to All That*, 16.

CHAPTER 6

1. Troubridge, *Life among the Troubridges*, 6; Nelson, *Family Ties in Victorian England*, 158–159; Elizabeth Buettner, *Empire Families: Britons and Late Imperial India* (Oxford: Oxford University Press, 2004), 110–145.

2. Davin, *Growing Up Poor*, 39–40.

3. Norman Longmate, *The Workhouse: A Social History* (London: Temple Smith, 1974), 169.

4. Frank Crompton, *Workhouse Children* (Stroud, Gloucestershire: Sutton Publishing, 1997), 36–42; Hopkins, *Childhood Transformed*, 174, 176.

5. Horn, *Victorian Town Child*, 186; George Haw, *From Workhouse to Westminster: The Life Story of Will Crooks, M. P.* (London: Cassell and Company, 1907), 8–15.

6. Hopkins, *Childhood Transformed*, 174; Horn, *Victorian Town Child*, 192.

7. Louise Westwood, "Care in the Community of the Mentally Disordered: The Case of the Guardianship Society, 1900–1939," *Social History of Medicine* 20 (2007): 57–58.

8. Ethel Mannin, *Confessions and Impressions*, 37.

9. Crompton, *Workhouse Children*, 46–50; Hopkins, *Childhood Transformed*, 175.

10. Longmate, *Workhouse*, 168–169; Hopkins, *Childhood Transformed*, 177–178; Horn, *Victorian Town Child*, 189–190; George Hewins, *The Dillen: Memories of a Man of Stratford upon Avon* (Oxford: Oxford University Press, 1982), 72.

11. Hopkins, *Childhood Transformed*, 177–178; Longmate, *Workhouse*, 52–57.

12. Shaw, *When I Was a Child*, 97–98.

13. E. L. Edmonds and O. P. Edmonds, eds., *I Was There: The Memoirs of H. S. Tremenheere* (Eton: Shakespeare Head Press, 1965), 51.

14. Haw, *From Workhouse to Westminster*, 105–127; Smith, *Cornish Waif's Story*, 22.

15. Hopkins, *Childhood Transformed*, 183–184.

16. Hopkins, *Childhood Transformed*, 184; Dorothy Hatcher, *The Workhouse and the Weald* (Rainham, Kent: Meresborough Books, 1988), 8.

17. Hatcher, *The Workhouse and the Weald*, 17.

18. Hopkins, *Childhood Transformed*, 188.

19. Horn, *Victorian Town Child*, 194; Hatcher, *Workhouse and the Weald*, 51.

20. Jeannie Duckworth, *Fagin's Children: Criminal Children in Victorian England* (New York: Hambledon and London, 2002), 48–56, 76; Heather Shore, *Artful Dodgers: Youth and Crime in Early 19th-Century London* (Woodbridge, Suffolk: Boydell Press, 1999), 55–74.

21. Horn, *Victorian Town Child*, 218.

22. Duckworth, *Fagin's Children*, 67–69, 91–111.

23. Ibid., 63–68.

24. Ibid., 68–74, quotes at 72.

25. Ibid., 81–134; Shore, *Artful Dodgers*, 132–136.

26. Louise Jackson, *Child Sexual Abuse in Victorian England* (London: Routledge, 2000), 132–137; Horn, *Victorian Town Child*, 205–206; Linton, *Not Expecting Miracles*, 15–16.

27. Mary Carpenter, *Reformatory Schools for the Children of the Perishing and Dangerous Classes* (London: C. Gilpin, 1851), 84.

28. Horn, *Victorian Town Child*, 204–205.

29. Ibid., 205–206.

30. Hopkins, *Childhood Transformed*, 206; George Behlmer, *Friends of the Family: The English Home and Its Guardians, 1850–1940* (Stanford, Calif.: Stanford University Press, 1998), 232–245.

31. Jackson, *Child Sexual Abuse*, 28–50; Hopkins, *Childhood Transformed*, 208.

32. Duckworth, *Fagin's Children*, 199–201.

33. Ibid., 205–209.

34. Smith, *Cornish Waif's Story*, 124–127, 136–137.

35. Jackson, *Child Sexual Abuse*, 133–137.

36. Samuel, *East End Underworld*, 68–160.

37. *Times* (London), March 24, 1854, 11; *Times* (London), July 23, 1866, 11.

CHAPTER 7

1. Horn, *Victorian Town Child*, 181–183.

2. Jordan, *Victorian Childhood*, 310; Behlmer, *Friends of the Family*, 46–50, 56–59.

3. Barr, *I Remember*, 42; Wheway, *Edna's Story*, 1–16, 62.

4. Wheway, *Edna's Story*, 11–12.

5. Smith, *Cornish Waif's Story*, 74.

6. Hopkins, *Childhood Transformed*, 197; Jordan, *Victorian Childhood*, 280.

7. Behlmer, *Friends of the Family*, 33–62; Hopkins, *Childhood Transformed*, 200.

8. Horn, *Victorian Town Child*, 195–196; Jordan, *Victorian Childhood*, 312.

9. Horn, *Victorian Town Child*, 198–199; Behlmer, *Friends of the Family*, 291.

10. Horn, *Victorian Town Child*, 199–200; Jordan, *Victorian Childhood*, 320.

11. Behlmer, *Friends of the Family*, 295–299; Horn, *Victorian Town Child*, 196–197.

12. Case 795, 1886–1927, Hidden Lives Revealed: A Virtual Archive—Children in Care, 1881–1918 (CEWSS records), http://www.hiddenlives.org.uk.

13. Lionel Rose, *Massacre of the Innocents: Infanticide in Great Britain, 1800–1939* (London: Routledge and Kegan Paul, 1986), 23.

14. Jordan, *Victorian Childhood*, 291–292; *Yorkshire Gazette*, February 17, 1885, 3; *Lancaster Guardian*, June 1, 1895, 2.

15. Carolyn Conley, *The Unwritten Law: Criminal Justice in Victorian Kent* (New York: Oxford University Press, 1991), 100–111; *Times* (London), July 25, 1853, 8.

16. Shani D'Cruze, *Crimes of Outrage: Sex, Violence, and Victorian Working Women* (DeKalb: Northern Illinois University Press, 1998), 28–29; Conley, *Unwritten Law*, 117–121.

17. "Horrible Child Murder," *Lancaster Guardian*, March 27, 1875, 2; Carolyn Conley, *Certain Other Countries: Homicide, Gender, and National Identity in Late Nineteenth-Century England, Ireland, Scotland, and Wales* (Columbus, Ohio: Ohio State University Press, 2007), 179.

18. Behlmer, *Friends of the Family*, 104–111; George Behlmer, *Child Abuse and Moral Reform in England, 1870–1908* (Stanford, Calif.: Stanford University Press, 1982), 67–73.

19. Behlmer, *Child Abuse and Moral Reform*, 70–77; *Friends of the Family*, 112–116.

20. National Archives, Old Bailey Sessions Papers, PCOM 1/154, 1101–1105; *Times* (London), October 17, 1902, 2; *Times* (London), October 31, 1902, 2.

21. Behlmer, *Child Abuse and Moral Reform*, 188–192.

22. Jackson, *Child Sexual Abuse*, 133–140.

23. Paula Bartley, *Prostitution: Prevention and Reform in England, 1860–1914* (London: Routledge, 2000), 94–103.

24. Jackson, *Child Sexual Abuse*, 137–140, quote at 139.

25. Smith, *Cornish Waif's Story*, 134.

26. Behlmer, *Friends of the Family*, 274–284, quote at 281; Behlmer, *Child Abuse and Moral Reform*, 156.

27. Behlmer, *Child Abuse and Moral Reform*, 98–110; Ross, *Love and Toil*, 234n40 (for quote).

28. Hopkins, *Childhood Transformed*, p. 203; Davin, *Growing Up Poor*, p. 212.

29. Davin, *Growing Up Poor*, 212–213; Ross, *Love and Toil*, 195–221.

30. Ellen Ross, "Mothers and the State in Britain," in *The European Experience of Declining Fertility, 1850–1970: The Quiet Revolution*, ed. John Gillis, Louise Tilly, and David Levine (Oxford: Blackwell, 1992), 48–65.

31. Farningham, *Working Woman's Life*, 254.

BIBLIOGRAPHY

Acorn, George. *One of the Multitude*. London: William Heinemann, 1911. Story of a deprived and abused child in London.

Anderson, R. D. *Education and Opportunity in Victorian Scotland*. Oxford: Clarendon Press, 1983. Overview of the effects of Victorian reforms on Scottish education.

Baillie, Eileen. *The Shabby Paradise: The Autobiography of a Decade*. London: Hutchinson & Co., 1958. Daughter of an Edwardian vicar serving in the East End of London; helpful on family life.

Barclay, Tom. *Memoirs and Medleys: The Autobiography of a Bottle Washer*. 1934. Reprint, Coalville, Leicestershire: Coalville Publishing Company, 1995. Poverty-stricken Irish Catholic family in England in the 1850s and 1860s.

Barr, Pat, ed. *I Remember: An Arrangement for Many Voices*. London: MacMillan, 1970. Collection of memoirs put together by the National Old People's Welfare Council in the late 1960s.

Bartley, Paula. *Prostitution: Prevention and Reform in England, 1860–1914*. London: Routledge, 2000. Concentrates on efforts to reform or prevent prostitution; part 2 focuses on protective legislation and care of wayward girls.

Behlmer, George. *Child Abuse and Moral Reform in England, 1870–1908*. Stanford, Calif.: Stanford University Press, 1982. In-depth study of the National Society for the Prevention of Cruelty to Children, both before and after the Prevention of Cruelty and Protection of Children Act of 1889.

———. *Friends of the Family: The English Home and its Guardians, 1850–1940*. Stanford, Calif.: Stanford University Press, 1998. Centers on the private and state intervention into family life; includes chapters on domestic violence, juvenile courts, and adoptions.

Bligh, Eric. *Tooting Corner*. London: Secker & Warburg, 1946. Son of a doctor; much material on religion and schooling.

Booth, Maud Ballington. *A Rector's Daughter in Victorian England: Memories of Child-hood and Girlhood.* Metairie, La. Volunteers of America, 1994. Born 1865 to a rector; useful for religious concerns and sibling relationships.

Buettner, Elizabeth. *Empire Families: Britons and Late Imperial India.* Oxford: Oxford University Press, 2004. Focuses on the effect of imperial service on family life, including literary narratives of empire.

Burnett, John, ed. *Destiny Obscure: Autobiographies of Childhood, Education and Family from the 1820s to the 1920s.* London: Routledge, 1994. Twenty-eight short autobiographies; topics include schooling, religion, and family.

————, ed. *Useful Toil: Autobiographies of Working People from the 1820s to the 1920s.* New York: Penguin, 1984. Collection of twenty-seven short autobiographies about work, with helpful introductions.

Carbery, Mary. *Happy World: The Story of a Victorian Childhood.* London: Longmans, Green, and Co., 1941. Upper-class family relationships and gender roles.

Chase, Ellen. *Tenant Friends in Old Deptford.* London: Williams & Norgate, 1929. Rent collector in working-class district from 1886 to 1891; several descriptions of street life and games.

Chitty, Susan, ed. *As Once in May: The Early Autobiography of Antonia White and Other Writings.* London: Virago, 1983. First five years of future novelist's upper-class childhood; very good on parent-child dynamics.

Conley, Carolyn. *The Unwritten Law: Criminal Justice in Victorian Kent.* New York: Oxford University Press, 1991. Chapter 4 concentrates on children as victims and perpetrators of crimes between 1859 and 1880.

————. *Certain Other Countries: Homicide, Gender, and National Identity in Late Nineteenth-Century England, Ireland, Scotland, and Wales.* Columbus, Ohio: Ohio State University Press, 2007. Comparison of homicide trials across the British Isles between 1867 and 1892; chapter 6 focuses on crimes against children.

Cookson, Catherine. *Our Kate.* London: Corgi, 1997. Deprived childhood of the famed novelist; much material on her illegitimacy and mother's alcoholism.

Crompton, Frank. *Workhouse Children.* Stroud, Gloucestershire: Sutton Publishing, 1997. Surveys the experiences of children in workhouses before and after the reforms of 1834.

Davies, J. H. *The Life and Opinion of Robert Roberts, a Wandering Scholar, as Told by Himself.* Cardiff: William Lewis, 1923. Early Victorian farm life and education in Wales.

Davies, Margaret Llewellyn, ed. *Life as We Have Known It by Co-operative Working Women.* 1931. Reprint, New York: W. W. Norton, 1975. Five short autobiographies of working-class women.

Davin, Anna. *Growing Up Poor: Home, School and Street in London, 1870–1914.* London: Rivers Oram Press, 1996. Excellent study of London childhood at the turn of the century; particularly good on education and the influence of empire.

D'Cruze, Shani. *Crimes of Outrage: Sex, Violence, and Victorian Working Women.* De Kalb: Northern Illinois University Press, 1998. Exploration of violence against women in northern England; includes some cases of adolescent girls.

Duckworth, Jeannie. *Fagin's Children: Criminal Children in Victorian England.* New York: Hambledon and London, 2002. Focuses on punishments and the change in approach toward young offenders.

Edmonds, E. L., and O. P. Edmonds, eds. *I Was There: The Memoirs of H. S. Tremenheere.* Eton: Shakespeare Head Press, 1965. Memoirs of a mine inspector and poor-law commissioner who fought for reforms to help poor children.

Elson, George. *The Last of the Climbing Boys.* London: John Lang, 1900. Gripping descriptions of the hazards of chimney sweeping.

Ezard, Edward. *Battersea Boy.* London: William Kimber, 1979. Edwardian who grew up by the railway; interesting account of the activities of Boy Scouts.

Farningham, Marianne. *A Working Woman's Life: An Autobiography.* London: James Clarke & Co., n.d. Deeply religious Baptist, born in 1833, who grew up to write articles for Baptist publications and teach Sunday school.

Fisher, H. A. L. *An Unfinished Autobiography.* London: Oxford University Press, 1940. Future Liberal cabinet member, born in 1865; gives overview of an elite upbringing.

Fletcher, Sheila. *Victorian Girls: Lord Lyttelton's Daughters.* London: Phoenix, 1997. Joint biography of the four daughters of Lord Lyttleton, a reformer of women's education.

Foakes, Grace. *Between High Walls: A London Childhood.* London: Shepheard-Walwyn, 1972. Poor family in London; concentrates on family relationships and children's play.

Foley, Alice. *A Bolton Childhood.* Manchester: North Western District of the Workers' Educational Association, 1973. Poor Catholic family in northern England; especially strong on family relationships.

Gautrey, Thomas. *"Lux Mihi Laus": School Board Memories.* London: Link House Publications, 1937[?]. Worked with school boards for more than thirty years; particularly useful for educational reforms between 1870 and 1900.

Gosse, Edmund. *Father and Son: A Study of Two Temperaments.* 1907. Reprint, London: Penguin, 1989. Thoughtful exploration of the tension between a mid-Victorian father, a member of the Plymouth Brethren, and his freethinking son.

Graves, Alfred Perceval. *To Return to All That: An Autobiography.* London: Jonathan Cape, 1930. Robert Graves's father; wrote his memoir as a reply to his son's.

Graves, Robert. *Good-bye to All That.* 1929. Reprint, New York: Doubleday, 1985. Classic account of late-Victorian, upper-class childhood and the end of illusions in the trench warfare of World War I.

Grundy, G. B. *Fifty-Five Years at Oxford: An Unconventional Autobiography.* London: Methuen & Co., 1945. Born in 1861, son of a headmaster; worked his way into a fellowship at Oxford after his father went bankrupt.

Harrison, Brian. "For Church, Queen and Family: The Girls' Friendly Society, 1874–1920." *Past and Present* 61 (1973): 107–138. Overview of the popular organization.

Hatcher, Dorothy. *The Workhouse and the Weald.* Rainham, Kent: Meresborough Books, 1988. Illegitimate child who grew up in the workhouse and foster care.

Haw, George. *From Workhouse to Westminster: The Life Story of Will Crooks, M. P.* London: Cassell and Company, 1907. Sentimental version of the life of an early Labour leader; has sections on the workhouse in two different periods.

Hewins, George. *The Dillen: Memories of a Man of Stratford upon Avon.* Oxford: Oxford University Press, 1982. Brought up by extended kin; became a building laborer.

Hicks, J. D., ed. *A Victorian Boyhood in the Wolds: The Recollections of J. R. Mortimer.* Hull: East Yorkshire Local History Society, 1978. Early-nineteenth-century rural childhood of future architect.

Hidden Lives Revealed: A Virtual Archive—Children in Care, 1881–1918, http://www. hiddenlives.org.uk. Digitized case records of the Church of England's Waifs and Strays Society at the turn of the century.

Hopkins, Eric. *Childhood Transformed: Working-Class Children in Nineteenth-Century England.* Manchester: Manchester University Press, 1994. Thorough study of working-class childhood; argues for a significant improvement in children's lives after 1870.

Horn, Pamela. *The Victorian Town Child.* Stroud, Gloucestershire: Sutton Publishing, 1997. Well-illustrated and accessible overview of town children's lives; especially strong on education.

Hughes, Molly. *A London Child of the 1870s.* 1934. Reprint, Oxford: Oxford University Press, 1977. First of four volumes of autobiography, centering on home education and relationship with four brothers.

———. *A London Girl of the 1880s.* 1946. Reprint, Oxford: Oxford University Press, 1978. Second of four volumes of autobiography, focusing on secondary education and adolescence.

Hunt, Agnes. *Reminiscences.* Shrewsbury: Wilding & Sons, 1935. Born in 1867 into an upper-class family; grew up to be a nurse.

Jackson, Louise. *Child Sexual Abuse in Victorian England.* London: Routledge, 2000. Analysis of the legal, medical, and social ramifications of Victorian child abuse cases; includes a chapter on reform homes for girl victims.

Jaspar, A. S. *A Hoxton Childhood.* London: Centerprise Publications, 1969. Edwardian childhood; son of a drunken delivery man and strong working-class mother.

Jermy, Louise. *Memories of a Working Woman.* Norwich: Goose & Son, 1934. Childhood with an abusive stepmother; labored as a dressmaker, laundress, and servant.

Jobson, Allan. *The Creeping Hours of Time.* London: Robert Hale, 1977. Late-Victorian son of a shoemaker with Methodist background.

Jones, Edgar, ed. *The Memoirs of Edwin Waterhouse: A Founder of Price Waterhouse.* London: B. T. Batsford, 1988. Life of the famous businessman; highlights relationship with his brothers and his Quaker religion.

Jordan, Thomas. *Victorian Childhood: Themes and Variations.* Albany: State University of New York Press, 1987. Covers all four British kingdoms and the whole Victorian period; though impressionistic in topics, author includes useful charts and graphs throughout.

Kerr, John. *Memories Grave and Gay: Forty Years of School Inspection.* London: William Blackwood and Sons, 1902. Memoir of a school inspector and education reformer.

Lieck, Albert Henry. *Narrow Waters: The First Volume of the Life and Thoughts of a Common Man.* London: William Hodge and Company, 1935. Born in Hackney to poor family; centers on his strong mother.

Linton, Alice. *Not Expecting Miracles.* London: Centerprise Trust, 1982. A poor but happy Edwardian childhood.

Littler, Walter. *A Victorian Childhood: Recollections and Reflections.* Belbroughton, Worcestershire: Marion Seymour, 1997. Born in the 1880s to a working-class family; rich depictions of school, play, and work.

Longmate, Norman. *The Workhouse: A Social History*. London: Temple Smith, 1974. Early study with a chapter on the treatment of children in the workhouse.

Lutyens, Emily. *A Blessed Girl: Memoirs of a Victorian Girlhood Chronicled in an Exchange of Letters, 1887–1896*. New York: J. B. Lippincott Company, 1954. Story of a diplomat's large family, told mostly through letters to a family friend.

MacDonald, Greville. *Reminiscences of a Specialist*. London: George Allen & Unwin, 1932. Memoir of a future doctor; useful material on all aspects of middle-class childhood in the 1860s.

Magnus, Phillip. *Gladstone: A Biography*. London: John Murray, 1954. Classic biography of the four-time Liberal prime minister.

Manchester, William. *The Last Lion: Winston Spencer Churchill*. Vol. 1, *Visions of Glory, 1874–1932*. New York: Dell, 1983. First volume of a biography of the future prime minister, centering on his home life, education, and early career.

Mannin, Ethel. *Confessions and Impressions*. London: Hutchinson & Co., 1936. Born 1900 to a poor family in South London; strong on parent-child relationship and schooling.

Manning, Leah. *A Life for Education: An Autobiography*. London: Victor Gallancz, 1970. Grew up with her grandparents; good for effects of the Boer War. Eventually became a teacher to working-class children.

Marshall, Mary Paley. *What I Remember*. Cambridge: Cambridge University Press, 1947. Born in 1850 in a rector's family; helpful on education of girls in the mid-Victorian years.

Mayhew, Henry. *London Labour and the London Poor*. 4 vols. 1861–1862. Reprint, New York: Dover, 1968. Compilation of Mayhew's journalistic articles on the poor of London, including many vignettes about child workers.

McCurdy, Sylvia. *Sylvia: A Victorian Childhood*. Lavenham, Suffolk: Eastland Press, 1972. Born in 1876 to a well-off family; centers on education and play.

McDermid, Jane. *Schooling of Working-Class Girls in Victorian Scotland*. London: Routledge, 2005. Recent study of educational reform for Scottish girls.

Mitchell, Hannah. *The Hard Way Up: The Autobiography of Hannah Mitchell, Suffragette and Rebel*. Edited by Geoffrey Mitchell. London: Faber and Faber, 1968. Farmer's daughter with violent mother who grew up to work for workers' and women's rights.

Mockford, George. *Wilderness Journeyings and Gracious Deliverances: The Autobiography of George Mockford*. Oxford: J. C. Pembrey, 1901. Early Victorian (b. 1826) son of a farmer; became a preacher and schoolmaster.

Nelson, Claudia. *Family Ties in Victorian England*. London: Praeger, 2007. Succinct and effective overview of Victorian family life and its literary representations.

Newbolt, Sir Henry. *Collected Poems, 1897–1907*. New York: T. Nelson and Sons, 1910. Contains more than seventy poems, including several that connect boys' games with warfare. Also available on line at http:infomotions.com/etexts/Gutenberg/dirs/1/3/9/0/13900/13900.

Okey, Thomas. *A Basketful of Memories: An Autobiographical Sketch*. London: J. M. Dent & Sons, 1930. Born 1852, son of a disabled father; later involved in socialism and education.

Ommanney, Francis Downes. *The House in the Park*. London: Longmans, Green, and Co., 1944. Writer's memoir; good on his relationship with his sister and his unhappy memories of public schools.

Paton, John. *Proletarian Pilgrimage: An Autobiography*. London: George Routledge & Sons, 1935. Story of the poor Scottish upbringing of a future Labour leader.

Ratcliffe, George. *Sixty Years of It: Being the Story of My Life and Public Career*. London: A. Brown & Sons, 1935[?]. Born in a Leeds slum in 1863; includes descriptions of numerous odd jobs and children's games.

Ridge, W. Pett. *A Story Teller: Forty Years in London*. London: Hodder and Stoughton, 1923. Child advocate in London; long descriptions of children's games.

Rogers, Frederick. *Labour, Life and Literature: Some Memories of Sixty Years*. 1913. Reprint, Brighton, Sussex: Harvester Press, 1973. Happy but poor childhood in London of a future Labour leader.

Rose, Lionel. *Massacre of the Innocents: Infanticide in Great Britain, 1800–1939*. London: Routledge and Kegan Paul, 1986. Pioneering study of the crime of infant murder and attempts to police it.

Ross, Ellen. *Love and Toil: Motherhood in Outcast London, 1870–1918*. Oxford: Oxford University Press, 1993. In-depth look at mother-child relationships in London during the transition to the twentieth century.

———. "Mothers and the State in Britain." In *The European Experience of Declining Fertility, 1850–1970: The Quiet Revolution*, ed. John Gillis, Louise Tilly, and David Levine, 48–65. Oxford: Basil Blackwell, 1992. Focuses on the challenge to working-class mothers from the high demands for cleanliness and nutrition in the Edwardian years.

Samuel, Raphael. *East End Underworld: Chapters in the Life of Arthur Harding*. London: Routledge and Kegan Paul, 1981. Small-time criminal in East London; sections on Sunday school, charities, and street life.

Shaw, Charles. *When I Was a Child by an Old Potter*. London: Methuen & Co., 1903. Firsthand account of child industrial labor and life in the workhouse.

Shore, Heather. *Artful Dodgers: Youth and Crime in Early 19th-Century London*. Woodbridge, Suffolk: Boydell Press, 1999. Traces the experience of child criminals from arrest through prison or transportation.

Smith, Emma. *A Cornish Waif's Story: An Autobiography*. London: Popular Book Club, 1956. Life of an illegitimate child; includes descriptions of the workhouse, a Salvation Army home, and a refuge for fallen women.

Smith, Samuel. *My Life-Work*. London: Hodder and Stoughton, 1902. Born in 1836 to a poor farmer in Scotland; worked for children's rights.

Smyth, Ethel, ed. *Little Innocents: Childhood Reminiscences*. London: Cobden-Sanderson, 1932. Short anecdotal memoirs of thirty middle- and upper-class Victorians.

Southgate, Walter. *That's the Way It Was: A Working-Class Autobiography, 1890–1950*. Oxted, Surrey: New Clarion Press, 1982. Poor family in London; numerous charming vignettes of family, school, work, and the Band of Hope.

Stanley, Maude. *Clubs for Working Girls*. London: MacMillan, 1890. Middle-class reformer sets out program for assisting worthy, poor young women.

Tosh, John. *A Man's Place: Masculinity and the Middle-Class Home in Victorian England*. New Haven, Conn.: Yale University Press, 1999. Monograph on the role of middle-class husbands and fathers; includes a study of generational tension.

Toye, C. Richard. *Sandy: The True Story of a Boy and His Friends Growing Up in Cornwall in the Late 1800s*. Milverton, Somerset: Great Western Books, 2003. Well-off farmer's son, born in 1877; good picture of rural life.

Troubridge, Laura. *Life among the Troubridges: Journals of a Young Victorian, 1873–1884*. London: Tite Street Press, 1999. Journal of second oldest of six upper-class orphaned children in the 1860s and 1870s.

Warburton, Katherine. *Soho Days and Other Memories*. London: A. R. Mowbray & Co., 1906. Part of a religious order that worked with children in mid-Victorian London.

Westwood, Louise. "Care in the Community of the Mentally Disordered: The Case of the Guardianship Society, 1900–1939." *Social History of Medicine* 20 (2007): 57–72. Rare study of the treatment of the mentally ill, including some afflicted children.

Wheway, Edna. *Edna's Story: Memories of Life in a Children's Home and in Service, in Dorset and London*, ed. by Gillian Hall. Wimborne, Dorset: World and Action, 1984. Daughter of a widow; put in an orphanage at age three.

Wilson, John. *Memories of a Labour Leader: The Autobiography of John Wilson, J. P., M. P.* 1910. Reprint, Firle, Sussex: Caliban Books, 1980. Born 1837, rich description of mining work and trade union struggles.

Woodward, Kathleen. *Jipping Street*. 1923. Reprint, London: Virago, 1983. Born in 1896, daughter of disabled father and washerwoman; grew up to work in the mills.

Wright, William. *From Chimney-Boy to Councillor: The Story of My Life*. Medstead, Hampshire: Azania Press, 1931[?]. Born 1846, became a chimney sweep at eight years old and eventually owned his own business.

INDEX

About the Author

GINGER S. FROST is Professor of History at Samford University in Birmingham, AL. She is the author of *Promises Broken: Courtship, Class and Gender in Victorian England* and *Living in Sin: Cohabiting as Husband and Wife in Nineteenth-Century England* as well as numerous articles. She has received fellowships from the National Humanities Center and the National Endowment for the Humanities, and served as President of the Southern Conference on British Studies from 2002 to 2003.